Union General John A. McClernand
and the Politics of Command

DATE DUE

Union General
John A. McClernand
and the Politics
of Command

CHRISTOPHER C. MEYERS

McFarland & Company, Inc., Publishers
Jefferson, North Carolina, and London

LIBRARY OF CONGRESS CATALOGUING-IN-PUBLICATION DATA

Meyers, Christopher, C.
  Union general John A. McClernand and the politics of
command / by Christopher C. Meyers.
     p.   cm.
  Includes bibliographical references and index.

  ISBN: 978-0-7864-5960-5
  softcover : 50# alkaline paper

  1. McClernand, John A. (John Alexander), 1812–1900.
2. Generals — United States — Biography. 3. United States —
History — Civil War, 1861–1865 — Biography. 4. United
States — History — Civil War, 1861–1865 — Campaigns.
5. United States — Politics and government — Civil War,
1861–1865. 6. Command of troops — History —19th century.
7. United States. Army — Biography. 8. Soldiers — Illinois —
Biography. I. Title.
E467.1.M23M49 2010
973.7'41092 — dc22 [B]   2010034806

British Library cataloguing data are available

Cover image: General John A. McClernand in his major
general's uniform (1862 or 1863, Library of Congress)

Manufactured in the United States of America

McFarland & Company, Inc., Publishers
  Box 611, Jefferson, North Carolina 28640

To my parents, Charles and Jill Meyers,
and
to my son, Jacob Meyers

Acknowledgments

One of the pleasant tasks of writing this book is thanking those who helped and assisted in completing the project, and I have many debts to recognize. Archivists and librarians at numerous repositories across the country are among the most important resources to historians conducting research. I particularly wish to thank Cheryl Schnirring of the Abraham Lincoln Presidential Library in Springfield. Also in Springfield, John Lupton, Martha Benner, and Susan Krause of the Lincoln Legal Papers helped me with aspects of McClernand's legal career. Cody Wright of the Illinois State Archives answered my many questions about Illinois history. Ingrid Nyholm of the Chicago Historical Society was especially helpful with my requests for documents related to John McClernand. I would also like to thank the staffs of the Library of Congress, National Archives, New York Historical Society, and the Delaware State Historical Library. Denise Montgomery in the Interlibrary Loan Department at Odum Library at Valdosta State University was able to get many books and rolls of microfilm for me. I would also like to thank Julie Smith for drawing the excellent maps for this book.

My graduate school professors in the History Department at Florida State University had a profound impact on how I think about and write history, and I particularly wish to thank Drs. James P. Jones, Donald D. Horward, William W. Rogers, Philip D. Morgan, and Valerie J. Conner. Many other persons provided assistance in many other ways. Henry and Margaret Kirschner opened their home to me when I was in Springfield; their hospitality is something I will not soon forget. Ed Pree, also in Springfield, showed me all the old Lincoln haunts around the city and discussed my research with me at the Sangamon Club. My colleagues in the History Department at Valdosta State University always had encouraging words, especially David Williams, who probably heard way more about John McClernand than he cared to. Moral support and encouragement came from friends too numerous to list, but I would like to specifically thank David Coles, Will Benedicks, Kyle Eidahl, Tracy Power, Chris Fonvielle, Paul Riggs, Cathy Oglesby, Mary Block, Dixie Haggard, Charles Johnson, Jimmy Taw, Alan Bernstein, Jim Martinello, and Shelley Stiver Brannon.

My family was a constant source of encouragement. My wife, Tracy, and son, Jacob, were incredibly tolerant of my preoccupation with this project. My sisters Caren, Nancy, and Julie at least feigned interest. My parents, Charles and Jill Meyers, provided encouragement throughout. My dad even read an early version of the manuscript! People too often don't say "thank you" enough to their parents, and I would like to take this opportunity to thank my parents for everything they have done for me.

Table of Contents

Introduction

The general commanding the expedition ordered a staff officer to climb a nearby tree from which to better view the assault on the Arkansas River fort. The fort was a Confederate bastion called Arkansas Post and the general was John A. McClernand, a Union officer from Illinois. After a several-hours-long battle the Confederate fort surrendered and General McClernand had won his greatest victory of the war. This was the zenith of his Civil War service. Although he expected to accomplish greater victories his war experiences started on a downhill slide to ultimate oblivion and banishment from any theater of action.

Before the Civil War, John McClernand had an extremely successful political career. He served in the Illinois general assembly for a number of years before being elected to the U.S. House of Representatives, where he spent a total of ten years. By the end of his political career he was one of the most powerful politicians in the state of Illinois. Despite his remarkable achievements, he always seemed to serve in the shadow of other more powerful and influential men. During his antebellum political career he worked in the shadow of one of the most powerful politicians in America in the 1850s, Stephen A. Douglas, who also happened to reside in Illinois. McClernand was Douglas' spokesman in the U.S. House, and McClernand worked hard for the "Little Giant." The two collaborated in getting the Compromise of 1850 passed through Congress and McClernand spared no effort for Douglas' presidential candidacy in 1860. Without a doubt Douglas was the dominant person in this political relationship. When Douglas died in May 1861 McClernand could rightfully expect to assume the mantle of leadership in the Illinois Democratic party, not to mention Douglas' Senate seat. But the Civil War broke out and a new set of prominent men dominated the political and military landscape.

During the Civil War two men overshadowed McClernand — President Abraham Lincoln and General Ulysses S. Grant. Lincoln was the most famous hero of the war and he overshadowed all Union officials, civilian and military. On the military side McClernand spent the war years in Grant's shadow, and because of Grant's military success there was little opportunity for McClernand to distinguish or separate himself from his superior. The Illinois general certainly reaped the benefits of fighting under Grant — winning virtually every engagement and earning quick promotion. Early in the war McClernand established himself as a rival to Grant, and because Grant was so successful McClernand could not emerge from his shadow.

John A. McClernand serves as a mirror through which historians can view other individuals. Through McClernand we can learn something about Stephen A. Douglas, Abraham Lincoln, and Ulysses S. Grant. Through McClernand one can again learn how politically astute Lincoln was and how Grant understood wartime politics. There is much we can learn from a study of John A. McClernand that balances politics and war.

The principal theme of this study of John McClernand is politics. Once he entered the political arena he could not separate himself from politics. Even during the conflict the Illinoisan politicized his Civil War experiences. He remained active in politics until near the end of his life; from 1836 until 1886 John McClernand was involved in politics in one way or another. McClernand's penchant for politics during the Civil War alienated many high-ranking officials and his scheming undermined the command structure in the Army of the Tennessee. And therein lies the paradox of McClernand's Civil War experience. On the one hand he fought tenaciously to defeat the Confederates, but on the other his intriguing undermined the federal command system. It is important to appreciate this paradox if we are to understand John A. McClernand.

The McClernand vs. Grant theme is an important part of the McClernand story and one question that must be asked is this: Is there anything new to offer to the story of this rivalry? The relationship has almost always been described from Grant's perspective, but in a study of McClernand we can view this rivalry from McClernand's position. To get a fuller understanding of the McClernand-Grant relationship we must have the opportunity to study it from both sides, which this book does.

Historians have not always been kind to John McClernand. He has been variously described as "dangerous," "ever ambitious," "a braggart and a blowhard," and "vain, inept, contemptuous of authority, disdainful of West Point trained officers, and toadying to home-state constituent troops."[1] Other historians have commented on McClernand's political shrewdness by describing him as "clever," "witty" or "flippant."[2] Herman Hattaway and

Archer Jones took a middle-of-the-road approach when they described General McClernand's plan to capture Vicksburg as "inspired political-military entrepreneurship."[3] This seems to be both a condemnation and a compliment. Steven Woodworth, in his recent history of the Army of the Tennessee, referred to McClernand as a "pathologically ambitious politician."[4]

Although fewer historians have recognized McClernand's competence and ability as a commander, Allan Nevins described him as "intrepid" and Edward Longacre suggested that McClernand "displayed soldierly characteristics of a high order."[5] Richard Kiper outlined McClernand's military leadership during the first half of the Vicksburg campaign and his evaluation was positive: "He exhibited broad military vision as he proposed alternatives to the initial plan of attack against Vicksburg. He skillfully directed the movement of his corps over forty miles of flooded terrain from Milliken's Bend to DeShroon's Plantation. His participation in the expedition to reconnoiter the road to New Carthage, where he came under Confederate fire is evidence of his bravery."[6] More recently William Shea and Terrence Winschel compared McClernand in the Vicksburg campaign favorably to both Generals Sherman and McPherson: "McClernand, however, was a capable officer who had performed admirably thus far in the campaign, more so than either Sherman or McPherson, and he enjoyed the respect of his soldiers."[7] These examples show that McClernand was not just an incompetent politician in uniform — he did possess leadership ability.

My portrait of John McClernand attempts to balance his war experiences with his largely neglected prewar political career and points out his shortcomings as well as his abilities. Because McClernand's commission in 1861 was predicated upon his status as a prominent Democrat, it is imperative to study and understand the man's prewar political career. The intention behind this book was to write an account that focuses on John McClernand the politician. During the war years I focus on how he politicized his military service, the politics of command; I never set out, for example, to reconstruct the movements of every unit under his command. Readers who are interested in a more detailed tactical examination of McClernand's war experiences should see Richard Kiper's *Major General John Alexander McClernand: Politician in Uniform* (Kent, OH: Kent State University Press, 1999). For my purposes, tracing the movements of every regiment, for instance, would make the manuscript unwieldy and it would lose its focus on the politics of command. I never intended to write a "behind this tree" battle narrative for McClernand's Civil War service. I wanted instead to stay more narrowly focused on the man and his actions and how he politicized the war.

1

Glory Hunting in Illinois

Brigadier General Alexander Posey's First Brigade was part of the pursuit of Black Hawk and his warriors as they withdrew toward the Mississippi River in 1832. General Posey ordered his thin, frail assistant brigade quartermaster to take a dispatch through the hostile countryside. A crude map the general furnished his quartermaster-turned-courier was virtually useless, but the general's order was to deliver the message as quickly as possible. With the successful delivery of the dispatch, the courier's mission was complete; he traversed one hundred miles through hostile, Indian-infested Illinois backwoods in the middle of an Indian war. And he survived.[1]

The courier, John Alexander McClernand, could allegedly trace his ancestry back to Malcolm I of Scotland, who became king in 943, to the clan of Mac of the Clearlands. From Scotland the family migrated to Ireland, to the county of Antrim, and the family name was eventually changed to McClernand. John's father, Dr. John McClernand, a native of Ireland, studied for the ministry at Dublin University. Not answering a minister's calling, he studied medicine at Edinburgh, graduated with honors, and began to practice medicine. The physician also allegedly became involved in several civil disturbances, and in order to escape capture and punishment by the British government he fled to America in 1801.[2]

Landing in Philadelphia, Dr. McClernand traveled westward and settled near Hardinsburg in Breckinridge County, Kentucky. There he met and married Fatina Seaton, a native of Prince William County, Virginia, and a recent widow.[3] Together they raised John Alexander McClernand, who was born on May 30, 1812, their only child to survive infancy.

Shortly after the birth of their son, Dr. McClernand moved his family just across the Illinois border to Shawneetown in Gallatin County. Here he established his practice. Tragedy struck the family when Dr. McClernand died in 1816. Though only four years old when his father passed away, the doctor's son must have been adversely affected by this event. John A. McClernand passed through his formative years without a father, raised by his twice widowed mother. Perhaps this absence of a father figure in his early life helped mold him into an independent, ambitious, strong-willed politician and Civil War general. Perhaps a lack of discipline as a youth sowed the seed for his alleged insubordination at Vicksburg in 1863.

McClernand's childhood was normal for a frontier village in the early 1800s. He received his education at the typical common schools of the village, which he attended irregularly. Two men have been credited with being particularly helpful with the boy's education — William F. Cassidy, described as "an Irish gentleman," and Illinois state senator William Jefferson Gatewood.[4]

Although an only child, the 1820 federal census suggested that eight-year-old John McClernand did not lack for playmates, either around the village or in his own household. The census return for Gallatin County, Illinois, in 1820 recorded many children his age. It also indicated there were as many as thirteen persons in his household. Four of these were children or young teenagers, while five were over the age of sixteen (two of whom were over the age of 45, one being his mother). These persons may have been cousins or other relatives, but only his mother was immediate family. The remaining four persons in the household, according to the census return, were slaves. This was not unusual since Shawneetown was just over the Illinois border, not more than five miles from Kentucky, a slave state. Southern Illinois had historically contained significant pro-slave sentiments.[5]

As he was a slight and skinny child — young John was described as being of a "delicate and slender habit of body" — an outdoors occupation did not seem suited for him, so he pursued a white collar career. After speaking with Judge Joptah Hardin, McClernand was convinced to undertake the study of law. In 1829, at the age of seventeen, McClernand began to read and study law in the Shawneetown law office of Henry Eddy. He studied for four years, completing his preparatory work in 1832, and was admitted to the Illinois bar that year.[6]

Other important events were happening in Illinois in 1832 that affected McClernand's life. Some Indians of the Sac and Fox tribes living in neighboring Iowa claimed that their cession of western Illinois land to the United States government in 1804 had been illegal. These Indians, under the Sac leader Black Hawk, wished to reclaim the ceded territory. In April 1832, after a winter of near starvation in Iowa, Black Hawk, along with approximately 800 warriors (about 300 of them from allied tribes) and some 1,000 women and children crossed the Mississippi River into Illinois. Their destination was the Rock River area of western Illinois. The presence of the women and children seemed to indicate two things — their move was intended to be peaceful and they meant to stay. Unlike Black Hawk's venture across the Mississippi in the spring of 1831 when settlers' houses were burned, the warriors committed no depredations in 1832.

The U.S. government quickly amassed troops to meet this Indian threat. The War Department ordered Colonel Henry Atkinson, commander at Jefferson Barracks in St. Louis, to gather as many regular troops as possible and move against Black Hawk (he rounded up about 500 men). General Winfield Scott was ordered to collect 1,000 men from the eastern United States and travel to Illinois through the Great Lakes. Illinois governor John Reynolds called up the state militia, and some 2,000 men volunteered, most of them mounted.

Against this array of American troops Black Hawk did not have much chance of success. Facing superior numbers, the Sac and Fox warriors were forced to withdraw, taking the women and children with them. Hoping to escape across the Mississippi River, they crossed over into the Wisconsin Territory. At a place called Wisconsin Heights there was a small engagement with a portion of the Illinois mounted militia. Tired, hungry, and leaving some 68 men dead on the battlefield, Black Hawk and his people continued for the Mississippi. On August 2, at the confluence of the Mississippi and Bad Axe rivers, they were caught. For three hours the Sac and Fox were driven into the river and mercilessly slaughtered in what became known as the Battle of Bad Axe. Only 300 of the original number succeeded in crossing the Mississippi. Black Hawk himself and 150 others were captured.[7]

Like many other Illinois men, John A. McClernand answered Governor Reynolds' call for volunteers. He enrolled at Fort Wilburn, which was located on the south bank of the Illinois River about one mile above Peru, on June 16, 1832. He enrolled for ninety days, although he did not serve that long, and was attached to Captain Harrison Wilson's company, 1st Regiment, 1st Brigade, Illinois Mounted Volunteers. Captain Wilson, like McClernand, was from Shawneetown. The brigade commander was General Alexander Posey. Shortly after enlisting, McClernand was appointed assistant brigade quartermaster with the temporary rank of colonel. His experience in the Black Hawk War was similar to that of most of the volunteer militiamen: they marched and camped, but they did little, if any, fighting. Only rarely did a company even happen upon Native American or militia casualties of the conflict. The only excitement for McClernand was when he acted as General Posey's courier and delivered a message one hundred miles through "a wild country infested by hostile Indians." The colonel and his company were mustered out on August 14, 1832, having served fewer than ninety days.[8]

Upon his return from the war, McClernand did not immediately take up his law practice. Instead the colonel became a trader working the Ohio and Mississippi rivers, gaining important knowledge of the western river systems. The fruits of this labor and knowledge were displayed during the Civil War when the Confederates closed the Mississippi to commerce. Relying on his familiarity with the river systems, McClernand proposed a campaign to reopen the "father of waters" in a September 1862 letter to President Lincoln. This proposal was undoubtedly based upon insight gleaned from his years as a trader.

John A. McClernand had worked as lawyer, soldier, and trader. In 1835 he added yet another title to his list of occupations — that of newspaper founder and editor — when he established the *Gallatin* (Illinois) *Democrat*. In addition to continuing his law practice, McClernand edited the fledgling weekly newspaper. The weekly newspaper was an early indication of his political principles, as a staunch Jacksonian, McClernand enunciated democratic beliefs in its pages. The December 5, 1835, issue promoted the presidential candidacy of Martin Van Buren and his running mate, Richard M. Johnson. The *Democrat*'s masthead read "Whatever is violent, is not durable," and trumpeted itself as "The voice of Illinois." The newspaper cost $3 if payment was made at the end of the year and $2 at the beginning of the year.[9] McClernand continued his editorial duties after winning election to the Illinois house of representatives, and the newspaper became a medium through which McClernand espoused his political ideology.

Early in McClernand's adult life he showed an interest in land speculation, a hobby that would be with him for some time. In November 1834 he purchased two lots, each six acres in size, in Shawneetown for $100. Three years later McClernand purchased an additional forty acres in Shawneetown, paying $50 for the land, and in 1836 he corresponded with a Mr. David in New York City about land purchases.[10] During his life John McClernand bought and sold thousands of acres of land throughout Illinois.

McClernand's political career began in 1836 when he ran for a seat in the Illinois house of representatives from Gallatin County. He was one of eight men contesting three seats in the state house on August 2, 1836. McClernand ran first, collecting 943 votes, while the next top finishers received 623 and 482 votes. He ran first in six of the eight precincts and in the other two he finished second.[11] This suggests that his popularity and appeal were widespread throughout the district. At 24, McClernand was the youngest man to serve in the Illinois general assembly up to that time. His political principles were that of a Jacksonian Democrat — he steadfastly defended President Andrew Jackson and Democratic convictions. The representative was described as "inflexibly Democratic," and a former Democratic U.S. Senator from Illinois made this pronouncement about him: "McClernand we can count upon; he is always for the Democracy and his friends."[12]

Yet another indication of his early political principles was a set of resolutions he authored in 1837 at the state Democratic convention. As chairman of the committee on resolutions he produced the following:

> Resolved, that the Democratic principle is founded on an imperishable basis of truth and justice, and is perpetually striving to sustain society in the exercise of every power which can promote honor or happiness, and elevate our condition; that instead of warring against order, and encroaching on the privilege of others, the spirit of Democracy maintains an active principle of hope and virtue.
>
> Resolved, that our first aim is to connect our party with the cause of intelligence and morality; to seek the protection of every right consistent with the genius of our institutions and the spirit of the age. We desire to extend moral culture, and to remove, as far as possible, all inequalities in our human condition, by embracing all improvements which can ameliorate our moral and political state.[13]

Committed to Democratic principles and the Democratic party, McClernand took his seat in the general assembly in 1836. The Tenth General Assembly of Illinois convened in Vandalia on December 5, 1836, amid anything but ideal conditions. The old statehouse had been abandoned and a new frame building was constructed to keep the capital in Vandalia. The rooms were damp and cold and the plaster was still wet. One legislator complained to his wife: "This is the dullest, dreariest place."[14] Despite the working conditions in the capitol, McClernand was among many men who would distinguish themselves in the political arena. McClernand worked with Stephen A. Douglas, Abraham Lincoln, future U.S. Senators James Shields and James Semple, and future U.S. Representatives Edward Baker, John J. Hardin, William A. Richardson, and Robert Smith. John A. McClernand made many important associations in the Illinois house of representatives, but none were more important than Douglas and Lincoln.

After James Semple was elected speaker, the house could begin its work. The first order of business was committee appointments, and this was done on December 10. McClernand was assigned to two committees, the Committee on Internal Improvements and the Committee on Salines.[15] To open the legislative session on December 9 the governor, Joseph Duncan, gave his state of the state address. In addition to the usual state business, Governor Duncan assailed the policies of President Andrew Jackson. He denounced Jackson for his veto of the Bank of the U.S. recharter bill, abuse of executive patronage, and violation of the Constitution.

In response, a committee was formed to investigate the governor's charges and prepare a reply. As a leader of the pro–Jackson faction in the Illinois

house, McClernand was appointed to this extraordinary legislative committee. Another member was Stephen A. Douglas. This was perhaps the first
meeting between these two men, the beginning of a political alliance that
lasted until Douglas' death in 1861. McClernand penned the committee's
response to the governor, and his strongly worded report defended President
Jackson's policies. The report, issued on December 23, 1836, proposed two
resolutions: (1) "That we approve the general course of the present administration"; and (2) "That we disavow the correctness of the charges preferred
by Governor Duncan."[16] Despite being the youngest man in the legislature
McClernand fared well in this confrontation with the governor. This was an
auspicious beginning to a promising political career for the legislator from
Shawneetown.

One of the most important topics of the legislative session was internal
improvements. As a member of the Committee on Internal Improvements,
McClernand contributed to this pivotal subject. The committee introduced
a bill that contained a wide-ranging program of improvements.[17] After long
debate in both house and senate, mostly on what provisions were pork bar-
rel, the legislation passed in February 1837. The bill contained two particularly notable provisions. One was the creation of the Illinois-Michigan Canal,
and the other provided for moving the state capital from Vandalia to
Springfield. The voting for the location of the new capital was done on February 28, 1837, and after four ballots Springfield was selected. McClernand,
showing loyalty to his constituents, voted for Shawneetown on the first ballot and Equality on the second. On the third and fourth ballot McClernand
cast his vote for Springfield.[18]

The Illinois-Michigan Canal had a greater impact on the legislator from
Gallatin County. As a member of the newly created Canal Commission,
McClernand had great influence on the progress of the canal. One hot topic
of debate was whether the canal should be of the "narrow cut" or "deep cut"
variety. McClernand favored the "deep cut" plan and was persistent in his
argument. The "deep cut" plan was finally adopted. Because of his great interest in the canal, on March 3, 1837, the house of representatives voted McClernand treasurer of the Board of Canal Commissioners, effective March 4, 1837.[19]
With this appointment, McClernand was in the forefront of Illinois internal
improvements. The position also kept him busy, as canal business took much
of his time and energy for the remainder of 1837.

In December 1837 the canal treasurer attended the state Democratic
convention in Vandalia and served as the chairman of the committee on resolutions. The convention served as an indication of McClernand's political
progress and his influence in the party. It was a testament to the respect
accorded him that he was named a committee chairman even though he was

a relative newcomer to politics. More proof of his growing political prestige was that at the convention he was offered the chance to run for lieutenant governor on the party's 1838 ticket. However, since McClernand had not yet reached the constitutionally mandated age of thirty for that office, he declined the offer. Six months later McClernand explained his position in a letter published by the *Illinois State Register*, Springfield's Democratic organ: "The reason upon which I predicate my declension of an honor, altogether so flattering to my pride, exists from a clause of our state constitution. By reference to that instrument it will be seen, that a citizen must be of or above a prescribed age, in order that he shall be eligible for the office of Governor or Lieutenant Governor. I do not come within the rule of that prescription — and consequently am not eligible under the constitution for the place mentioned in connection with my name."[20]

At the end of the convention McClernand again turned his attention to canal business, and this kept him busy through much of 1838. In fact, canal activities and other business kept McClernand so busy that he decided against running for reelection in 1838. However, other results of that election held considerable significance for McClernand. Thomas Carlin, a Jacksonian Democrat, was elected governor of Illinois. After taking office in December 1838 Carlin wished to test the state doctrine of "life appointment" for the Illinois secretary of state. The state constitution left the tenure of office undefined, and the new governor wanted the right to select his own advisers from his own party. The secretary of state at the time was Whig Alexander P. Field, who had been appointed to that post in 1829 by Governor Ninian Edwards. At the time of his appointment Field was a Jacksonian Democrat, but later switched party affiliation. Carlin approached canal treasurer McClernand and offered him the office of secretary of state, an offer McClernand could not refuse. McClernand explained his acceptance of the offer this way: "I resigned my connection with the Canal to receive the appointment of Secretary of State.... The motive which impelled this sacrifice, was not one of hostility to the then incumbent, but a desire to test the great question of whether his tenure of office was *for life*— whether it was a *franchise* irresumable by the constituted authority — and to allow the Governor a Secretary of his own choice."[21] Although merely a test of the "life appointment" doctrine, Carlin's offer to McClernand was another indication of McClernand's growing influence in Illinois politics. The Whig-controlled state senate rejected the appointment by a vote of 22–18, holding that there was no vacancy to fill. The secretary of state controversy proved that McClernand was becoming an important man in state affairs.

In the spring of 1839 Governor Carlin again attempted to replace secretary of state Field with John A. McClernand. The governor's motive seemed to be to test the "life appointment" doctrine until he got a favorable outcome, and this time the controversy entered the court system. McClernand had a team of legal representation, among them Stephen A. Douglas, which demonstrated a strong political alliance between the two men.[22] One of the attorneys opposing McClernand and the governor was Abraham Lincoln. The case first went to the Fayette County court, which affirmed Governor Carlin's right to replace the secretary of state. Field appealed the decision to the state supreme court, but before this court made its decision Field moved his office, including all official files, to Springfield, the new capital. McClernand immediately filed a writ of replevin in the circuit court of Sangamon County and posted a $10,000 bond with Garrett Elkin, the Sangamon County sheriff, to recover the files of the secretary of state. These papers, including the state seal, had been stored with the mercantile trading company of Robert Irwin & Co. for safekeeping.[23] Abraham Lincoln, counsel for Robert Irwin & Co., succeeded in getting the writ of replevin quashed. All that remained was the decision of the Illinois Supreme Court, and it was simply a question of party politics. After several days of argument the court voted 2–1 (one justice did not vote because he was a distant relative of McClernand) to strike down the action of Governor Carlin and uphold Secretary Field. This was a bitter defeat for the Democrats, and the party started a movement to reform the state judiciary.[24]

With the controversy over, McClernand turned his attention to the upcoming 1840 elections, in which he played a large role. At the state Democratic convention in December 1839, McClernand was chosen to be an elector at the 1840 Democratic National Convention.[25] The Gallatin County Democratic Party nominated McClernand for the state legislature, which gave him an added incentive to actively campaign.

Most Democrats, including McClernand, took to the stump to support Martin Van Buren's effort to retain the White House. McClernand was a strong campaigner, having already gained a reputation as a fine speaker, and was sometimes called the "Grecian Orator." The Democrats' difficulty in the West lay in Van Buren's image as a big business easterner and how to identify him with the West. Also, the Panic of 1837 was an event from which the Democrats had to disassociate themselves. It was a formidable task, but one McClernand took up with enthusiasm. He spoke all over southern Illinois on Van Buren's behalf, often debating Whig politicians, and in August and September 1840 he took on the Whig's effective campaigner Abraham Lincoln. An Illinoisan himself, Lincoln was trying to win the state for the Whig candidate, William Henry Harrison. McClernand and Lincoln traveled all over southern Illinois and debated the campaign issues. The newspapers for both parties claimed victory, but it was difficult to determine a winner in these debates.[26] If one decided a winner based solely on the outcome of the election there was a split decision — Lincoln's man won the White House, while

McClernand's candidate won the state's electoral votes. Nevertheless, they debated the issues throughout the campaign, and a political association was forming between these two political opponents that lasted until Lincoln's death in 1865. McClernand's own election bid was rather easy. The Whigs put up only token opposition, printing some handbills for distribution. In the end McClernand was returned to the Illinois general assembly.[27]

When the 1840–1841 session of the general assembly opened, McClernand was named chairman of the Committee on Canals and Canal Lands. In this committee assignment McClernand was again reacquainted with Abraham Lincoln, who was named a member of the same committee.[28] The Democrats made a determined effort to reform the judiciary system in this session and had several motives for this action. First, the Democrats claimed the Illinois supreme court delayed or prevented the distribution of spoils from the previous legislative session. Second, the party believed the Court had "played politics" with a decision in a case dealing with the voting rights of aliens — the "Galena aliens" case. McClernand had a more personal reason for reforming the Supreme Court — he wanted reform as revenge for the secretary of state case in 1839 — and he became a leader in this movement.

The first act in this supreme court drama was the beginning of the "Galena aliens" case. Under consideration was the question of whether aliens could vote, and the focus of the case was in Galena, where about 10,000 aliens lived. Since most of these 10,000 would vote Democratic, that party believed the aliens could vote. The Whigs, on the other hand, contended that only citizens had the right to vote. The state constitution gave the right to vote to all white male inhabitants over the age of 21 who had resided in the state for six months. In June 1840 the court delayed a decision until after the fall elections, seemingly a political move since three of the four justices were Whigs. Delaying a decision until after the election served two purposes: (1) It prevented the aliens from voting in the election; and (2) It eliminated the possibility of the decision being an issue in the election. After the election the Democratic leaders in the general assembly proposed a bill to reform the supreme court. The justices then made a narrow decision in the case that affected only the aliens in the Galena area, avoiding a broad decision. This was apparently an attempt to halt the impending reform bill.[29]

John McClernand was a leader in getting this reform bill passed. He charged the supreme court with collusion in an attempt to stop the bill. On January 26, 1841, McClernand made a speech in the general assembly in which he suggested that the justices had already made a decision in the "Galena aliens" case but changed their decision after the judiciary reform bill was proposed. In the speech he also proposed a wide range of reform in the operations of the Illinois supreme court.[30] All the justices denied the collusion charge and one,

Justice Theophilus W. Smith, the only Democrat on the supreme court, became so angry over the ordeal that he challenged McClernand to a duel. The challenge was accepted and McClernand, the challenged party, had the choice of weapons, location, and other particulars. He chose rifles at forty paces and stipulated that the duel was to be fought in Missouri. Illinois attorney general Josiah Lamborn heard about the affair, and placed Smith under a peace bond. The duel was off.[31] The reform bill passed in February 1841, and it added five new justices to the Illinois supreme court. All of the new justices were Democrats, and among the new appointees were Stephen A. Douglas and Walter B. Scates, who later served on McClernand's staff during the Civil War.[32]

After handily winning reelection in August 1842 against only nominal opposition, McClernand was named chairman of the Committee on Finance and appointed a member of the Committee on Banks and Corporations when the general assembly reconvened.[33] The issue of banking in Illinois dominated this legislative session, and McClernand was right in the middle of this often acrimonious, bitter debate. The new governor, Thomas Ford, wrote a banking bill that he believed would solve Illinois' financial woes and showed the bill to McClernand since McClernand chaired the Finance Committee. McClernand called a meeting of the Democratic members of the committee along with Judge Douglas, James Shields, an influential Illinois Democrat, and the governor. The Whig members of the committee were not invited to this meeting. All parties at the meeting agreed that Ford's bill was good and that it should be introduced as a Democratic measure. As the bill came out of the Finance Committee McClernand was its primary sponsor.

The principal opponent of the banking bill was secretary of state Lyman Trumbull. While he may have had reservations about the bill, Trumbull disliked McClernand and this legislation gave him a chance to lash out against the Finance Committee chairman. Among other things, Trumbull labeled McClernand a "milk and water democrat," which was an attack on his allegiance to the Democratic party and its principles.[34] McClernand answered Trumbull's accusations and got the better of the secretary of state. Governor Ford wrote this about McClernand and his speech: "McClernand, who possessed a kind of bold and denunciatory eloquence, came down upon Trumbull and his confederates in a speech in the House; which for argument, eloquence, and statesmanship, was far superior to Trumbull's. This speech silenced all opposition thereafter to the bill."[35]

This feud between McClernand and Trumbull originated with the judiciary reform in 1841. When Stephen A. Douglas was appointed one of the new supreme court justices, he vacated the secretary of state's office. When an opening such as this occurred it traditionally fell to the state legislature to nominate one or more candidates for the post. Since the governor did not want to antagonize the legislature, especially on the eve of a session, he usually appointed the person the general assembly nominated. However, Douglas vacated his office at the end of a session. Since Governor Carlin had nothing to fear from the legislature, he ignored its recommendation, which was to appoint either McClernand or James Shields, and named Trumbull to the post. McClernand and Shields then attempted to have Trumbull's appointment blocked by the senate, but failed. This was the gist of the McClernand-Trumbull quarrel, and it played itself out in the middle of the debate on the banking bill.[36]

In December 1842 Illinois had a U.S. Senate seat to fill as Senator Richard M. Young's term had expired. With a strong Democratic majority in the general assembly — the result of the 1842 elections — the choice would obviously be a Democrat, but who would it be? The Democratic caucus narrowed the field to three candidates: Stephen A. Douglas, Illinois supreme court justice Sidney Breese, and John A. McClernand. The caucus nominated the candidate to the general assembly, and that body formalized the decision. Early on it became apparent that McClernand was eliminated from serious consideration, and the real choice was between Douglas and Breese. Finally, after nineteen ballots on December 16, 1842, the caucus nominated Breese over Douglas 56–51, with McClernand receiving three votes to the end. Even though he did not win the nomination, the fact that he was considered spoke volumes about McClernand's position in Illinois politics: only six years in the political arena and he was accorded great respect by his colleagues in the party.[37]

It was indisputable that in the early 1840s the Democratic party was the dominant political organization in Illinois. It controlled the governor's office, the general assembly, and federal appointments from Washington, D.C. Even though the Whigs won the national election in 1840, Illinois was comfortably in the Democratic fold. This choke hold only got stronger as the years passed. Contributing to the Democrats' power was a decline in the opposition party — the Whigs, who held virtually no power in Illinois.[38] In February 1845 Whig legislator David Davis wrote, "I have hardly the faintest hope of this State ever being Whig." By the end of the year Davis decided that "there is precious little use for any Whig in Illinois to be wasting his time and efforts. The state cannot be redeemed. I should as leave think of seeing one rise from the dead."[39] Even when the Whigs elected Zachary Taylor to the presidency in 1848 Illinois' nine electoral votes went to the Democratic candidate, Lewis Cass. A Whig was never elected governor in the Prairie State; the Democrats held a monopoly on that office until the first Republican governor was elected in 1856. It was undeniable that the Democratic party held the upper hand in Illinois politics.[40]

The Democrats' control over Illinois politics got even stronger as a result of the 1840 federal census. Illinois received four additional seats in the U.S. House of Representatives, increasing its delegation from three to seven. In 1843, congressional districts in the state were redrawn, and as a result the Whigs could count on winning only one of the seven House seats (the district that represented central Illinois). The remaining six House seats and the two Senate seats would be won by Democrats in the 1843 elections. The Democratic nominee for the Second Congressional District (the Southern District) was Gallatin County's John A. McClernand.

The Second District was made up of the southernmost fourteen counties in the state, one of which was Gallatin.[41] County Democratic conventions were held in April 1843, and the overwhelming choice was John A. McClernand. The convention in Hamilton County, in fact, announced that "His election may be considered certain."[42] At the district convention in May, McClernand received the official nomination from the Democratic Party. His opponent was a former Methodist minister, Zadoc Casey, who ran as an independent. Casey had been elected lieutenant governor of Illinois in 1830 and had served in Congress from 1833 to 1843. He did not have a party affiliation and was described as "the democrat, the whig, the conservative, the all-things-to-all-men."[43] The campaign was spirited and the two men shared the platform on many occasions. The *Illinois State Register* recorded one of these campaign stops in Albion, Illinois, on June 30, 1843: "McClernand according to his custom, led off in a speech of about an hour and a half. He leaped into the arena with characteristick [sic] boldness. Those who were opposed to him were struck with admiration at his manly and fearless manner ... Zadock! poor Zadock! He suffered tortures under the edged weapons that were employed against him."[44] The Democratic party was simply too strong and McClernand too fine a speaker for an opponent without the support of a party. McClernand won handily on election day, August 7, 1843: the final vote was 6,364 to 3,629.[45] McClernand's years of hard work at the state level had paid off. He was going to Washington!

McClernand was an ambitious man and this was evident early in his political career. His first election to the Illinois house was satisfying, and once he arrived in the capital he wanted more power and influence. This was apparent in the secretary of state controversy. After being rebuffed by the Illinois senate the first time, McClernand was willing to take another chance, even pursuing the matter as far as the Illinois supreme court. His first participation in national politics, when he was a Van Buren elector in 1840, must have whetted his appetite for bigger and better things. McClernand was certainly honored that he was one of three candidates for a U.S. Senate seat in 1842. It was also undeniable that he wanted the appointment badly, and he was sorely disappointed when he did not receive it. He was positively overjoyed when he was nominated for a U.S. House seat the next year. John A. McClernand was indeed an ambitious man, and he longed for power, influence, and notoriety. With hard work and shrewd politicking, those were available in Washington.

McClernand's successful bid for Congress in 1843 ended the prologue period of his political career. His years in the Illinois general assembly were a learning time, and McClernand learned his lessons well. He left for Washington as one of the most powerful Democrats in the state. McClernand, along with Douglas and the other Democratic congressmen, controlled Illinois politics. They supervised federal patronage, governed the Democratic party in the state, and directed the election of Stephen A. Douglas to the U.S. Senate.[46] While McClernand was an influential politician in his own right, he made many powerful acquaintances and allies, most importantly Abraham Lincoln and Stephen A. Douglas. Lincoln especially, at the outset of the Civil War, did not forget his Democratic associate from the Illinois general assembly.

2

Congressman from Illinois

In 1843 Washington, D.C., was a dichotomy — it contained elements of both big city and small town. As the nation's capital it sometimes resembled a bustling metropolis, but only when Congress was in session. At other times it took on characteristics of a small southern town. Historian Allan Nevins called it a "fourth-rate town," while Robert Johannsen wrote that it "lacked the proper earmarks of a national capital."[1] True it was dirty, crude, and incomplete, with both the Capitol and Washington Monument unfinished (as they remained until the Civil War). It appeared to be several small villages connected by dusty, dirty streets. During the oppressive summer heat and humidity Washington became a virtual ghost town as congressmen, diplomats, and bureaucrats fled to cooler climes. However, when Congress convened every December Washington again became the focus of attention. As the heat abated people converged on the capital as boardinghouses filled to capacity and the city bustled once again.

European visitors to Washington gave conflicting descriptions of the capital. Frances Trollope, who visited in 1830, characterized the city as "light, cheerful, and airy." Charles Dickens was not so kind after visiting in 1842: "Spacious avenues that begin in nothing, and lead nowhere; streets, miles long, that need but a public to be complete; and ornaments of great thoroughfares, which only lack great thoroughfares to ornament ... make it scorching hot in the morning, and freezing cold in the afternoon, with an occasional tornado of wind and dust ... and that's Washington." Alexis de Tocqueville visited America in 1831 and was, like Dickens, unimpressed with Washington. He wrote: "The Americans have traced out the circuit of an immense city on the site which they intend to make their capital.... They have already rooted up trees for ten miles around lest they should interfere with the future citizens of this imaginary metropolis. They have erected a magnificent palace for Congress in the center of the city and have given it the pompous name of the Capitol."[2]

Without a doubt Washington was more exciting every December when Congress convened. Streaming into the city were congressmen and their families (if they chose to bring them), diplomats, lobbyists, and newspaper reporters. Boardinghouses filled up, merchants stocked their stores with all sorts of wares, and the capital once again became a busy city. The center of all the hustle and bustle was Congress.

The Senate lent dignity to the confusion and craziness of lawmaking. It was small enough to allow for quiet civilized deliberations, and the galleries were usually filled with visitors trying to get a glimpse of some of America's great orators. In 1843 when the Twenty-eighth Congress opened there were 51 U.S. senators representing the 26 American states (there was a vacancy in the Maryland delegation). Some of the more distinguished members of this body included James Buchanan of Pennsylvania, a future president, Robert Walker of Mississippi, soon to be treasury secretary for President Polk, Thomas Hart Benton of Missouri; and John J. Crittenden of Kentucky. None of the "Great Triumvirate" of John C. Calhoun, Henry Clay, and Daniel Webster was in the Senate in 1843.

The House of Representatives was larger than the Senate and the debate there tended to be more boisterous. The House met in a beautiful semicircular hall that impressed even Charles Dickens, who described it as an "elegant chamber," and as "a beautiful and spacious hall of semicircular shape, supported by handsome pillars."[3] Each member had a writing desk and chair on the floor, and there was a raised, canopied chair at the front for the Speaker. The gallery seated approximately 1,000 and the acoustics were not good. Deliberations in this lower chamber were not as dignified as in the Senate, as the noise and applause from the gallery occasionally played a role in debate. There were 221 representatives in the Twenty-eighth Congress (8 of these seats were vacant, however), which convened on Monday, December 4, 1843. Members included a former president — John Quincy Adams; a future president — Andrew Johnson; Hannibal Hamlin, vice president for Abraham Lincoln; Hamilton Fish, who served President Grant as secretary of state; and the "Little Giant," Stephen A. Douglas of Illinois.

While various groups of representatives were busy strategizing, others might be lounging on the sofas, reading, talking, or passing time until the next vote. When an important discussion began, lawmakers halted their extraneous gabbing and listened intently. When a boring speaker arose, the sofas filled up, newspapers suddenly appeared, and the buzzing began.

Congressmen's duties sometimes were not as glamorous as the legislators might have expected. Early into the session most new representatives developed a routine that probably resembled the schedule of most House members. They ate breakfast early in the morning then set off on a variety of tasks that included reading newspapers, writing letters to family and constituents, visiting government departments, and attending committee meetings. The House convened at noon and adjourned most days between four and eight in the evening, although some sessions lasted until midnight and beyond. The evenings were devoted to informal caucuses among representatives, writing letters, or sampling Washington's social life. This schedule left much to be desired, as meals were often taken on the run and there was little private time. Many new lawmakers quickly learned that a congressman's life was sometimes sheer drudgery.[4]

John A. McClernand joined this group of lawmakers in December 1843, but before traveling to Washington the new congressman got married. Sarah Dunlap, his bride, was the daughter of Colonel James Dunlap, a respected and powerful Jacksonville businessman. As a state assemblyman McClernand had probably dealt with Dunlap in 1837 when the state opened a branch of the Bank of Illinois in Dunlap's hometown. This was likely how John first met Sarah. Later in the 1840s Sarah Dunlap moved to Springfield, undoubtedly to sample the social scene at the state's capital, where she was often in the company of not only John McClernand, but also Stephen A. Douglas.[5] A wedding in Jacksonville in early November 1843 united John McClernand and Sarah Dunlap. This marriage, which produced three children, lasted until Sarah died of consumption (tuberculosis) in May 1861.[6]

As McClernand and his new bride prepared to travel to Washington, the congressman was described as "a young looking man, in the prime of life, of genteel appearance — fine size, six feet in height; with an elastic figure of the finest western mould. He has a thin keen, Cassius face and a Grecian chin, with pleasing regular features, of the noblest cast. His forehead is deep, firm, and polished, with a high set, calm, brow, beautifully arched — a small fine head — dark hair, and a fair complexion. But his fine full eye, it is, that depicts the man, and forms the leading point in his countenance. His eye is a deep, liquid blue, almost black; and emits one stream of happiness and philanthropy."[7]

Sarah McClernand was described as being "very young, quite a girl, about common height, of the DeMedicis size, and form, and has much ease and elegance in her walk and gestures. Her face is exceedingly fair, round, and full, and richly shaded with the rose, while her neck and forehead, are fair as an alabaster. Her eye is a light blue, rich, and dazzling, over-shaded by a light floating brow of inimitable beauty, while her forehead, sweet and innocent, is large and polished.— Her hair is fair and shining ... so modest, so meek, and so chaste it defies description."[8]

The first session of the Twenty-eighth Congress opened on Monday,

December 4, 1843, and the House of Representatives was called to order "precisely at twelve o'clock." McClernand was one of seven Illinois U.S. House members, six of whom were Democrats. Those six were McClernand (2nd District), Douglas (5th District), Robert Smith (1st District), Orlando B. Ficklin (3rd District), Chicago's John Wentworth (4th District), and Joseph Hoge (6th District). The lone Whig was John J. Hardin, who represented the 7th District. This Democratic majority in the Illinois delegation was representative of the House as a whole. Of the 221 House seats, 144 were occupied by Democrats, 68 by Whigs, 1 by a "Tyler man" (Virginia's Henry A. Wise) and eight seats were vacant. Three of the Democrats represented Wisconsin, Florida, and Iowa, states not yet admitted into the Union.[9]

After being sworn in as a member of the House on December 4, McClernand's first official act was to vote for a Speaker. A day earlier Democratic members of the House met in caucus to decide their choice, and as they held almost a two-thirds majority whoever they chose would win the speakership. McClernand, along with the entire Illinois delegation, agreed at the caucus to support Virginia's John W. Jones. When the official vote was taken on December 4, McClernand cast his ballot for Jones, as did the other five Illinois Democrats. Jones won the Speaker's chair with 128 votes, while Kentucky's John White, the Whig candidate, was a distant second with 59.[10]

With the Speaker's post decided the Democrats worked on organizing the House, which meant making appointments to standing committees. When assignments were announced on December 12, McClernand learned that he was a member of the Committee on Public Lands. This was his only committee assignment and he remained on it throughout both sessions of the Twenty-eighth Congress. His work on this committee was recognized, and when the House was organized for the Twenty-ninth Congress McClernand was rewarded with the committee chairmanship.

In 1843 sectional tensions were not as grave as they became in the 1850s, but the House of Representatives was beginning to show the strains of sectionalism. The lower chamber was starting to divide into two camps — southerners huddling to plot legislative strategy against northerners and vice versa. McClernand later wrote that he recognized the impending sectional crisis as early as 1843 and that he did all he could to stave off civil war. In 1865 he wrote about these observations: "In 1843, when I first took a seat in Congress, I became convinced that the agitation of the slavery question would engender civil war, but my convictions of public duty led me to do all in my power, throughout a period of near ten years Congressional service, to stay the impending catastrophe as long as possible."[11] Whether he actually foresaw the "impending catastrophe" as early as 1843 is impossible to verify; however, much of congressional debate after 1843 had a sectional slant.

By 1843 the Second Party System of Democrats and Whigs had been operational for about fifteen years. Since its inception, national crises had been effectively handled within the framework of this political system without resorting to military conflict. The system continued to work for another ten years, containing the growing sectional conflict. A realignment of voters occurred between 1853 and 1856 that swept away the Second Party System. Once the mechanism for containing the sectional conflict disappeared, political debates became more sectional issues than party issues. A new two-party system was created that was based upon sectional competition between the northern Republican party and southerners in the Democratic party. Because this new system was based upon a sectional alignment it could not contain the sectional conflict, and a few years later civil war broke out.[12]

The 1844 presidential election was less that a year away when the Twenty-eighth Congress convened in December 1843, and a great deal of time was used jockeying for position for November 1844. As a result, work in this session was frustratingly slow, and much Congressional debate, House and Senate, was spent discussing the best possible combination(s). Because of the impending election, little work was accomplished in this stormy session. It frustrated McClernand, who, like most new congressmen, was eager to accomplish great things for his state and himself. Amid the electioneering and general confusion in the House McClernand did not get to speak on the floor for over a month. Part of this delay was undoubtedly his status as a freshman; newcomers were often overlooked in favor of more senior representatives.

McClernand delivered his maiden speech in Congress on Saturday, January 7, 1844. Just as his first major action in the Illinois state assembly was a defense of President Andrew Jackson, his first congressional speech was also in this vein. In 1815 General Andrew Jackson was fined $1,000 by a Louisiana judge for contempt of court, a case that grew out of Jackson's declaring martial law during the British invasion that ended with the Battle of New Orleans. The bill under consideration in this session of the Twenty-eighth Congress, introduced by Pennsylvania's Charles J. Ingersoll, provided for refunding the amount of the fine plus interest. This legislation was considered during the prior Congressional session, but Whig majorities prevented its passage. Reconsidering the bill allowed Democrats the opportunity not only to pay homage to Jackson, but also to do some Whig-bashing on the eve of the election. McClernand was willing to perform both tasks.

He got the floor late in the day on January 7 "amidst much confusion" and calls for adjournment. McClernand wished to speak and promised not to take long. He unconditionally defended General Jackson's actions in 1815:

"I ask whether it is better that martial law should prevail, or the law of British bayonets? ... There was martial law at New Orleans, and the city was successfully defended, and the honor of the country nobly vindicated." Continuing, McClernand announced that the American people overwhelmingly supported the General's declaration. In fact, a majority of state legislatures instructed their Representatives to vote in favor of this bill (McClernand, as a member of his state's assembly, voted to instruct the Illinois delegation to support the measure). McClernand also suggested that it was treasonous for him to vote not to refund: "...[I]f I did not vote for it, I would consider myself as an abettor of treason — if not by commission, at least by omission."[13]

McClernand simultaneously supported Jackson and denounced the Whigs as traitors, particularly Daniel D. Barnard of New York, who opposed the bill. Although singling out Barnard, McClernand fired a series of verbal salvos at the Whig party in general. Besides accusing his opponents of treason, he charged the Whigs with election fraud in Martin Van Buren's defeat in 1840: "A conspiracy leveled at the ark of our political safety — the ballot box — is the explanation of the defeat of the Democratic candidate for the presidency in 1840." Anticipating that the Whigs would run Henry Clay in 1844, McClernand took some shots at the Kentuckian: "Has Mr. Clay been beaten so often and so long — has Mr. Clay and defeat become so hackneyed an identity, that the circumstances has lost all its novelty, and has failed to attract attention?" The freshman from Illinois was more than willing to sling some mud in the face of the expected Whig candidate, even if it was the venerable Henry Clay.[14]

McClernand ended his first set speech in the House by suggesting this refund question would be an issue in the 1844 election: " Whether shall we vindicate the war-worn veteran from an act of injustice, or whether shall we turn a deaf ear to the voice of the country, and let him go down to the grave wronged and injured in his good name? The Democracy have taken their position; Those who are opposed to them have taken theirs also; and let the country judge between us." With that parting shot McClernand finished his address. Besides defending the general, he sounded the traditional theme of Jacksonian Democracy by declaring that the American people supported the refund. He also did some early campaigning for the upcoming election by denouncing the Whigs and their expected candidate, Henry Clay. With floor time so scarce for a freshman, McClernand made the most of his hour. The refund bill passed the House the next day, January 8, ironically, and perhaps deliberately so, on the anniversary of the Battle of New Orleans, with all Illinois representatives voting aye. Despite a Whig majority in the Senate, the measure passed that body with unexpected ease.[15]

A new congressman's first speech must be distributed for his constituent's consumption, and McClernand did just that. He mailed copies of the speech to Illinois, and the state's major Democratic newspaper in the capital published it.[16] McClernand distributed his speech so widely that the *Quincy Whig* complained, but the Democratic *State Register* came to his defense: "The *Quincy Whig* is loud in its lamentations over the number of speeches sent by Messrs. Douglass and McClernand through the mails. This is as it should be; it is the best evidence that the speeches are having a good effect among the people, and winning for their authors golden opinions among their constituents."[17] The state newspapers were not the only ones to congratulate McClernand on his speech. The Washington correspondent for the *New Hampshire Argus* described his address as "pointed and eloquent," and summarized the speech in this manner: "The arguments of Mr. McClernand were to the point, and his language always eloquent sometimes beautiful, and altogether his speech was highly creditable to its author."[18] In addition to mailing copies of speeches to constituents, McClernand wrote letters to local newspapers describing his activities. One such letter appeared in the *Illinois State Gazette*, a Shawneetown newspaper. In this letter McClernand informed the voters in his district that he "spared no exertions" to have a federal armory placed at Massac.[19]

One topic that was especially important to the Illinois delegation was internal improvements, and the House was considering a bill to fund improvements on various western water systems. McClernand was particularly interested in this measure, as he was heavily involved with internal improvements as a state assemblyman. Additionally, the years he had spent as a trader on the Ohio and Mississippi rivers in the 1830s gave him unique insight on the subject. The act provided for $100,000 to improve the upper Ohio River system (from Pittsburgh to Louisville), while the lower Ohio system (the Mississippi, Missouri, and Arkansas rivers) was to receive $180,000. This came to $20,000 per one hundred miles for the upper Ohio and $2,500 for the same distance along the lower Ohio. McClernand objected to this unfair appropriation of money, and the bill passed the House over his objection. This bill seriously split the Illinois delegation. Four members voted for the measure (Douglas, Hardin, Hoge, and Wentworth), while the other three (McClernand, Ficklin, and Smith) voted against it.[20]

As the first session of the Twenty-eighth Congress drew to a close speeches centered on the upcoming 1844 elections. McClernand joined in the campaigning when he took the floor on June 4, 1844, ostensibly to speak on the appropriations bill before the House. He did not address the bill, noting that representatives before him set the precedent, and started in on the campaign speech. Both parties had already nominated their candidates when he took the floor, the Whigs naming Henry Clay and the Democrats running James K. Polk.

The Illinois freshman had attempted to get the floor for two days before the chair finally recognized him. After haranguing the House for several minutes on his inability to get the floor, McClernand then defended Martin Van Buren's record even though the New Yorker was not a candidate. McClernand's devotion to Van Buren was a result of his dedication to President Andrew Jackson. McClernand then briefly spoke on the Democratic nominee, but spent most of his hour assailing Henry Clay's record. The gist of the speech was that the Whig candidate waffled on the issues, specifically Texas and Oregon. McClernand summarized his views on the Kentuckian Clay with these words: "These are the few of the many political eccentricities and erratic wandering of Mr. Clay. On the score of inconsistency, there is no prominent politician in the country more vulnerable.... He has veered and vacillated to every point of the political compass, according to the impulses of hate and ambition."[21]

Thus ended the Illinoisan's first session as a United States representative. While he did nothing extraordinary, McClernand left a solid record of loyalty to the Democratic party and his constituents. He took this record home with him and began to campaign for the August and November elections. Not only did McClernand campaign for Polk, but for his own reelection. His nomination in the 2nd district had been secured at the Democratic congressional convention held in Shawneetown on May 6, 1844.[22] McClernand's hometown Democratic newspaper, the *Illinois State Gazette*, placed his reelection on its masthead and during the campaign printed his June 4, 1844, address.[23] The incumbent faced two challengers in this election, Rowland H. Bell and James Danah, both without a party affiliation. McClernand's victory in the August 5 election was completely one-sided. Out of 8,047 votes cast, McClernand collected 7,968 — over 99 percent of the votes.[24] All six of the Illinois Democratic Representatives were returned to the House. The only change in the Illinois delegation was in the 7th district, where Whig John J. Hardin lost his seat to Edward D. Baker, another Whig.

In the presidential race the Democrats ran on a program of continued American expansion. Specifically, the platform called for the annexation of Texas and the reoccupation of Oregon. By making Texas and Oregon twin issues the Democrats avoided the slavery issue; the possession of both as states would bring both free and slave territory into the Union. Expansion was presented as a national, not sectional, issue. The candidate was in complete accord with the platform — Polk supported American expansion to the Pacific Ocean. Concerning Oregon Polk campaigned on the premise that the boundary would be settled at 54°40' latitude and regarding Texas he supported immediate annexation and admission as a state. Polk's victory at the polls seemed to be a mandate from the voters — they favored expansion.[25]

With his own reelection assured, McClernand did all he could to help Polk's campaign. Shortly after the nomination was made McClernand wrote an open letter to the *Illinois State Register*, the Democrat newspaper in Springfield. In this letter McClernand described Polk as "the leader through whom we are to rescue Oregon in its length and breadth, from the clutches of British spoilation, and to restore Texas to our Union."[26] The Illinoisan also stumped the state on behalf of the "Young Hickory." In early September he spoke in Jacksonville, located in Morgan County in central Illinois. By early October he had addressed crowds in his hometown of Shawneetown, then moved on to Marion, Jefferson, and Hamilton counties. In Shawneetown McClernand spoke to the Democratic crowd from the Kentucky Hotel, and his speech was characterized as "particularly felicitous in the withering sarcasms and scorching rebukes he uttered in relation to the inconsistencies of the Coon Idol — Henry Clay."[27]

Serious division along sectional lines was just beginning to rear its ugly head in the mid–1840s. One catalyst for this growing sectionalism was the question of slavery in the territories. In the 1844 election the Democrats suggested that expansion was a national rather than sectional issue. Together the Texas and Oregon questions garnered bipartisan support since many Americans favored possession of both, but there would be trouble if one was pursued and the other abandoned. In the interests of sectional harmony, all issues related to expansion had to be handled delicately.[28]

The first potentially dangerous issue to reach Congress was the annexation of Texas, which turned out to be an important party issue.[29] The questions of annexation and admission to the

John A. McClernand as a member of Congress in the 1840s (Abraham Lincoln Presidential Library and Museum).

Union were hot topics of debate and first reached Congress during the 1843–1844 session. The Senate debated a resolution in February 1844 that allowed for the admission of Texas, but did not act upon it. President-elect Polk ran on a platform that supported Texas annexation, and he planned to pursue this after his inauguration. Lame duck President John Tyler interpreted the 1844 election as a mandate and requested Congress to accomplish annexation by joint resolution before Polk took office. Congress acceded to the president's wishes. The Senate passed a joint resolution on February 27, 1845, and the House approved it the next day.[30]

John McClernand adamantly supported American expansion, as he made clear by backing Texas annexation, the extreme claims to Oregon, and the U.S.–Mexican War. He believed the annexation of Texas was an important question, as he informed his fellow representatives after congressional Whigs suggested that the Democrats used the Texas issue as a "political humbug" for the election. Rebutting charges by Illinois Whig John J. Hardin, McClernand stated that he considered Texas "a great question, vital to the welfare of this country and its republican institutions."[31]

Having laid the foundation that the Texas question was important and not merely an election issue, McClernand expounded on his views. "I am for extending the shield of the American Union over our kindred of Texas; they are bone of our bone, and flesh of our flesh," he proclaimed. To what extent would the Illinois representative support annexation? He favored war if necessary. War seemed to be the principal Whig obstacle to acquiring Texas; but that did not bother McClernand, and he addressed this Whig objection: "Among the most prominent [Whig objection], is the argument that the annexation would be to adopt the war between Texas and Mexico — at the most, a mere nominal and constructive war."[32] He concluded this portion of his June 1844 speech by suggesting that Congress not delay in acting on the Texas issue. Congress did, in fact, delay annexing Texas until its next session.

When Congress pursued annexing Texas during the second session of the 28th Congress, McClernand, like most Democrats, showed his support with his votes. The joint resolution annexing Texas passed the House on January 25, 1845, by a margin of 120 to 98, with McClernand and all other Illinois Democrats voting aye. The lone Illinois dissenter was Whig John J. Hardin. After the Senate considered, amended, and passed the resolution, the measure was back in the House for its concurrence in the Senate's amendments. The lower chamber received the amended joint resolution on February 28 and approved it the same day. Again McClernand and all Illinois Democrats voted in favor of the measure while Hardin disapproved. In an almost strictly party vote the resolution passed the House by a 132–76 margin.[33] Clearly Texas annexation was a party, not a sectional, issue, and served to polarize the parties. This also confirms that Texas annexation invigorated the party system rather than destroyed it.[34]

The annexation of Texas was a major step toward accomplishing the national agenda of manifest destiny. The next step was settling the Oregon boundary dispute with England. The debate was over the boundary between American and British territory, and most expansionists supported the extreme U.S. claims. England claimed all Oregon territory north of 49° latitude (the 49th parallel), while the U.S. asserted its ownership of all land south of the 54°40' line. As with Texas, expansionists were willing to go to war over Oregon.

The United States and England had negotiated several agreements concerning the Oregon country. Those most often cited in congressional debate dated from 1818 and 1827. The 1827 pact contained a provision for its abrogation stating that one year's notice was required if either country wished to nullify the treaty. Once the agreement was voided negotiations could begin on a new settlement. One important question concerned who possessed the authority to rescind treaties, the president, Senate, House, or some combination of these. McClernand believed this responsibility belonged to Congress, and his justification was the Constitution. Congress had the power to legislate, according to the Constitution; therefore, since abrogating a treaty fell under the scope of legislating, Congress was constitutionally empowered to repeal the 1827 treaty. McClernand considered this method less aristocratic and more democratic.[35]

McClernand was opposed to negotiating a settlement with England. He saw no reason to forfeit America's claim to 54°40', and he spoke forcefully on that position. McClernand was "utterly and inexorably opposed to the compromise of the 49th parallel." He also stated that "Oregon is ours, every inch ours, from 42 degrees to 54 degrees, 40 minutes, north latitude, inclusive."[36] As with Texas, McClernand was willing to risk war to get Oregon. He stated his position at the very beginning of the debate on Oregon: "If war should come out of this measure, let it come."[37]

The first order of business was to abrogate the 1827 treaty, a task Congress accomplished by joint resolution. McClernand supported the joint resolution on the presumption that negotiations with England would be based upon the 54°40' line. The resolution first passed the House on February 9, 1846, with McClernand's support. The wording of the resolution was such that the Illinoisan believed further agreements would be centered on the 54°40' line. The other six Illinois representatives believed likewise as the entire delegation, Democrats and Whigs, supported the resolution. However, they all reversed course when the measure came out of the Senate in April. There were only minor changes in the wording, but the words implied that President Polk was free to negotiate a settlement on any terms. In other words the Senate backed down. McClernand was especially incensed: "Sir, I am opposed to the report, because it is deceptive; because it, in effect, instructs the President to avert war by any sacrifices of territory or territorial right."[38] Many westerners in the House felt deserted. The entire Illinois delegation voted against the resolution, but it passed by a considerable margin anyway, 142–46. That President Polk and secretary of state James Buchanan would negotiate away Oregon was inevitable.

As expected, the agreement set the Oregon boundary at 49 degrees. The treaty was finalized in Washington, D.C., in June, accepted by England in July, and presented to Congress in August 1846. It was a bitter defeat for many western representatives. McClernand termed the settlement "irresponsible" and suggested that Oregon was "sacrificed." He compared Oregon to Texas and concluded: "Contraction on the North and West, expansion on the South, seems to be the order of the day." Another Illinois representative, John Wentworth, suggested that the South used the West to get Texas, then abandoned it on Oregon.[39] Many westerners, including the entire Illinois delegation, felt betrayed on the Oregon question.

The twin questions of Texas and Oregon and how they were settled began a rift in the Democratic party. Northern Democrats expected President Polk to support the Oregon claim as vigorously as he pushed for Texas. Disillusionment started when the Oregon issue was delayed so Texas could be settled. Again Oregon was postponed in January 1846 when American troops were sent into the disputed area between the Rio Grande and Nueces rivers in Texas. When war broke out in May 1846 northern Democrats supported it, expecting reciprocal support with Oregon. Disappointment was complete in June 1846 when the Oregon agreement was finalized in Washington. The Oregon settlement destroyed the bisectional basis for expansion and was the first open break between northern and southern Democrats.

3

The Sectional Conflict

Even as national politics raged over the Texas and Oregon issues John A. McClernand was mindful of his responsibilities to his constituents at home. He sent his January 30, 1845, speech to the Democratic Shawneetown newspaper, which promptly printed it for local consumption.[1] Shortly thereafter a rumor swirled around the state that McClernand would be a candidate for governor. In an open letter printed throughout Illinois he declined to run, explaining that he had "no disposition whatever to aspire to or occupy the station in question."[2] The station he wished to occupy was his own House seat from the Second Congressional District of Illinois, and in August 1846 he was overwhelmingly reelected. McClernand's popularity and power were such that the district did not even hold a convention to consider candidates and he had no formal opposition in the August election.[3] The incumbent received 7,151 votes (a scattering of opposition received 204), or 97 percent of the votes cast — overwhelming support from his constituents.[4]

With this mandate McClernand continued to represent his district in the business of running the nation. In the debate over Texas annexation he was one of many who supported the measure even if it meant war. He also supported going to war over Oregon. America could not fight two wars at the same time — one against Mexico (over Texas) and one with England (over Oregon), so the administration had to decide which potential war to pursue and which to settle. A war against Mexico seemed winnable, while fighting England carried a greater risk of defeat. Given this choice it seemed prudent to negotiate a settlement with England and risk war with Mexico, especially since that country had severed diplomatic relations with America in March 1845. And so it was done. Even as the Oregon question was settled war broke out in Texas.

The American claim in Texas stretched to the Rio Grande River, while Mexico claimed the boundary was the Nueces River. In January 1846 President Polk sent United States troops under General Zachary Taylor to occupy a position along the Rio Grande, which he considered American territory. Since this was in the disputed area the American presence would almost certainly provoke a response from Mexico. Many people who opposed war accused Polk of baiting Mexico into inciting war, while expansionists ignored the possible provocation. Those who supported war believed these American troops occupied American soil. As expected Mexican troops clashed with General Taylor's men on April 25, 1846, and President Polk could therefore take the high ground — America was invaded and American blood was shed on American soil. He could get his declaration of war.

President Polk sent his war message to Congress on May 11, 1846, and requested that the House and Senate declare war. The House approved a declaration of war on May 11 by the lopsided vote of 174–14. McClernand, along with the entire Illinois delegation, voted in favor of the declaration. The Senate passed a similar measure the next day and Polk had his declaration of war. A short time later Congress passed a supplemental war bill that allowed the president more resources to prosecute the war. This was approved overwhelmingly by the House on June 4, 1846, with McClernand again backing the war effort. The Illinoisan, in the debate over Texas annexation, stated that he supported war to gain the territory in dispute, and his voting record proved he was as good as his word.[5]

In his remarks and addresses in Congress McClernand's record was consistent — he supported the war and its vigorous prosecution. In a speech barely a month after war was declared he stated that, "the present war against Mexico should be prosecuted vigorously and effectually."[6] He also scolded Whigs who opposed the war, complaining that they had "uniformly opposed this war."[7] The U.S.-Mexican War, like Texas annexation, sharply divided the two parties, Democrats generally supporting and Whigs generally opposing the conflict. McClernand favored the war, as he made clear on numerous occasions, building an untarnished record of support for American expansion.

McClernand's speeches and addresses also indicate his complete support of the war and the soldiers fighting the war. In January 1847 he addressed the House on the issue of support for the soldiers, advocating increasing the soldiers' pay, and he came out in favor of granting land bounties to the soldiers when they arrived home after the war. This speech was published in local newspapers for his constituents.[8] At home McClernand also demonstrated his support for the war and the soldiers. In June 1847, at a ceremony for the return of some Illinois volunteers from the war, he spoke about the soldiers in glowing terms. In this address he explained his continued support of the war while in Congress: "As your representative in Congress, I have voted all the supplies demanded, to give success to our arms; perhaps, no one has labored more earnestly to secure the soldier a just compensation for his patriotic services than myself."[9]

The fruits America reaped from the U.S.-Mexican War — the acquisition of a large amount of territory — tore it apart and the most important issue was the status of slavery there. This problem was introduced into Congress less than three months after war was declared against Mexico. In August 1846 the House received a bill that provided for an appropriation of $2 million to defray the costs to further prosecute the war (called the Two Million Bill). David Wilmot, a Pennsylvania Democrat, wished to add an amendment to the bill. Commonly called the "Wilmot Proviso," the amendment excluded slavery from any territory gained as a result of the war. This amendment, eight lines added to an appropriations bill, was the center of the storm that became America's greatest sectional crisis to that time. The Wilmot Proviso became the centerpiece of American politics until secession.

There was virtually no middle ground when it came to the Wilmot Proviso. Most northerners supported it while southerners generally condemned it as abridging their Fifth Amendment rights to due process.[10] McClernand opposed the Wilmot Proviso and voted against the measure every time it appeared in the House. From August 1846 until February 1850 the Wilmot Proviso, or a bill or resolution similar to it, was discussed and voted on no less than eleven times. Each and every time, McClernand voted to table the bill or voted against it.[11]

What was McClernand's position on slavery in the territories? In 1847 he favored Congress legislating over slavery in the territories because, he believed, the power to acquire involved the power to govern. By 1848 McClernand advocated noninterference by Congress in the territories "for the reason that the people of a territory ought to be left to judge for themselves," as he explained. The Illinoisan wanted the country to "avoid ultra pro slaveryism on the one hand, and Wilmot Provisoism on the other."[12] He also believed that Congress had no constitutional power to interfere in states where slavery already existed.[13] McClernand later proclaimed that he was "as much opposed to the existence of slavery as any one," that he would "be glad to see slavery prohibited everywhere, with the consent of those interested in the institution."[14] These remarks indicate that by 1848 McClernand had come to be a proponent of the doctrine of popular sovereignty.

Popular sovereignty was a policy first espoused by Lewis Cass in 1847. Illinois representative and senator Stephen A. Douglas became the champion of popular sovereignty in the 1850s when he applied it to the organization of the Kansas and Nebraska territories. Popular sovereignty was the belief that the residents of a territory possessed the power to decide for themselves, by way of the ballot, the condition of their territory, i.e., whether it would be free or slave. It was a system that seemed more democratic, as the voters chose for themselves. One controversy surrounding this doctrine was at what time in the political evolution of a territory the residents acquired the right to regulate slavery. Was it during the territorial stage? Or was it after statehood was conferred?[15]

Lewis Cass hoped to ride his theory of popular sovereignty into the White House in 1848 and McClernand was willing to help him. His own reelection a certainty, the Illinois representative stumped the state on behalf of the Lewis Cass/William Butler ticket. On October 11, 1848, he spoke in Springfield at a political rally at the capitol. In this speech he ironically compared the Whigs' 1848 campaign to the one they ran in 1840, when they successfully elected William H. Harrison. McClernand criticized the Whigs so severely that a local newspaper called this address "the neatest coon-skinning performance we have witnessed this season."[16] A few weeks later McClernand ventured to Chicago and spoke there, but it was all for naught, however, as the Whigs captured the White House.

Having failed to secure the presidency for the party's candidate, McClernand hoped to elevate himself to the Senate. Sidney Breese's term expired and his seat had to be filled. There were three Democrats vying for the office — Sidney Breese, the incumbent; James Shields, the U.S.-Mexican War hero; and John A. McClernand. The Democratic caucus was held in January 1849 and the candidate chosen would be a lock when the general assembly made its choice. After two ballots the caucus chose James Shields, with McClernand third.[17] The general assembly made it official, formally electing James Shields as a U.S. Senator, but there were questions about Shields' residency in the state. These concerns prompted an investigation by the Senate, which determined that Shields was not eligible for the post and voided the election. The Illinois governor, Augustus French, chose not to appoint anyone to fill the vacancy, but rather to wait for a special session of the general assembly, which he scheduled for October 1849. This time the same three men stood as candidates, and this time the caucus took 21 ballots before settling again on James Shields. McClernand again ran third, but he collected much more support than in January.[18] By that time Shields had met the residency requirement, so he could legally take his seat. Although he failed to win the Senate position, McClernand still had good work to accomplish in Washington from his office in the House of Representatives.

When the Thirty-first Congress convened on December 3, 1849, its principal task was to address the slavery question in the territories, specifically California, Utah, and New Mexico. The chore of electing a speaker of the House indicated a contentious session. There was no clear-cut majority in the House, as Democrats occupied 112 seats, Whigs 105, and Free Soilers the remaining 13.[19] Since no party held a majority the election of a speaker hinged on the votes of the thirteen Free Soilers, and as a result, the House did not organize for three weeks. In those three weeks the House took 63 ballots before electing a speaker and even then no candidate had a majority of the votes. After its 63rd ballot the House passed a resolution to elect Howell Cobb by a plurality rather than a majority. The speakership battle indicated that the House would have trouble legislating with no clear majority.

In the Democratic caucus to nominate candidates for the speakership McClernand was nominated, but he "immediately declined" and asked that his name be withdrawn.[20] He supported Cobb for speaker although the Illinoisan himself received votes on 24 of the 63 ballots. As late as the 59th ballot McClernand received 50 votes and ran second in the race. However, he withdrew from the contest before the 60th ballot and continued to support Cobb. Perhaps because he backed Cobb, McClernand was named chairman of the House Committee on Foreign Affairs. This was an important committee assignment and illustrated the respect McClernand received from his colleagues. He had become a nationally important politician just as he had on the state level ten years earlier.[21]

By the time Congress convened, California had written a constitution and wished to be admitted as a state. Its constitution prohibited slavery and President Zachary Taylor recommended its immediate admission as a state, bypassing the territorial stage. Therein lay the basis of the sectional difficulties. The immediate admission of California as a free state would upset the delicate balance in the Senate between "free" and "slave" states. California would become the sixteenth free state, while the number of slave states remained at fifteen. This was unfair, claimed southerners, because the free majority could pass legislation that would hurt the minority South, particularly limits on slave expansion, not to mention possibly eliminating the institution itself. For that reason southerners generally opposed the immediate admission of California without some concession.

McClernand favored the admission of California as soon as possible in order to provide federal protection for Americans there. This he stated as early as February 1849. Although opposed to the Wilmot Proviso, he was willing to support a bill admitting California with it rather than continue debating the issue. The Illinois representative declared that he would "vote for any practicable measure proper to extend governments to our exposed brethren."[22] Although he preferred to settle the slavery in the territories issue once and for all, he was unwilling to delay admitting California in order to continue the endless debate.

The admission of California resulted in an executive-legislative stand-off. President Taylor was unwilling to negotiate on immediate admission, while southern congressmen were unwilling to admit California without some compensation in return. It was a crisis of the first order. Southerners called for a convention in Nashville in June 1850 to draft a unified southern response to congressional action on California. There was a real threat of secession if some compromise was not negotiated. Enter Henry Clay.

Kentucky senator Henry Clay saved the country from the brink of sectional conflict with compromise measures in the periods 1820–1821 and 1832–1833. It was time for him to save the nation once again. On January 29, 1850, Clay took the Senate floor and offered a set of resolutions upon which the California question could be settled.[23] His solution was debated in Congress for the next six months. The compromise measures were the subject of some of the finest oratory ever delivered in Congress: Clay's major address on the issue February 5–6, 1850; John C. Calhoun's address to the Senate on March 4, read to the chamber by James Mason as Calhoun was too sick to speak; Daniel Webster's famed "Seventh of March Speech"; and William H. Seward gave his "Higher Law" speech on March 11.[24]

The compromise debate was the last hurrah for Clay, Webster, and Calhoun, America's "Great Triumvirate." It was time for younger men to take control, and among those were Stephen A. Douglas and William H. Seward in the Senate and Speaker Howell Cobb, Alexander H. Stephens, Robert Toombs, and John A. McClernand in the House. One obstacle to progress on the compromise measures was the endless speechifying by both pro- and anti-compromise congressmen. In the midst of these speeches a bipartisan House conference was held on the evening of February 19, 1850, at the residence of Speaker Howell Cobb. The conference had been initiated the day before when McClernand, during House debate, went over to the Whig side and approached Stephens and Toombs about resolving the differences. These two southern Whigs stated their position, after which the conference was arranged for the evening of the nineteenth.[25]

Present at this conference were Georgia's Howell Cobb, Alexander H. Stephens, and Robert Toombs, Linn Boyd of Kentucky, McClernand and William A. Richardson of Illinois, and John K. Miller of Ohio. Stephens and Toombs were Whigs, while all the others were Democrats. McClernand informed the southerners that his colleague in the Senate, Stephen A. Douglas, was ready to cooperate with anything agreed to at the conference. Douglas did not attend because he was under the impression that the meeting was for House members only. Since Douglas and McClernand worked closely together, McClernand could speak for Douglas' position. The southerners stated their position: they would accept the immediate admission of California

as a free state, but only after the question of slavery in the territories was settled. They wanted no Congressional exclusion of slavery, but rather to allow
the voters of the territory to decide the question. To this McClernand agreed.
He also agreed to the proposition that slavery should not be abolished in
Washington, D.C. These agreements were put on paper and McClernand
promised to convey them to Douglas.[26]

As a result of the conference Douglas offered a set of compromise resolutions to the Senate on March 25. McClernand was to present the same proposal in the House, but could not get the floor until April 3. He offered a
plan to settle the sectional question, "which has for so long a time, and so
deeply and widely agitated, and divided the public mind." In essence the
plan, which McClernand stated was "not of my authorship," called for the
following: immediate admission of California as a free state; organization of
the Utah Territory; organization of the New Mexico Territory; and resolution of the Texas boundary dispute with New Mexico.[27] It was a common
compromise plan, similar to those of Clay and Douglas, and when he introduced them McClernand admitted the plan was not his. It was also not the
first compromise measure, although he later claimed it was.[28]

On the Senate side, that body debated Henry Clay's plan through July
1850. President Taylor's proposal was still in the mix. All compromise measures seemed to be hopelessly deadlocked with little chance of passage. Then
two unhappy yet fortunate (for the compromise) events occurred. The first
was the death of President Taylor on July 9, 1850. He died of gastroenteritis
(cholera morbus) from an overindulgence of ice water, milk, and cherries
during Independence Day ceremonies on July 4. Taylor's successor was Millard Fillmore, who was sympathetic to the compromise measures and would
aid in their passage. The second event was Henry Clay's illness. After working from January to July to get his compromise passed, Clay was physically
exhausted. Added to that was the defeat of his proposal in the Senate on July
31. Two days later, on August 2, 1850, seventy-three-year-old Henry Clay left
Washington for Newport to recover from exhaustion.

With those two obstacles out of the way, the compromise had a better
chance of passing through Congress. McClernand was one who grew weary
of the endless debate on the compromise measures. On August 29, 1850, he
scolded the House for not acting: "We have now been in session some nine
months, and the time for action has arrived, and shall we not act? For one,
sir, I am for a decision — a final decision of the several questions before us."[29]
By then the Senate had already passed five of the six compromise bills, and
they had been sent to the House. McClernand did not have to wait long for
the House to take action, as that body started voting on these bills during
the first week in September. From September 4 to September 17 the House

deliberated and voted on the compromise bills. All passed the lower chamber, with McClernand supporting every one, and awaited only President Fillmore's signature for final approval.[30]

The Compromise of 1850 was the last gasp of this congressional session and the whole country could breathe easier. It was time to celebrate and many believed that it was the duty of every patriot to get drunk. Many in Washington did. Senators and representatives went home tired, but knowing they had staved off disunion, at least temporarily. Although this was the most serious sectional confrontation yet, the compromise debate also indicated that party competition was still vibrant. An analysis of the roll calls on the compromise measures in the House and Senate suggests that Whigs and Democrats still opposed each other regardless of sectional identification. The most astute observer of party politics in the 1850s summarized the compromise and parties in this manner: "The dynamics of the Second American Party System are readily apparent in the party alignments that developed over the Compromise.... [M]ost Northern Whigs opposed the Compromise even after Taylor's death. Most Northern Democrats backed it. Most Southern Whigs favored the Compromise. Most Southern Democrats opposed it."[31] Even though there was an obvious sectional nature to the compromise, in the sections party conflict and competition remained vigorous.

McClernand's role in the compromise was significant. Although not outspoken, he played a prominent role in helping the two sides find common ground. When Douglas took control of the compromise measures in the Senate, McClernand became his spokesman in the House. As early as February he helped bring northern and southern representatives together; he and Douglas were two of the primary figures of the Compromise of 1850. During the compromise debates, McClernand was allegedly prepared to defend himself if the political conflict became physical. One historian reported that during the acrimonious compromise debates he was armed with two pistols and a bowie knife.[32] Did McClernand stand to benefit politically from his role in the compromise proceedings? Perhaps. Did he wish to ride the success of the compromise and his role in it to higher office? Perhaps. At least one constituent, A.G. Sloo, believed McClernand could ride his success to the vice presidency and ultimately the highest office in the land. Sloo outlined for McClernand his "recipe for making a President": "Mr. McClernand will offer a bill on his own responsibility to cede the entire public domain to the states and Territories in which it lies. Mr. King of Alabama or some other good Southern democrat by way of amendment will attach the Missouri Compromise line (extended to the Pacific), therefore Mr. King would be President in 1852. Mr. McClernand vice — with a certainty of the succession."[33] McClernand certainly had the ambition to attempt to fulfill the "recipe," but only the future would tell if he would succeed.

The compromise measures were McClernand's swan song in this stint in Congress. Although he still had the second session of the 31st Congress ahead of him, it was the short session and he had already decided against running for reelection. He had decided to go home to Illinois and make some money in land speculation, proposing to Charles Lanphier, editor of the Democrat *Illinois State Register*, that they "go to Cairo and make each a big fortune."[34]

The second session of the 31st Congress had none of the excitement of the first. As chair of the House Committee on Foreign Affairs, McClernand had a special interest in the workings of the State Department. His committee conducted an investigation of the Clayton-Bulwer Treaty of 1850 and McClernand corresponded with former secretary of state James Buchanan to get his views on the treaty.[35] In addition to this investigation, McClernand proposed a reorganization of the State Department. Although termed a "reorganization," the proposal merely added employees to the department — an assistant secretary of state and four clerks. As justification for the new clerks, McClernand pointed out that the War Department employed 332 clerks, the Department of the Interior 125, and the State Department only 14.[36] This was the only significant work he sponsored. Little if any important legislation came out of this session, and McClernand ended his congressional service on a quiet note.

John A. McClernand spent eight years in Congress (1843–1851). During those years Manifest Destiny was achieved, and McClernand fully supported it and built a reputation as a loyal party man. Though willing to negotiate on some issues, as the Compromise of 1850 illustrated, he was firm in his convictions. When the Polk administration negotiated the Oregon boundary McClernand opposed any settlement that strayed from the 54°40' line. He opposed the Wilmot Proviso from beginning to end and never compromised on that. He came around to support popular sovereignty, a doctrine that appeared almost Jacksonian. In that sense McClernand had come full circle. He started in the Illinois house in 1836 as a Jacksonian Democrat and left the U.S. House in 1851 with the same political philosophy.

McClernand returned home to Shawneetown, but he did not stay long. He had decided that his association with southern Illinois was hurting him politically — the power base in Illinois politics was not in the south. In 1852 he moved to Jacksonville, about 30 miles from Springfield, to be closer to the political power. Jacksonville was also the home of his wife's family.

McClernand occupied himself with his law practice, land speculation with his father-in-law, James Dunlap, public service, and keeping informed on state and national politics. His interest in land took him back to southern Illinois, specifically Cairo, through which the Illinois Central Railroad was supposed to pass. McClernand stood to make a considerable sum from his investments in land when the railroad came. In later years McClernand speculated in land in and around Springfield. By the end of the decade he had purchased over 250 acres in addition to many individual lots in Springfield and Sangamon County.[37] By 1858 McClernand also owned over 550 acres in Monroe County, and by 1862 over 1,568 acres in Pulaski County and over 550 acres in Massac County in southern Illinois.[38] Besides his land purchases McClernand was appointed director of the Institute for the Deaf and Dumb in 1853 for a four-year term.[39]

Despite not holding a political office for the first time in a decade, McClernand could not stay out of politics, state or national, and 1852 was an election year. After eight years in Congress McClernand was a recognized power in Illinois politics, a fact the Democratic party recognized at its state convention in April 1852 when he was named president. Although not a candidate for office himself, McClernand helped engineer the nomination of Joel A. Matteson for governor and Gustave Koerner for lieutenant governor.[40] On the national scene McClernand was named a delegate to the Democratic national convention, which nominated Franklin Pierce and William R. King.

McClernand campaigned vigorously for the Democratic ticket, a task made more significant when he was named a member of the electoral college for the state of Illinois. As an elector, McClernand campaigned in nearly every part of the state. A speech in Springfield on June 19, 1852, was described as a "soul-stirring effort" that was "exceedingly well received."[41] By August 16 he was in White County in southern Illinois, where he reportedly "skinned the varmints well — routed the enemy, horse, foot, and dragoon."[42] Two days later he addressed a Democratic crowd in nearby Wayne County. On December 1, 1852, the members of the electoral college met in Springfield to cast the state's electoral votes. McClernand was named president of that body, which proceeded to cast the state's votes for the Pierce/King ticket.[43] After Pierce's election there was a strong feeling that Illinois deserved a place in the cabinet, perhaps for one of the state's U.S. senators, Stephen A. Douglas or James Shields, but both declined any consideration. Because of his strong support for Pierce, McClernand might have expected some consideration; but when Pierce assembled his cabinet Illinois was left out.[44]

Pierce's administration brought much turmoil to the country and to America's political parties. The Democrats and Whigs experienced a transformation that ultimately divided one party and destroyed the other. Consensus, or the absence of party competition, was encouraging the disintegration of the party system.[45] Because there was little that distinguished the two parties, the differences between them became blurred. Stephen A. Douglas, U.S. senator from Illinois and longtime political ally of John A. McClernand, was at the flash point of party realignment that followed the period of consensus. In November 1853 Douglas wrote that the Democratic Party was in a "distracted condition & it requires all our wisdom, prudence, & energy to consolidate its power and perpetuate its principles."[46] Douglas recognized that something must be done to distinguish the Democratic party from the Whigs. In order to further his own program and reinvigorate the Democratic party, Douglas reported the Kansas-Nebraska Act out of his senate Committee on Territories in January 1854. He described the significance of this legislation: "The principle of this Bill will form the test of Parties."[47] This bill ultimately divided the Democrats, destroyed the Whigs, and helped create the new Republican party.

The Kansas-Nebraska Act provided for the organization of the Kansas and Nebraska territories and popular sovereignty would be applied to determine their status, free or slave. Douglas believed this legislation would unify the Democratic party and wanted the bill to be a test of party orthodoxy. Many Democrats instead broke from the party, some going over to the Whigs, some to the Free Soilers, while still more banded together to form the new Republican party. McClernand opposed the Kansas-Nebraska Act but did not bolt from the party. He supported the principles of the legislation, but did not believe it should be a test for the Democratic party. He repudiated the act as "unauthorized and inimical to the harmony and success of the democratic party."[48] His opposition to the bill was that it would repeal the Missouri Compromise line of 36°30', something he deemed "uncalled for." McClernand believed that slavery could not exist in the Kansas and Nebraska territories, so repeal of the Missouri Compromise line was a "mere abstraction."[49] His opposition also strained his relationship with Douglas. McClernand claimed that making the bill a party test had "prostrated the Democratic party," and he allegedly followed Douglas around the state speaking against him.[50] Though McClernand opposed the Kansas-Nebraska Act, he eventually reconciled with Douglas and even appeared with him at the Illinois State Fair in the autumn of 1854.[51] They had repaired their political alliance, and by 1856 Douglas wrote McClernand that he "would have been glad of the opportunity of advising with you in regard to political movements, both State and National. If there is anything in which I can gratify yourself or friends you must not hesitate to confer with me freely and in entire confidence."[52]

Although the Kansas-Nebraska Act divided the Democratic party McClernand maintained his status in it. He was named chairman of the State Democratic Committee, and in that capacity sent out a call in December 1855 for the State Democratic Convention. Coming into the convention there had been some discussion of nominating McClernand for governor. He was passed over, however, in favor of William Richardson of Quincy. Shortly thereafter the national Democratic convention in Cincinnati nominated James

Buchanan and John Breckinridge to run against John C. Frémont and William L. Dayton of the new Republican party and Millard Fillmore and Andrew J. Donelson of the American/Know Nothing Party. In this campaign McClernand stumped the entire state on behalf of Buchanan and Richardson, often accompanying Richardson.[53] The results were a mixed bag for McClernand and the Democrats. Buchanan captured the White House, but Republican William Bissell won the gubernatorial election. There was again an expectation that McClernand would receive an appointment from Buchanan for his support during the campaign and this time the rumor was that he would be named minister to Russia.[54] Stephen A. Douglas in fact requested this appointment from President Buchanan in March 1857.[55] McClernand was kept informed of the status of his appointment, but he did not receive the post.[56]

In the middle of the 1856 campaign McClernand again moved his residence, this time to Springfield. It was his last move, and the capital became his final home. Politically it was a good move for McClernand as he could stay better informed of political movements in the state. Douglas suggested he do just that: "Your position at the Seat of government will enable you to cast your eye over the whole State and by your advice to give the right direction to the efforts of all our friends."[57] This McClernand was more than willing to do.

Once settled in Springfield McClernand opened his law practice and took a partner, Elliot B. Herndon, who was the brother of William Herndon, Abraham Lincoln's law partner.[58] The law firm of McClernand & Herndon advertised that they practiced in the U.S. circuit and district courts for Illinois and the circuit courts of the Eighth Judicial Circuit, Springfield, Illinois.[59] The Sangamon County court soon appointed the new firm as the county attorney, with a salary of $100.[60] Having established himself in Springfield, McClernand was in frequent contact with Abraham Lincoln. Their association had started when both were elected to the Illinois House of Representatives in 1836. Lincoln also served one term in the U.S. House while McClernand was in Washington, and the two renewed their acquaintance.

The barristers McClernand and Lincoln clashed on many cases and served as co-counsel on numerous others in and out of Sangamon County. As early as 1840, in a Jefferson County case, *Holt v. Dale*, the two men sat on opposite sides of the bench. In this case McClernand got the better of Lincoln.[61] McClernand and Lincoln handled many types of cases, and on one occasion they worked together in defending a man on a murder charge. In the case of *People v. Bantzhouse,* McClernand, Lincoln, and the Herndon brothers defended John Bantzhouse against charges that he shot and killed Walter Clark. The incident took place on February 21, 1857, and went to trial that August in the Sangamon County court. The defense, for a number of reasons, requested a change of venue, which was granted. The trial was rescheduled for October in Carlinville, Macoupin County, just south of Springfield. Lincoln had recently returned to Springfield from Chicago, so McClernand made the trip to Carlinville for the trial. On October 1 McClernand moved to quash the indictment on grounds that Bantzhouse did not receive a speedy trial. The judge, David Woodson, sustained the motion and the case ended.[62] The high point in their parallel legal careers was probably when they appeared as opposing counsel in a case that went to the United States Supreme Court. The case was *Van Brunt & Watrons v. Madux* (1859) and McClernand again bested Lincoln.[63] Through their legal careers McClernand and Lincoln maintained their professional association.

Meanwhile, trouble was brewing in Kansas over its organization as a United States territory. By the Kansas-Nebraska Act, Kansas was to be formally organized, and President Pierce appointed Andrew Reeder as territorial governor. Under Reeder a proslavery legislature was elected, which sat at Lecompton. This body wrote a proslavery constitution in September 1857, a document that President Buchanan approved and sanctioned. Many people, McClernand and Douglas included, denounced the Lecompton constitution as fraudulent and unrepresentative of the residents of Kansas. This Douglas explained to McClernand in November 1857: "The only question is whether the constitution formed at Lecompton is the acts & will of the people of Kansas, [or] whether it is the act and will of a small minority, who have attempted to cheat & defraud the majority by trickery & juggling."[64] McClernand agreed that fraud played a role in the framing of the constitution and urged the senator to "Agitate! Rouse the people!" and claimed that "never before did any political struggle so thoroughly possess and sway the hearts of the masses."[65]

Responding to the constitution, McClernand wrote a public letter that was printed in the *Illinois State Register*, the Democratic organ in Springfield. Although it was a public letter it appeared to be a policy statement of the Douglas faction of the Democratic party on Lecompton. McClernand assailed President Buchanan for supporting Lecompton, suggesting that Buchanan had "lost the position of a mediator and pacificator by becoming a mere partisan." He suggested that Congress "cut loose from the entanglements of the Kansas question by rejecting the Lecompton constitution" and that the constitution be returned "for approval or rejection by the people of Kansas." Should the constitution be rejected, McClernand suggested that Congress "*never*" receive it.[66] The specific section the Illinoisan opposed dealt with slavery in Kansas. The constitution allowed slavery though a majority of persons residing in Kansas disapproved of the institution.[67] It was first approved in a questionable election, and many antislavery residents demanded its recall.

Buchanan suggested the document be sent to Congress for approval, and then changed in Kansas if necessary. McClernand's public letter was a blistering attack upon the administration, and it proved McClernand was in the Douglas camp in its opposition to Buchanan. Douglas, of course, approved of McClernand's address and wrote to congratulate him. The Little Giant called the letter "a noble production" and wrote that he was with McClernand "heart and soul in this great struggle."[68]

McClernand returned the favor later in 1858 when he was "heart and soul" with Douglas in his bid for reelection to the U.S. Senate. Though Douglas faced McClernand's hometown associate, Republican Abraham Lincoln, there was no doubt McClernand would support Douglas and he traveled around the state speaking for the Little Giant. The campaign was nasty. At one point the editor of the *Illinois State Journal*, E.L. Baker, accused McClernand of lying about him. The two men by chance met on the streets of Springfield and a fight ensued, which ended with McClernand aiming a pistol at Baker. The election ended with a Democratic majority in the general assembly, and Douglas was duly reelected.

McClernand got a chance to return to Washington himself the next year when the representative from the Illinois Sixth District, Thomas Harris, died and a special election was ordered to fill the vacancy. In September the district convention nominated McClernand on the eighteenth ballot. After no other candidate could muster a majority McClernand allowed his name to be put forth on the sixteenth ballot, and he was nominated.[69] His opponent was Republican John M. Palmer, a longtime friend, with whom McClernand had almost become a law partner. McClernand set a speaking schedule in early October, and he planned to canvass the entire district.[70] The two candidates debated several times, once on the Alton & Terre Haute Railroad in late October. Douglas wrote and offered to help in any way he could, although sickness in his family reduced him to writing letters rather than making personal appearances. He also emphasized the importance of a decisive victory: "I have no fears about your election, but it is desirable that your majority should be large, overwhelming, on account of its effects at this time on other States."[71] When John Brown raided the Harpers Ferry arsenal in the middle of the campaign McClernand used the event to his advantage, associating Palmer with Brown's abolitionist conspiracy. In later years Palmer wrote that he expected to be beaten by one or two thousand votes.[72] On the eve of the election Democrats were confident of victory, one newspaper proclaiming that "McClernand will lay Palmer as cold as an iron wedge."[73] The final tally for McClernand was over twice as large as Palmer expected — he rolled up a majority of 4,619.[74] John McClernand was going back to Washington!

When the Thirty-sixth Congress convened in December 1859 John

McClernand and his congressional colleagues had an opportunity to utilize their political skills to shepherd the country through its most serious crisis to that time. During the two sessions McClernand demonstrated that his closest political associates could count on his continued support. Throughout McClernand's political and public life in the 1840s and 1850s he made acquaintances and associations that effected his service. More often than not these associations were beneficial to McClernand's career, something that did not escape his notice. These men dominated the relationship and John McClernand served in the shadow of each man. The Illinoisan was astute enough to trade on these associations to help his own career, but seldom could his relationships with these men be termed "friendship." The most important political associations and acquaintances were those McClernand made with Abraham Lincoln and Stephen A. Douglas.

The earliest of these political acquaintances was with Stephen A. Douglas. The first contact between these two men was probably in the Illinois General Assembly in 1836 when both were freshmen representatives. Both were assigned to a special legislative committee to respond to Governor Duncan's remarks on President Jackson. This provided the first opportunity for the two to work together. Another opportunity came during 1838 and 1839 when McClernand was the centerpiece in a test of the Illinois state constitution. Douglas served as counsel for McClernand in this secretary of state case. Though the two men failed to achieve their objectives, a political bond was formed.

McClernand and Douglas rose swiftly through the ranks of the Democratic party in Illinois and when the results of the 1840 census provided the state with four additional seats in the U.S. House of Representatives, both were prepared to legislate on the national level. These two western men shared similar political sentiments during their years together in the House. One of the few times they differed was over the internal improvements bill Congress debated in 1844, which also divided the Illinois delegation. This split seemed to irritate John McClernand, who was accused of encouraging Senator Thomas Hart Benton's attacks on Douglas. This incident did nothing to damage the alliance between McClernand and Douglas, and the two were then accused of conspiring to get themselves elected U.S. Senators.[75]

With Douglas' election to the Senate in 1846 he dominated the relationship, and McClernand became the Little Giant's spokesman in the House. McClernand served in the shadow of Douglas until the latter's death in 1861. Between 1846 and 1861 the two men seldom found themselves on opposite sides of a political debate. McClernand was a careful observer and certainly recognized Douglas' growing stature in national politics, and was astute enough to link his political fortunes with Douglas. Together these two men played a dominant role in the Illinois Democratic party and national politics.

This Illinois tandem demonstrated their unity during the national crisis in 1850 over the admission of California. The negotiations surrounding the Compromise of 1850 demonstrated that Douglas dominated the alliance. While the Little Giant worked for compromise in the Senate, McClernand operated in the House under Douglas' guidance. At the House conference arranged for the evening of February 19, 1850, McClernand represented Douglas' position and spoke for him. The bill Douglas proposed in the Senate on March 25 was the result of the conference the previous month, and McClernand played a pivotal role in the bill's passage in the House. The Prairie State duo of Douglas and McClernand, under Douglas' leadership, helped broker the compromise that ended the crisis.

The most severe test of the political alliance between Douglas and McClernand centered on the Kansas-Nebraska Act of 1854. Though McClernand agreed with the principles of the bill he opposed Douglas' idea that it ought to be a test of party orthodoxy. This disagreement caused a split between the two, which was repaired before any serious damage was done. McClernand must have realized that he would have lost any power struggle with Douglas and made amends. The two had no serious political disagreements after that.

The alliance ended with Douglas' death in 1861. While it is undisputed that there was a political association between McClernand and Douglas, the two probably were not "friends." There is little evidence that the two socialized together. The contact between the two seems to get heavier based upon political necessity, such as Douglas' run for the presidency or when his status in the party was under attack. In each and every case McClernand answered Douglas' call and supported his positions. The two most notable examples were Douglas' run for the White House in 1860 and the Lecompton constitution controversy. McClernand spent his pre–Civil War political career working in unison with, and in the shadow of, Stephen A. Douglas. When Douglas died in 1861 McClernand was poised to take the mantle of leadership in the Illinois Democratic party, but the Civil War started and others dominated the political landscape.

Like his relationship with Douglas, McClernand's association with Abraham Lincoln dated to his years in the Illinois General Assembly. One important difference in McClernand's relationship with Lincoln was that the two men initially were political opponents. From 1836 to 1861 they were on opposite sides of most political discussions, but once the Civil War started in 1861 the two both believed in preserving the Union. McClernand's first important encounter with Lincoln was probably the secretary of state case of 1838–1839.

Lincoln served as counsel for secretary of state Alexander Field, whom McClernand was appointed to replace. In succeeding years these two debated many times during many elections, neither gaining a decisive advantage over the other, although McClernand's Democratic party was much stronger in Illinois than Lincoln's Whig party. In the courthouse, however, the pair often combined their considerable talents — in many legal cases McClernand and Lincoln served as co-counsel. In just as many cases the two were on opposite sides of the bench. Again, neither gained a decisive advantage over the other in their legal battles — both won as many times as they lost.

In McClernand's relationships with Douglas before the war and with Lincoln during the war he served in the shadows of both men. Lincoln and Douglas dominated, even controlled, the relationship each had with McClernand. In neither case could the men be termed "friends," but the associations had many benefits for McClernand. His association with Douglas made McClernand a nationally known and powerful politician, prompting at least one suggestion that McClernand would one day be president. His work with Lincoln brought him much fame and glory on the battlefield, which proved to be his downfall.

4

The Secession Crisis

John McClernand traveled to Washington for the start of the Thirty-sixth Congress against the backdrop of the most serious sectional tensions to date. Congress went into session on December 5, 1859, just three days after John Brown was hanged by the state of Virginia in Charlestown." Brown's raid and subsequent hanging caused much angry dissention. America seemed to be on the brink of sectional conflict. Congress was similarly divided along sectional lines when the session started, and it did little to quell the fears of civil war. In fact, the election of the speaker of the House of Representatives further incited antagonisms between North and South. The speakership struggle was symbolic of America's sectional quagmire. Although previous speakership battles took more ballots (1849–1850 took 63; 1855–1856 took 130), none was more divisive than 1859–1860.

No party held a majority in the House when Congress convened. The Republicans claimed 109 seats, the Democrats 101, while the remaining 27 members were of the American party, mostly former Whigs. Since most of the Americans were southerners, they would probably support a proslavery candidate and reject any Republican. If all Democrats and Americans united they could elect the speaker; but the Democrats were divided, so that caused some anxiety for the party. Added to this was the looming 1860 presidential election, which made the speakership battle a positioning campaign for presidential hopefuls. If the speakership contest was a preview of the November elections, a monumental struggle was in the offing.[1]

Perhaps no presidential hopeful needed to gain more support before the election than Stephen A. Douglas. His opposition to the Lecompton constitution antagonized both the Buchanan administration and many southerners. While his estrangement from Buchanan was not fatal to his presidential aspirations, losing southern support was, because Douglas absolutely had to have southern votes to win the 1860 nomination from a united Democratic party. He pursued a conciliatory policy to gain the lost southern support and used the speakership contest in 1859 to mend these fences. The speakership was important because the speaker made all committee assignments, and a Douglas man could possibly unite those factions of the party that were aligned against him, especially moderate southerners. If John McClernand, Douglas' spokesman in the House, could engineer a speakership victory for a Douglas advocate without further splitting the party, the Little Giant had a much better chance of receiving the Democratic presidential nomination.

In caucus the House Democrats chose Virginia's Thomas S. Bocock as their nominee for speaker. This was a victory for the Douglas forces, since Bocock was a moderate southerner; the Little Giant stood to gain considerably if the Virginian became speaker. McClernand, a member of the five-man steering committee to direct the campaign, approved the selection. He wrote that Bocock was not "one of the fanatical class of political recusants who are pledged to oppose Judge Douglas, for president, should he be nominated at Charleston."[2] As historian Victor Hicken has pointed out, McClernand had to overcome two problems: "First, he had to win the speakership for Bocock by uniting both southern 'radicals' and American party elements with the moderate Democrats in order to overcome Republican numerical superiority. Second, he had to accomplish this in a manner that would best help Douglas get the presidential nomination in 1860, without splitting the party."[3]

The speakership battle was nasty. Since neither party had a majority — the 27 Americans held the balance — the balloting was not a simple formality. With 109 seats, the Republicans needed to pick up only a few votes to reach a majority for their candidate, John Sherman of Ohio. Because of the split in the Democratic party, its candidate could count on receiving only about 85 of its 101 votes. Bocock needed most if not all of the American votes to win. Simple arithmetic indicated that the contest would be a long battle. And it was.

After the first inconclusive ballot, southern Democrats attempted to poison Sherman's candidacy. They offered a resolution that any man who had endorsed Hinton R. Helper's book *The Impending Crisis* was unfit to be speaker. Although the resolution failed, Sherman was damaged because he had signed a circular endorsing the book (even though he never read it). The resolution was aimed not only at Sherman but also at any northern candidate for speaker who endorsed the book.[4]

The Helper resolution was just the first act in a two-month long drama. Debate in the House had always been somewhat boisterous, but during the speakership battle it turned ugly. Most if not all congressmen were armed with pistols and knives and there were many confrontations on the House floor.

According to Senator James Hammond of South Carolina, the only congressmen who did not carry a revolver were those who had two.[5] Even a former New England clergyman then in the House broke down and bought a weapon for defense; and supporters of both southerners and northerners in the galleries were also armed and ready to fight. Many anticipated bloody fighting before the House was organized: "One southerner reported that a good many slave-state congressmen expected and wanted a shootout on the House floor."[6] It seemed clear that many southerners preferred bloody revolution to accepting an antislavery Republican in a high government office.

Luckily there were no shootouts, but southerners early recognized their minority status and did all they could to delay the election of a speaker. The House was in a state of paralysis. A resolution to halt all discussion until after a speaker was elected failed, and likewise a suggestion to elect the speaker by plurality vote failed. Obstruction became a powerful political weapon. Southerners were willing to paralyze the government until the new president took office on March 4, 1861, if they could not have their way in the House. This was an example of the South's "rule or ruin" doctrine — if they could not rule (the House, the party, or the government) they would ruin it. In mid–December McClernand wrote dejectedly, "I hope the threatened dangers may be averted."[7]

With the delaying tactics in full force ballots were seldom taken; in the first two weeks there were only thirteen votes. Only on rare occasions was more than one ballot taken on any day. After two weeks the Democrats determined they could not elect Bocock and shifted their support to several men. One of these was men John McClernand, who claimed he was not a candidate. More important for McClernand was gaining presidential support for Douglas. McClernand simply was not free to be a candidate and twice on the House floor he implored his supporters not to vote for him: "Sincerely thanking these gentlemen for this mark of their respect and confidence, I beg of them to cease voting for me, and to vote for another. I am not a candidate for the Speakership."[8] In response to letters of support for the position, McClernand wrote that he wished to "set an example of denial."[9] Again, the strategy was for McClernand to be free to work at conciliation and push the Douglas candidacy from behind the scenes.

This worked only temporarily and shortly after requesting his name be withdrawn McClernand again began receiving considerable support for the post. By early January he had climbed to a distant second behind Sherman. McClernand also began to get southern support, as South Carolina representative J.B. Ashmore spoke on his behalf. Mississippi senator Jefferson Davis appeared on the House floor to rally support for McClernand, Howell Cobb of Georgia, who along with McClernand helped bring North and South together in February 1850, also supported the Illinoisan.[10] McClernand commented hopefully to Charles Lanphier, "We have gained something by our conciliatory course towards our fellow democrats."[11]

Despite this southern support, McClernand did not have the speakership post wrapped up. There were three groups within the House that opposed his candidacy, and they worked hard against him. First, the southern Americans opposed McClernand simply because he was a Democrat. Second, because he opposed the Lecompton constitution, McClernand earned the enmity of the Buchanan administration, and therefore did not get the support of the administration Democrats. Third, some southern extremists were unwilling to compromise and would not accept a man who endorsed popular sovereignty.[12] Jefferson Davis' support got McClernand within 26 votes of the speakership, but other forces scuttled his bid. As the McClernand bandwagon gained strength Missouri senator James Green, an established Douglas foe, convinced enough Alabama and South Carolina representatives to vote against McClernand. This cost him the speakership.

After McClernand failed to garner enough votes, the Democrats shifted support to other candidates. They backed Andrew J. Hamilton of Texas, then almost won with William N.H. Smith, a North Carolina Whig. McClernand was still preaching conciliation between northern and southern Democrats. On January 18, 1860, he suggested that the differences between the party factions were abstractions, "and should not be allowed at this time to divide and distract the energies of the Democratic party."[13] After Smith's near victory John Sherman withdrew his name and the Republicans supported William Pennington of New Jersey. Because he had supported the fugitive slave law a decade earlier Pennington garnered the votes of border state men. To counter Pennington the Democrats again concentrated their efforts on McClernand. On February 1, 1860, the House elected William Pennington as speaker on the 44th ballot, and he became the highest placed Republican in the government.

McClernand, Douglas, and their supporters recognized that even though the crisis of the speakership was over, sectional hostility remained strong, not only in Congress but throughout the country. McClernand saw the hostility and believed civil war possible: "The divisions in the House are typical of the divisions in the country, and in that sense are most deplorable. Our country for the first time is in serious danger of civil commotions." An influential politician was needed, thought McClernand, to peacefully solve America's sectional dilemma. He lamented the absence of "the great men of the last generation." He believed that the country could be saved from "civil commotions" if a great compromiser was alive: "[I]f a Clay was now alive his voice might be potent enough to quell the spirit of disunion in the South. That if a Webster was alive his counsels might stay the Land of aggression in the north."[14] But alas, neither Webster nor Clay was alive to save the country.

So what was the answer? According to McClernand, the answer lay in the 1860 election — a compromise candidate must triumph in order to save the nation. He believed if the wrong man won the presidency disunion would result. During the speakership battle he stated his opinion: "Unless the triumph of conservative and patriotic sentiment in the approaching presidential election delivers us from danger, the result must be disastrous." He found this "conservative and patriotic sentiment" in the candidacy of Stephen A. Douglas. Looking toward the 1860 election, McClernand worked to mend the Little Giant's fences during the speakership contest. He proclaimed that his fellow Illinoisan was the answer to America's sectional woes: "Douglas' election to the presidency would give us a new lease of peace and concord."[15] To that end McClernand worked feverishly.

One method of advancing the Douglas candidacy was to defend him against all charges. An allegation frequently brought on the House floor was that Douglas conspired with Horace Greeley to win the 1858 senatorial election, an accusation made solely to destroy Douglas' presidential hopes. Illinois Republican representative William Kellogg made this charge in early December 1859, in the middle of the speakership struggle. McClernand addressed the accusation at that time, as did fellow Illinois Democratic representative John A. Logan, a freshman in the House. John McClernand's relationship with Logan at this time was that of "mentor." After Logan's address defending Douglas — his maiden speech — McClernand stood by him "like a man," as Logan reported to his wife, Mary Logan.[16] Kellogg was determined to sabotage Douglas' candidacy and brought it up again in March 1860. McClernand lashed out at Kellogg, suggesting he was "mad, sir, stark mad." This was an act of desperation claimed McClernand, and would succeed only in making Kellogg "notorious, since he cannot become famous." Continuing, McClernand defended Douglas' relative silence in response to these allegations: "Fortunately for both him and the country, he is far above the reach of the bats and owls that would carp and hawk at him." Concluding, he sounded a common Douglas theme — his nomination for the presidency in April 1860 in Charleston, South Carolina.[17]

The Douglas nomination process began at the state level in January 1860. At that time each state Democratic committee held a convention to appoint delegates to attend the Democratic national convention in April. At the state conventions delegations could be instructed to support a particular candidate or they could be "uninstructed" delegations. Uninstructed delegations were free to support any candidate, and Douglas' men targeted these delegations during the convention. It was a long and arduous task. The Douglas campaign officially started at the Illinois state convention, which began on January 4, 1850, and the Little Giant had lieutenants working for him in Washington and Springfield. In Washington Douglas had McClernand, Logan, and other Illinois Democratic congressmen pressing his cause. In Springfield Charles H. Lanphier, editor of the Democratic *Illinois State Register*, directed arrangements for the state convention. If the Douglas campaign was to be successful Illinois must come out strongly supporting its favorite son — there should be no doubt about where the Prairie State stood.

To that end McClernand collaborated with Douglas on writing the platform for the state convention. In December 1859 McClernand forwarded the platform to Lanphier in Springfield for presentation to the convention. Since this was Douglas' home state, the entire country looked to the Illinois state convention for the candidate's position on the issues. For that reason special care was taken in writing the platform and there were no surprises — it reaffirmed all of Douglas' political principles. It supported popular sovereignty, a more effective fugitive slave law, expressed horror at John Brown's raid, and criticized the Republican party and Douglas' opponents in the Democratic party. The platform emphasized the Supreme Court as the final authority on all questions concerning the territories, a gesture aimed at getting southern support at the national convention. The Illinois delegates were instructed to support Douglas, but in the event he did not receive the nomination they were to back the party nominee. Lastly, it endorsed the Democratic platform from 1856, the Cincinnati Platform, which supported popular sovereignty.[18] The platform, written in part by John McClernand, was the basis for Douglas' 1860 campaign.

John McClernand was not named a delegate to the national convention, but the chairman of the Illinois State Democratic Committee requested his presence in Charleston to work for Douglas' nomination.[19] Illinois representative John A. Logan attended to help Douglas as well. Chicagoan Thomas Dyer, Douglas' agent, and Illinois Congressman William Richardson were designated as the Little Giant's floor leaders. McClernand, Logan, and others left the Douglas headquarters in Washington, where it was reported that "whisky flows like a river," and arrived in Charleston a few days before the April 23 start of the convention.[20] As a proper candidate waiting to be called to the office, Douglas remained in Washington while his lieutenants worked for his cause in Charleston.

In hindsight, Charleston, South Carolina, seemed uniquely unqualified to host the 1860 Democratic national convention. Charleston was the center of ultra southern fire-eaters, and almost eliminated any chance for bisectional harmony, which was precisely what was needed to keep the party united and to avert disunion. The convention was held in Institute Hall near the center of the city, and a block and a half away was Hibernia Hall, where Douglas established his headquarters. There were three rooms on the first floor, each well stocked with copies of James W. Sheahan's campaign biography of Douglas, *The Life of Stephen A. Douglas*. On the second floor, reported Murat Halstead, were several hundred cots, arranged and numbered, for the northwestern delegations.[21]

The day before the convention started all Douglas men were confident of success. Southern caucuses had met for the previous two or three days and were unable to unite on a candidate to oppose Douglas. This gave the Douglas campaign more hope. However, Halstead wrote that the Little Giant's stock had "drooped" by the evening of April 22. He observed three Illinoisans "seated mournfully" on the steps of Hibernia Hall, "pensive and silent." Besides Logan and Richardson he spied McClernand, his "peaked face running to a hooked nose, sadly playing with his watch-guard."[22] Was this silence bred of confidence or fear of impending doom?

The convention started at high noon on April 23 with Thomas B. Flournoy of Arkansas, a Douglas supporter, temporary chairman. Early convention business favored Douglas. Several states, most notably Illinois and New York, sent two delegations, pro– and anti–Douglas in sentiment, to Charleston. The committee on credentials seated the pro–Douglas delegation in each case. The first real setback for Douglas came on the second day, April 24, when Caleb Cushing of Massachusetts, an anti–Douglas man, was named permanent chairman.

The biggest obstacles facing the convention were constructing a platform acceptable to both North and South and settling on a candidate. If successful in this the party had an excellent chance to win the election. Most southern Democrats went to Charleston intent on destroying Douglas, as some had done to McClernand four months before in the speakership battle. Southerners wanted no part of his doctrine of popular sovereignty as it provided no guarantees of protection of personal property. They were determined to write a platform that protected slavery in the territories and to nominate a candidate who agreed with this platform. If that did not happen they threatened to walk out of the convention, fatally dividing the Democratic party. The message southerners gave to the convention was this: submission (to them) or secession.

The convention first tackled the platform. A committee, composed of one representative from each state, wrote this document. On April 27 the platform committee reported. With California and Oregon taking southern positions, a slave-code plank was written into the majority report (the vote was 17–16). A minority report that endorsed popular sovereignty was also issued. The battle lines were drawn. Which report would the delegates accept? It took the convention three days to vote on the platform. April 27 and 28 were taken up in fiery speeches from both sides, and April 29, a Sunday, was a day of rest. On Monday, April 30, the eighth day of the convention, the party crossed its Rubicon and voted on the platform. In an almost strict sectional vote the minority platform was accepted 165–138.[23] After a flurry of resolutions seven southern states, Alabama, Mississippi, Louisiana, South Carolina, Florida, Texas, and Arkansas, withdrew from the convention.[24]

The southern doctrine of "rule or ruin" was carried out and the Democratic party was irreparably fractured. Since the Democrats had a two-thirds rule for nomination, the walkout doomed any chance of nominating a candidate, especially Douglas. For 57 ballots the delegates tried. When it was apparent that nobody could be nominated, the Democrats adjourned on May 3 to meet in Baltimore six weeks later. The party's demise in this election was accomplished; with the division of the Democrats the election of a Republican in November was virtually assured.

Between the Charleston and Baltimore conventions the Constitutional Union and Republican parties held their nominating conventions. The Constitutional Union party was a collection of border state men who hoped to prevent any candidate from receiving an electoral majority, thereby forcing the House of Representatives to decide the election. They held no hopes of winning the election outright and nominated John Bell of Tennessee. The Republicans convened in Chicago and nominated McClernand's legal associate Abraham Lincoln.

In addition to national conventions, Illinois Democrats held their state convention in early June. John McClernand was mentioned as a candidate for governor, but that nomination went to James C. Allen. McClernand was overwhelmingly renominated for his Sixth District seat in the U.S. House of Representatives.

In mid–June the Democrats assembled in Baltimore to again attempt to nominate a candidate. The first test was over the seating of delegates. Should those southerners who walked out of the Charleston convention be allowed to take their seats in Baltimore or should opposing, pro–Douglas delegations be seated? This was a crucial question, for if the bolters were seated the Baltimore convention could be simply a repeat of Charleston. The issue was debated from June 18 to June 22, and in the evening of the 22nd it was decided that the pro–Douglas delegations would be allowed. John McClernand, in attendance at Baltimore, immediately wired the good news to Douglas.[25] The next day Douglas finally won the presidential nomination of the Democratic party, albeit a split party. Southern Democrats who could not support Douglas met in Richmond, Virginia, later in June and nominated their own candidate — John C. Breckinridge of Kentucky. The candidates in one of America's most exciting and most important elections were set and all that remained were the campaigning and voting.

After the Baltimore convention John McClernand did not return to Congress, but proceeded to Illinois to campaign for Douglas' election and his own. His Republican opponent was Henry Case, who challenged McClernand to a series of debates throughout the late summer. The Republicans attacked McClernand on several issues. They revived the old question of McClernand's brief split with Douglas in 1854 over the Kansas-Nebraska Act. They claimed that he held pro-southern views and based this accusation on his southern support during the speakership contest. In Springfield the Democratic *Illinois State Register*, edited by McClernand's friend Charles Lanphier, pushed for his reelection. The rival *Illinois State Journal*, Springfield's Republican organ, assailed McClernand almost daily.

On election day, November 6, all of McClernand's hard work paid off for himself, but not for Douglas. Though McClernand ran in Lincoln's hometown, he was able to win by a comfortable margin. Douglas was not as fortunate. After never having lost an election, Douglas did not even win his own state. Lincoln won Illinois' electoral votes on his way to collecting a majority and winning the presidency. With the election of a Republican president the eyes of the nation turned to the South. Would it uphold its threat to secede, or would southerners back down?

John McClernand left Springfield for Washington in early December and arrived in time to speak at a rally of the Douglas Club of Washington. In this speech he praised the northwest, and advised adhering to the Union if the South seceded, clearly establishing McClernand's opposition to secession. He announced, "As for myself, I am a Union man and the democracy of the northwest are all union men." He also stated his belief that Lincoln's election alone was not reason enough to secede: "Nevertheless I cannot agree that his election is sufficient cause for breaking up the country. On the contrary, I deny that it is."[26]

The second session of the Thirty-sixth Congress opened on December 3, 1860, with the very real threat of secession hanging over it. McClernand observed, "the absorbing, almost exclusive question of discussion here is 'secession' and 'disunion.'" He continued, to his friend Charles Lanphier: "A fanaticism — an infatuation has seized the minds of many, I believe most of the Senators and Representatives from the South. They are fatally bent on disunion."[27] South Carolina had already called for a state convention, to begin on December 17, to consider secession.

Throughout the troubled winter McClernand worked to prevent secession — to find a solution to save the Union. On the second day of the congressional session, December 4, he proposed the creation of a special "select committee" to consider the divisive issues facing the country. These were, according to McClernand's proposal, the president's annual message as it related to "matters of grievance between the slaveholding and non-slaveholding States," the "question of State secession from the Federal Union," and the return of fugitive slaves. There would be one member from each state on the committee, and the speaker would make the appointments.[28] McClernand again, as in the speakership contest a year before, worked for conciliation. "Let us then hasten," he announced on the House floor on December 10, "while it is not yet too late, to avert so lamentable a result, and to save the Union, if possible, by mutual conciliation and concession. Let us adjust all the jarring differences of the sections, forever."[29] He realized that civil war was inevitable if the South seceded, and he wished to prevent that.

Although McClernand withdrew his proposal, a similar measure differing only in wording passed just minutes later by a vote of 145–38, with McClernand supporting it.[30] Speaker William Pennington appointed the members of this panel, called the Committee of 33, and he angered many people with his choices. Not a single Douglas Democrat was named to the committee, a move McClernand called "offensive discrimination" and a "parliamentary atrocity."[31] Historian Allan Nevins described Pennington's selections as "maladroit" and "far more likely to quarrel than agree."[32] The committee entertained many resolutions and plans in its month-long existence, none of which bore fruit to prevent a crisis.

While the Committee of 33 plodded along, the lower south seceded. South Carolina left the Union on December 20, 1860, followed by Mississippi (January 9, 1861), Florida (January 10), Alabama (January 11), Georgia (January 19), Louisiana (January 26), and Texas (February 1). Later in February southern delegates met in Montgomery, Alabama, wrote a constitution, and elected Jefferson Davis president of the Confederate States of America. Secession had become a reality. Congressman McClernand believed war necessarily followed secession, and he made an accurate prediction to Charles Lanphier: "South Carolina will then seize the United States forts and Custom House, within her borders." After the North recruited troops, he continued, "war will be lighted up along the borders of the free and slave states from Maryland to Missouri inclusive. This is a prediction. Keep it. See if it does not become history." McClernand concluded with this warning: "Don't be deceived — don't be deceived civil war is immediately impending."[33]

McClernand continued to oppose secession while at the same time working for conciliation and compromise. In mid–January, after four states had already seceded, he made a lengthy speech on the House floor in which he once again took his stance against secession. "First, I deny the right of any State to secede from the Union," he announced. "The idea is absurd," he explained. "It would lead to a subversion of all order, government, and stability. It would inaugurate a reign of anarchy, confusion, and chaos."[34] He based his opposition on his understanding of the Constitution. He believed the Union was a contract that could not be broken, that the contract was made by the people, not the states.[35]

While McClernand obviously opposed secession he was willing to compromise to avoid war. "Let us, therefore," he implored his House colleagues, "in a spirit of conciliation and concession, compromise our existing differences upon just and equitable terms; let us do all this for the good of all." He in no way wanted civil war and made that perfectly clear: "Let me not be misunderstood. I do not desire war. I would avoid it by all honorable means, particularly a civil war between any of the States of this Union."[36] His solution, he wrote later in January, would be "to keep fanatics and factionalists — whether proslavery or antislavery — at a distance, and appeal to the conservative sense of the country." He repeated his desire to "stand by the Union," and to "offer generous terms of concession, conciliation and compromise."[37]

McClernand did not approve of the course taken by either President Buchanan or President-elect Lincoln. Claiming that nobody knew what Buchanan would do next he lamented, "Poor 'Old Buck' is still wavering between manhood and imbecility — between courage and cowardice." Along with other northwestern Democrats McClernand visited the president to urge against "acquiescence and disunion." Although he did not clarify what he expected Buchanan to do, McClernand clearly believed the lame duck president should do something.[38]

In Lincoln's case McClernand thought he should offer some terms of compromise, which would have "thrown the onus upon the fire eaters." Because Lincoln did nothing, McClernand questioned his patriotism: "True greatness would not stickle upon pride of opinion or of consistency, in a crisis like the present, but in a forbearing spirit, would yield something — enough, at least, to prove his sensibility to the welfare of his country." In not offering some compromise McClernand suggested Lincoln had "narrow views." Lastly, McClernand believed that Lincoln should have been in Washington "in personal communication" with persons of all political parties, not holed up in Springfield surrounded only by his advisers.[39]

On February 1 McClernand believed he learned something of Lincoln's plans and ideas when Republican William Kellogg offered a resolution that he wished the Committee of 33 to consider. Among other provisions Kellogg's proposal would amend the Constitution to allow slaves to be taken into any territory south of the 36°30' line. McClernand hailed the proposal as a "peace offering," and was "happy to see that proposition coming from the source it does." Based on the close political association between Kellogg and Lincoln, McClernand implied on the House floor that the plan was Lincoln's or that the president-elect knew about the resolution. Kellogg immediately denied that Lincoln had any knowledge of the proposal.[40]

This proposal accomplished two things, one definite, the other conjecture. As McClernand intimated, if Lincoln hatched the plan, it would give the country some insight into his thought process. It could be the first step toward a formal compromise offer from the president-elect. That, however, was only speculation. The proposal had at least one concrete achievement even though the plan was never implemented — winning Democrats over to the Lincoln administration. McClernand described this to Lanphier: "I dramatically struck hands with Kellogg at a climax, when he said he was willing to join conservative men of all parties to save the country."[41] Lincoln desperately needed Democrats to support him and his program, and he won over McClernand. Now other Union-loving Democrats could support Lincoln in good faith without feeling they had deserted the party. Lincoln biographer Carl Sandburg wrote, "A dozen McClernands, who leaned to the Union, were strengthened."[42]

Congress entertained numerous compromise proposals, but all were either rejected or stalled from indecision. The crisis continued, and Lincoln was inaugurated on March 4, 1861. Since the short session of Congress was over, Lincoln called for a special session of the Thirty-seventh Congress to convene on July 4, 1861. With no official business in Washington McClernand went home to Springfield to await the extra session. While home McClernand's position on the crisis evolved from compromise to war. He wrote Lincoln in April and asked, "Is not civil war unavoidable unless the United States surrender what would compromise their honor and safety to the so called Confederate States?" The Congressman answered his own question by urging the president to "take up arms."[43]

By April McClernand had come to realize that war was the best method to put down this domestic rebellion, and he had a plan to accomplish this, a plan he shared with Lincoln. McClernand envisioned Texas as the central point in the war effort, claiming that Texas was "the strategical point for initiating resistance to the existing revolution." He believed Texas was easily accessible, "by passage through friendly local jurisdictions." He also seemed to think that Texas governor Sam Houston would cooperate with this military operation. "As Texas was pressed by a land force upon her inland border and a naval force upon her Gulf coast," McClernand believed the rebellion there could not "long sustain itself." Texas would then detach itself from the Confederacy, and contact between the remaining rebellion states and Mexico would be cut off.[44]

This was a remarkable plan, notable only for its lack of strategic insight. Texas may have been easily captured in the early stages of the war, but to use it as a springboard to conquer the rest of the Confederacy was virtually impossible. The heart of the Confederacy was east of the Mississippi River, and crossing that river would be no easy task. Besides, Texas did not even border the river, so any Union army would first have to cross Louisiana before encountering the Mississippi. This was the first of several schemes for military operations that McClernand devised throughout the war, and his immature concept of strategy was clearly evident.

Still in Illinois, McClernand worked to keep his state secure from Confederate invasion. The most vulnerable spot was Cairo, which was located in a triangle-shaped area at the southern tip of Illinois called "Egypt." It was an area of divided loyalties during the Civil War — a northern center of Confederate sentiment. The Mississippi and Ohio rivers converge in Egypt at Cairo, and the town bordered the slave states of Kentucky and Missouri. One important aspect of Cairo was commercial trading on the river systems. On April 22, 1861, Illinois governor Richard Yates sent McClernand and John M. Palmer, as private citizens, to Cairo to stop all vessels passing Cairo on the rivers and to inspect their cargo. They were authorized to "take such measures as they might deem advisable for the purpose of controlling commercial intercourse upon the Ohio and Mississippi Rivers at that point." The fear was that arms and ammunition might be shipped past Cairo on their way to the South. McClernand and Palmer did not remain at Cairo long, but they seized "a large quantity of warlike stores."[45]

Until the special session of Congress met in July McClernand busied himself pressing the Union cause. He and Governor Yates encouraged secretary of war Simon Cameron to allow the enlistment of Illinois regiments to protect the state, especially the vulnerable Egypt. Yates appointed McClernand as a special envoy to Washington to plead Illinois' case and in this capacity he consulted with both President Lincoln and Secretary Cameron.[46] In early June McClernand's efforts on behalf of the Union were interrupted when Stephen A. Douglas died. As Douglas' leader in the House of Representatives and a close political associate, McClernand served on a committee to make arrangements for the funeral. With Douglas' death McClernand became the Democratic leader in Illinois.

McClernand's support for the war was strong, and on June 28 he spoke to the 21st Illinois Regiment, commanded by Colonel Ulysses S. Grant. On that day the regiment had to decide whether to reenlist in U.S. service for three years or go home. From May 15 to June 16 the unit had shrunk from 1250 to barely 600 and its colonel was worried. Colonel Grant met McClernand and John A. Logan in Springfield and the two politicians agreed to speak to the regiment and urge it to reenlist. McClernand spoke first then gave way to Logan. The effect was amazing, as the 21st Illinois reenlisted "almost to a man," as Grant later remembered.[47]

By the time Congress convened on July 4, 1861, Fort Sumter had fallen, President Lincoln had called 75,000 men to suppress the rebellion, and the upper South had seceded. War matters dominated the special session, and McClernand did his share. He proposed a resolution that showed his support for the war — that the House pledge "any amount of money and any number of men" to put down the insurrection. In other words McClernand favored using all means necessary to oppose secession and prosecute the war. The resolution passed by the overwhelming vote of 121–5.[48] McClernand also proposed to Lincoln the creation of a Department of Police. This organization, ostensibly under the direction of a cabinet level minister of police, would prevent communication leaks to the enemy.[49]

Meanwhile, Lincoln was granting commissions in the army for general officers. The two Illinois senators, Lyman Trumbull and Orville H. Browning, met with Lincoln on several occasions to discuss Illinois men. Among those considered were Ulysses S. Grant, John M. Palmer, and John McClernand. When the list of new generals was issued in early August, both Grant and McClernand were on it. Grant ranked seventeenth on the list, with McClernand just behind. McClernand's commission came through on August 7, 1861, to date from May 17. All of McClernand's loyalty and hard work to save the Union had paid off in the form of this commission. He visited Lincoln on August 12 before he left for Illinois to chase fame and glory on the field of battle.[50]

5

"Three Cheers for the Union"
Belmont

Brigadier General John A. McClernand was one of many men who received a general's commission because of political considerations. He had not attended West Point or served in the peacetime army. Except for two months of marching around Illinois in 1832 during the Black Hawk War, McClernand had no military training or experience. But Lincoln needed men like John McClernand, a Democrat, to set examples and perform important duties; in return the president rewarded them with generalships. McClernand had a reputation as a fine speaker, so he was a valuable tool as a recruiter, especially in southern Illinois with its divided loyalties. When McClernand visited Lincoln before returning to Illinois, the president admonished the new general to "keep Egypt right side up."[1] Lincoln expected McClernand and John A. Logan to keep southern Illinois, largely Democratic, loyal to the Union and raise troops for the cause. It seemed to be a safe bet since both men had large followings there.

As a political appointee with great ambition McClernand had to be managed carefully and in this respect Lincoln was masterful — he knew exactly how to massage McClernand's ego. The president knew how important it was to keep all Democrats in the Union fold. To an extent, Lincoln had to "handle" McClernand, and the president knew that he was succeeding when later in the war he said this about his Springfield associate: "There is General McClernand from my state, whom they say I use better than a radical."[2]

McClernand was assigned to the Western Department, which was commanded by Major General John C. Frémont, who had his headquarters in St. Louis. The department, ill-defined at the time, included Illinois and that part of the U.S. between the Mississippi River and the Rocky Mountains.

McClernand was assigned to command a brigade, which ideally was composed of four regiments. Lincoln suggested they be the Illinois units of Colonel John A. Logan, Colonel Philip Fouke, Colonel J.N. Coler, and Colonel B.C. Cook.[3] With the agreeable assignment of commanding Illinois units, the new general turned his attention to assembling a staff and arming his brigade.

In building a staff McClernand used personal acquaintances and family. His staff included his father-in-law, James Dunlap, as quartermaster; Mason Brayman, an acquaintance from Springfield, as chief of staff and assistant adjutant general; and Walter B. Scates, an Illinois supreme court justice. McClernand also wrote to General Winfield Scott in Washington to fill out his staff, requesting that Alexander Bielaski be appointed his aide-de-camp. When there was some confusion over Bielaski's commission, McClernand pleaded with Governor Yates to intervene. Finally, after Lincoln interceded the appointment was made. Lincoln also helped Josiah M. Lucas be named commissary of subsistence to McClernand's brigade. One appointment that was denied, however, was McClernand's request for Lieutenant James H. Wilson, from Shawneetown.[4]

Perhaps McClernand's greatest task was obtaining supplies for his brigade, especially weapons. To accomplish this the general turned to both the federal government and the state of Illinois. The Illinois adjutant general authorized McClernand's brigade quartermaster, Captain James Dunlap, to procure supplies for the brigade from the state. At the same time, McClernand wrote to Montgomery C. Meigs, U.S. quartermaster general and Georgia native who had remained loyal to the Union, requesting money to purchase the necessary supplies.[5] In order to procure weapons for his brigade, the general used any personal or political connection at his disposal. When the state and federal quartermasters did not respond rapidly enough to his requests McClernand wrote directly to Governor Richard Yates. He asked the governor to send him arms: "Send me four thousand stands of the Enfield rifle, which I understand have been or will be sent to you."[6] McClernand also relied on one of his regimental commanders, Colonel Fouke, who was in Washington. Fouke reported on the possibility of obtaining weapons, rifles and artillery pieces directly from the manufacturers.[7] One way or another McClernand tried to get adequate supplies for his brigade.

By early September McClernand was in Cairo with his brigade and in temporary command of the post there. Cairo was part of the District of Southeast Missouri, which was commanded by Brigadier General Ulysses S. Grant. The district encompassed troops at Cairo and Mound City in Illinois, Bird's Point and Cape Girardeau in Missouri, and Fort Holt in Kentucky. On September 4 Grant ordered McClernand, the second-in-command, to take charge of the post at Cairo. McClernand remained at the Cairo post while Grant

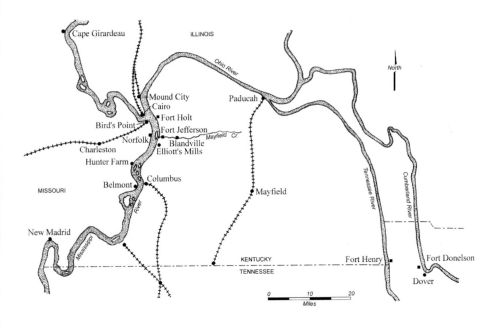

Cairo, 1861 (map by Julie Barnes Smith).

commanded the district from the same place.[8] The tri-monthly report dated
October 31, 1861, reported the total strength of the district as 11,161.[9]

Cairo was located at the southern tip of Illinois jutting down into
both Kentucky and Missouri, two states that sympathized with the Confederacy. Lincoln wished to prevent the two from seceding. The governors of
both states were secessionists, but could not force their states into the
Confederacy. Though Missouri had already plunged into military conflict,
Kentucky was neutral. A military incursion into Kentucky by Union troops
could force the state to secede or actively cooperate with the Confederacy.
Although neither seceded, the situation demanded a man with a calm demeanor.

At Cairo that man was the district commander, Brigadier General U.S.
Grant. A visitor to the camp described his character traits as "stoicism, tenac-
ity of purpose.... Nothing could surprise, excite or daunt him: he was imper-
turbable in all situations." He seemed to be the ideal man for Cairo. In contrast
to Grant's calm posture was that of McClernand. He was an ambitious political general thirsting for military glory who the same visitor described as "ner-
vous and fidgety."[10] These two different personalities might have
complemented each other, McClernand quick to act and Grant the cool collected leader. But that was not the case. Their differences only led to antag-

onism that eventually developed into full-blown hatred, but early in the war the two men cooperated well with each other.

In early September 1861 Kentucky was still a "neutral" state but both North and South soon broke this neutrality. The targets in Kentucky were Columbus and Paducah, strategically located on the Mississippi and Tennessee rivers. Columbus was on the Mississippi about 20 miles south of Cairo, while Paducah was on the Tennessee, approximately 40 miles east of Cairo. Confederates under General Leonidas Polk struck first and occupied Columbus on September 3. In response Grant and McClernand planned an expedition to Paducah that was carried out on the evening of September 5. McClernand made the preparations for the expedition and remained in command at Cairo while Grant sailed with the troops to Paducah.[11] Grant complimented his second-in-command "for the active and efficient co-operation exhibited by him in fitting out the expedition."[12]

Although the occupation of Paducah was important strategically, a campaign this early in the war was an aberration, as military activity was mostly confined to drilling and training the troops. It was mundane but important work. One consequence of the monotony of drilling was restlessness on the part of the men, as new soldiers did not adapt quickly to camp life. There were some discipline problems, and among the most common were the men's drinking and carousing. One Harry B. Smith of Cairo complained to General Frémont that "rows, fights & Murders are of almost daily Occurrence. at all hours of the Day & Night Multitudes of soldiers can be seen in the Pestiferous Dens, drinking Bellowing, Cursing & Fighting."[13] Frémont referred the problem to Grant, who in turn passed it on to McClernand with the suggestion that a provost marshal be appointed at Cairo to maintain order. McClernand promised to prepare general orders to enforce discipline.[14] This behavior was relatively common early in the war because most men wanted to fight immediately and became bored with drilling and the routine of camp life.

The rank and file men were not the only ones in camp to get restless or lonely away from home — these feelings also struck the high command, Grant and McClernand included. Neither was far from home and they wanted to have family with them. McClernand's wife, Sarah, died in May 1861, but he had his son in camp with him. Since that arrangement seemed to work well, Grant sent for his son.[15]

While the men drilled, McClernand continued to locate and procure weapons for his brigade. When the state of Illinois and the U.S. quartermaster failed to produce weapons, McClernand appealed to department commander Frémont for guns.[16] When this produced no weapons McClernand explained the situation to Grant in great detail, hoping the district commander could get the needed armaments. McClernand stated that not more than 2,000 of the 3,068 effective men in his brigade were armed, and that those weapons were fit only for drill, not combat. He suggested that sufficient ammunition, clothing, and equipment for 4,000 infantry and 500 cavalry would suffice for his brigade. This lack of weapons was discouraging enlistment, claimed the general, and he hoped Grant would "represent this matter to Genl. Frémont in a strong light."[17] Frémont's assistant adjutant general, Chauncey McKeever, promised Grant that he would send arms for McClernand's brigade.[18]

The monotonous and redundant work of drilling and training was only occasionally broken by a scouting trip or stopping commerce on the Mississippi. One such occasion came when a steamer was sent under a white flag of truce by General Leonidas Polk to discuss an exchange of prisoners. Grant refused the proposal on the grounds that accepting would have been a recognition of the Confederate government. When the boat appeared McClernand ordered three regiments of infantry and a body of cavalry out as a demonstration of the camp's strength. He wanted the enemy on the steamer to see the assembled power, displayed to appear like ten or fifteen thousand men, and report it to Polk. McClernand's men were eager to do something besides drill and, hoping for a fight, moved with "incredible alacrity," reported the general.[19]

The men were obviously bored with camp life and ached to do something combative, if only a demonstration of power to deceive a passing steamer. Finally, in early November Frémont ordered Grant to make a real demonstration. On November 1 Frémont ordered Grant to move up and down both sides of the Mississippi, making demonstrations toward Charleston and Norfolk in Missouri and Blandville in Kentucky. Grant was to keep his men "constantly moving back and forward against these places, without, however, attacking the enemy."[20] These demonstrations were to mask Frémont's own movements into Missouri to catch Confederate general Sterling Price, who had besieged and captured Lexington on September 20 with his 18,000-man army.

After receiving this command Grant issued a flurry of orders that ultimately put every force assigned to the district in the field. On November 3 Grant ordered Colonel Richard J. Oglesby, commanding at Bird's Point, Missouri (just across the Mississippi River from Cairo), to take his brigade and chase and destroy the Confederates under Jeff Thompson, about 3,000 men strong. On the 4th he ordered Colonel Joseph B. Plummer with the 10th Iowa Regiment out from Cape Girardeau (located up the Mississippi River from Cairo in Missouri) as a diversion for Oglesby. Frémont learned that Price was to receive reinforcements from Columbus, so on November 5 he ordered Grant to demonstrate against that place.[21] Grant then ordered C.F. Smith, at

Paducah, to make the demonstration against Columbus. Finally, on November 6 he ordered Colonel W.H.L. Wallace, at Bird's Point, to take a regiment and redirect Colonel Oglesby toward New Madrid, Missouri (on the Mississippi, southwest of Columbus). This redirection would ultimately threaten Belmont, located directly across the Mississippi from Columbus, from the south and west while Grant himself advanced upon it from the north.[22]

Grant took his men at Cairo to make the demonstration against Columbus. His forces consisted of two infantry brigades, two companies of cavalry, and some artillery batteries, totaling 3,114 men. McClernand commanded the First Brigade, made up entirely of Illinois men. It included the 27th Illinois, commanded by Colonel Napoleon B. Buford; the 30th Illinois, under Colonel Philip B. Fouke; Colonel John A. Logan's 31st Illinois; two companies of Illinois cavalry (one under Captain J.J. Dollins and the other commanded by Captain Delano); and Ezra Taylor's battery of the Chicago Light Artillery (the battery contained four 6-pounder guns and two 12-pounder howitzers). The First Brigade numbered 2,072 men, fully two-thirds of the entire expeditionary force.[23] Colonel Henry Dougherty commanded the Second Brigade, which consisted of the 22nd Illinois and 7th Iowa regiments. The flotilla included two gunboats, *Tyler* and *Lexington*, and five or six transports. McClernand, along with the 30th and 31st Illinois regiments, boarded the transport *Aleck Scott*, while the 27th sailed on the *James Montgomery*. The 7th Iowa joined the 27th Illinois on the *Montgomery*, and the 22nd Illinois accompanied Grant on his "large and luxurious" *Belle Memphis*. The cavalry embarked onboard either the *Rob Roy* or *Chancellor*, while the wagons went on the *Keystone State*.[24]

The Confederate force arrayed against Grant at Columbus numbered some 10,000 men under General Polk. Just across the Mississippi from Columbus was a rebel observation camp at Belmont, located on an eastward bend of the river. It was occupied by one regiment of infantry, a battery of artillery, and one squadron of cavalry. The trees along the riverbank at Belmont had been removed so that the artillery at Columbus could protect the camp. These trees were placed to form an abatis to thwart an enemy advance on the position. Polk had learned of the disposition of the various federal troops sent out by Grant. The rebel general also expected Grant to attempt to drive him out of Columbus, and he believed this move to be it.[25]

The Union troops left Cairo at 5:00 P.M. on November 6 and sailed down the Mississippi toward the intended target. The flotilla stopped for the night eleven miles above Columbus on the Kentucky side of the river. At 2:00 A.M. on the 7th Grant received a communication from Colonel W.H.L. Wallace that the Confederates were crossing troops over to Belmont from Columbus in order to trap Colonel Oglesby's force.[26] This changed Grant's plan.

Although specifically prohibited from attacking the enemy, Grant determined to do just that at Belmont. His justification was two-fold: first, he recognized that the men were "elated" at the opportunity to fight and believed they would become demoralized if not given that chance, and second, he planned only to break up the camp at Belmont and quickly return.[27] The Battle of Belmont was thus planned.[28]

After receiving Wallace's communication Grant redirected the expedition to the Missouri side of the river. The flotilla was to sail at 6:00 A.M. with the gunboats in the lead followed by McClernand's then Dougherty's brigades. The landing was to be effected at the lowest point of the Missouri shore that was safe from the rebel batteries at Columbus. The naval commander, Captain Henry Walke, chose the location.[29]

The troops disembarked at 8:30 A.M. at Hunter's Farm two and one-half to three miles above Belmont. McClernand formed his brigade in a cornfield preparatory to an advance, and ordered the cavalry under Captains Dollins and Delano to scout the woods along the road to Belmont. The march to the enemy camp began with McClernand's First Brigade in the lead in this order: the cavalry, 27th Illinois, 30th Illinois, a section of the artillery, Logan's 31st Illinois, and the remaining guns. Dougherty's Second Brigade followed with the 7th Iowa in front of the 22nd Illinois. McClernand rode ahead of the column to scout the camp and to locate the best ground to form his men for battle. The gunboats *Tyler* and *Lexington* fired on the Confederates at Columbus to distract the rebels there.[30] In Columbus General Polk learned of the Federal landing and dispatched General Gideon J. Pillow with four regiments, totaling 2,700 men, to reinforce Belmont. Shortly thereafter Polk sent over yet another regiment of about 500 men, who landed at about 10:30 A.M. Confederate artillery in Columbus soon opened fire on the Union column.[31]

About a mile and a half from the camp the Union troops deployed for battle. McClernand's brigade was on the right of the line; the 27th was on the right flank, the 30th on its left, and the 31st next, in the center of the entire line. The Second Brigade formed the left wing. General McClernand then ordered two companies from each regiment forward as skirmishers, encouraging them to "see the enemy" and to seek out their positions. As the skirmishers moved forward they encountered the enemy and sharp fighting soon began.[32] By that time the rebel reinforcements from Columbus had arrived and the number of troops on each side was roughly equal.

McClernand then ordered his brigade, along with the artillery, forward to support the skirmishers. The uneven terrain, described as a "marsh through this dense forrest with plenty of underbrush and dead wood," along with a pond in front of the 27 Illinois, made this task difficult.[33] Colonel Buford's men marched around the pond and were temporarily separated from the main line. The 27th got around the body of water and ultimately approached the rebel camp from its left. This movement, although completely unintentional, served as a flanking maneuver.

In re-forming his lines to move forward McClernand expected the alignment to remain the same, i.e., his brigade holding the right and Dougherty's the left. This, the general believed, would enable the Union army to encircle the camp and capture all the enemy troops.[34] When the movement got underway the 7th Iowa and 22nd Illinois crossed over and took positions on the right of the line, putting McClernand's brigade on the left, with Logan's 31st Illinois anchoring the flank.

As the Union line moved forward the Confederates poured a withering fire into it. The exchange lasted for about half an hour and temporarily threw the troops into disorder. This was short-lived, as the troops "rallied under the gallant example of Colonels Fouke and Logan," wrote their brigade commander.[35] The Confederates also attempted to turn the Federal left flank, a position Colonel Logan held. McClernand thwarted this effort by "ordering Colonel Logan to extend the line of battle by a flank movement, and bringing up a section of Taylor's battery ... to cover the space between the Thirtieth and Thirty-first."[36]

This emergency met and defeated, the Union continued the attack on the Confederate camp. In leading this assault McClernand was hit by a rebel ball, but luckily it struck one of his pistols and did no harm. While artillery shells from Columbus whistled through the trees McClernand, Logan, and Fouke encouraged the men to continue forward. Waving his cap in the air, McClernand led the final charge into the rebel camp. Here an enemy bullet grazed his head and his horse was shot from under him.[37]

The Federal surge was too much for the Confederates and they abandoned their camp. One of McClernand's staff officers, Captain Bielaski, who became separated from the general during the battle, was shot down as he planted an American flag in the rebel compound. After taking control of the camp Yankee soldiers displayed little discipline and began to pillage and plunder. In the midst of this rampage McClernand gave the word for "Three cheers for the Union."[38] The men, though tired from the fight, responded with great applause. Grant could not gain control of the looting soldiers, so he ordered his army to withdraw and the camp set afire.

While the camp burned the Confederates regrouped between the Union force and the transports. In order to return to the ships the Federals had to re-form their units and fight their way back. Besides these obstacles, Polk sent additional reinforcements that landed between the Union army and its flotilla. In response McClernand ordered his artillery to open on the rebel lines. While the artillery rained its destructive fire on the Confederates

McClernand ordered Logan to cut his way through the enemy line with his 31st Illinois. This Logan accomplished, and the rest of the Federal forces, except the 27th Illinois, followed close behind.

Logan led most of the force back to the safety of the transports over ground it had covered earlier in the day. Only the 27th, under Colonel Buford, took another route. It followed the road it had taken earlier in the morning, and it was again separated from the main force. While Buford and the 27th Illinois took a circuitous route to the ships, the rest of the army withstood fire from the Confederates. During this withdrawal McClernand's horse was again shot from under him. When a company grade officer was wounded near McClernand, the general's body servant, William Stains, offered his horse to the injured captain. Stains then put a bullet through the head of a Confederate who attempted to capture the officer.[39]

Upon reaching the landing the troops boarded the transports for the trip back to Cairo. Except for those of the 27th, still in the field, McClernand and two staff officers were the last to board the ships.[40] After sailing only a short distance up the river McClernand stopped his transport, the *Chancellor*, and picked up Buford and his regiment. Once the 27th boarded the entire force, after a six-hour battle, headed back to Cairo, which they reached about midnight.[41]

Both Grant and McClernand wrote congratulatory orders when they reached Cairo. These orders mirrored each man's personality. Grant's was short and to the point, while McClernand wrote a long-winded flamboyant account of what was a relatively minor engagement.[42] This was a habit McClernand continued throughout the war — he wrote lengthy congratulatory orders following virtually every battle. It was a habit that would come back to haunt him later at Vicksburg.

Immediately following the return to Cairo Grant and Polk agreed to a truce to bury the dead. One of those was McClernand's aide Captain Alexander Bielaski, who reportedly was a friend of President Lincoln. Bielaski's sword and overcoat were returned to McClernand but his body was never recovered, presumably buried in a mass grave. On two occasions McClernand wrote to Polk in attempts to find the body. When neither Union nor Confederate search parties located the remains, McClernand wrote to his aide's widow with the sad news.[43]

In evaluating and analyzing Belmont one must consider the nature of the engagement. Was it a full-blown battle or was it merely a distraction? If it is considered a battle then surely Belmont was a Confederate victory since the Union troops withdrew and abandoned the battlefield to the rebels. If it is considered simply a maneuver to prevent Polk from reinforcing General Sterling Price then it was a successful Union expedition. Whether Belmont was a battle or demonstration, there was one unmistakable benefit — it gave the soldiers experience under fire. According to Logan, Belmont also gave Union soldiers confidence in themselves and in their officers.[44] Experience and confidence were the most important results of Belmont for Grant, McClernand, and their men. This experience was costly, as the Union army suffered 120 killed, 383 wounded, and 104 captured or missing.[45]

Grant and McClernand cooperated well with each other in their first Civil War combat. Grant commanded the entire field while McClernand led the largest brigade, which included all of the artillery and cavalry. Both leaders were visible to the men throughout the conflict, and, with the exception of the looting, kept fairly good control over them. Grant complimented his brigade commander in his official report to the War Department: "General McClernand was in the midst of danger throughout the engagement, and displayed both coolness and judgment."[46] Grant repeated this evaluation in a letter to his father after the battle, stating that McClernand "acted with great coolness and courage throughout, and proved that he is a soldier as well as statesman."[47]

A habit McClernand started after Belmont and continued throughout the war was disregarding the official chain of command and communicating directly with superiors. The day after the engagement he wrote to General George B. McClellan in Washington, who had recently been named general-in-chief of the armies. In this communication McClernand briefly outlined the expedition and battle and promised to "report at large by mail."[48] He did not follow this letter with a larger account, but rather filed his official report with Grant as was proper. It was, nonetheless, a disturbing practice that antagonized Grant, his immediate superior.

When bypassing the chain of command McClernand most often corresponded with President Lincoln. They were both Illinois politicians from the general assembly and McClernand owed his commission to Lincoln. McClernand probably believed direct contact with the White House would ensure quick action or possibly approval of some campaign plan. The general did not write the president immediately following Belmont; but after meeting with Illinois congressman Elihu Washburne, Lincoln wrote to McClernand. Calling it a social letter, Lincoln thanked McClernand for his service at Belmont and promised to do all he could to get arms for the troops. It is interesting to note that Lincoln did not send similar congratulations to Grant. Did Lincoln slight Grant or did he realize McClernand needed constant positive reinforcement? Was this note part of Lincoln's "handling" of McClernand? If so, the president apparently did not realize what a dangerous precedent he set. By not going through proper military channels himself he subtlety implied it was proper for McClernand to do likewise. In reply McClernand sent the president a copy of his official battle report.[49] In addition to this correspondence, the general separately wrote Lincoln about requisitions for his troops.[50]

The return to Cairo also meant a return to the boredom and monotony of camp life. With spare time in abundance McClernand again corresponded with his patron in the White House. In late November the general saw fit to advise the president on war strategy, suggesting that the system of district commands lacked military unity. He proposed the creation of a new military department to comprise the lower Mississippi Valley, southern Missouri, and southwestern Kentucky. With this new organization, a coordinated attack on Columbus and Belmont could drive the Confederates from both places. This new department would have to be commanded by an "energetic, enterprising and judicious commander" and "supplied with an adequate army." Although he did not specifically request the assignment, it appeared McClernand had just created an independent command for himself.[51]

As he had done in previous letters to the president, McClernand again requested that Lieutenant James H. Wilson be assigned to his staff. A week and a half later McClernand repeated the request for staff officers and he advised Lincoln as to war sentiment in Illinois. The general described two political factions in the state — "ultra discontented Republicans" and "*quasi* secessionists being apostate democrats." He defined the position of both groups: "The former seek to substitute a new issue for the war: viz; The abolition of slavery. The latter desire to see the Rebel Arms prevail." As a solution to this divided opinion McClernand suggested that Colonels Logan and Fouke, still members of Congress, take their seats to demonstrate Democratic support for a vigorous prosecution of the war.[52]

McClernand learned of those political matters during a trip to Springfield in late November. Grant ordered him to the Illinois capital to see Governor Yates about filling out regiments at Cairo and to seek arms and weapons for the entire district. On arriving in Springfield he met with Colonel A.C. Fuller, Illinois adjutant general, and explained the conditions at Cairo. Although noncommittal Fuller promised to do what he could.[53] In addition to McClernand's trip to Springfield, Logan and Fouke went to Washington and New York to secure weapons for the brigade.[54]

On returning from Springfield McClernand reported to his friend, Mason Brayman, a rebel spy, Lieutenant Colonel William C. Chapell, from Columbus, who spent about ten days in Cairo. While there Chapell allegedly spoke freely with many people, apparently gathering information for General Polk. Besides tracking spies the troops passed the time training and drilling, preparing for the next movement. Occasional scouting expeditions were planned and sometimes cancelled. The troops tracked illegal rebel trade on the Mississippi,

Tennessee, and Ohio rivers and watched for possible Confederate attacks. That was how the First Brigade spent the remainder of 1861.[55]

The year ended with McClernand commanding a brigade at Cairo and Grant commanding the district. Although he temporarily lost control of his men at Belmont, McClernand acquitted himself well in his first combat experience. He began some rather disturbing trends after that battle, such as penning self-adulatory congratulatory orders and writing directly to Lincoln, circumventing the chain of command. Always looking for glory, the general began a self-promotion campaign after the battle, a skill he perfected in a short time. The ever attentive politician, he took time out from fighting the rebels at Belmont for some political remarks. Although constantly looking out for his own welfare, McClernand demonstrated he was a competent brigade commander. He led two-thirds of Grant's troops at Belmont, was grazed by a bullet, and had two horses shot from under him. Grant praised him for his conduct. Could this politician-turned-general take his experience at Belmont and become a successful Civil War general officer? Would he be just another politician in a uniform or a truly dependable and competent leader? If the latter, when and where would the next opportunity occur? Just down the Tennessee River from Cairo was a Confederate garrison unexpectedly weak and vulnerable — Fort Henry.

6

"The Death-Knell of Rebellion Is Sounded"

Forts Henry and Donelson

The southern defense of the Confederate heartland was weak. The leaders of this Western Department did not formulate a coordinated defensive strategy for their command. General Leonidas Polk, the first department commander, focused his efforts on defending the Mississippi River and did not concentrate troops in Tennessee.[1] Polk's successor, General Albert Sidney Johnston, assumed command of the department on September 15, 1861, and employed a cordon defensive system for the department. This was a strategy designed to defend vast territory, but by its very nature it prevented rapid concentration of troops. By January 1862 Johnston had about 50,000 men spread out over a defensive line 400 miles long. The left (western) wing of this line was at Columbus, Kentucky, on the Mississippi River, where Polk had approximately 17,000 men. About seventy miles directly east were some 5,500 troops at Forts Henry and Donelson, located on the Tennessee and Cumberland rivers, respectively. Northeast of Fort Donelson about ninety miles was Bowling Green, Kentucky, where Johnston himself commanded 25,000 men. The right (eastern) wing of this defensive line was at Knoxville, Tennessee, where General Felix Zollicoffer had 3,000–4,000 men.[2] The strength of this line was at both wings, so the middle, the Confederate heartland, was vulnerable.

Meanwhile, the Federal troops at Cairo were growing restless, and among the impatient was McClernand. With time on his hands the general began to write letters, and in early January he renewed his correspondence with President Lincoln. This time the general complained that he lacked both cavalry and artillery, and he requested special permission to recruit one company of each. He asked for extraordinary recruiting privileges because, he explained, "If I am left to the process of recruiting through general offices assigned to that service, I may never succeed in securing the two companies requested." If the president would grant this special permission, McClernand claimed that he had "an opportunity to do it now." This correspondence demonstrates again that McClernand hoped to use his association with Lincoln to receive special favors.[3]

That letter was to be delivered to President Lincoln personally by Colonel John A. Logan, who was in Washington as a member of Congress. McClernand directed Logan to support the request "by such views as may present themselves to your mind." He reported to Logan on the condition of the colonel's 31st Illinois Regiment, noting that the unit distinguished itself in a "sham battle."[4] A few days later McClernand again wrote Logan and again asked him to deliver a letter to the president. The general also complained to the colonel of the apparent lack of high ranking officers in the army from Illinois and the northwest generally. He believed that men from other areas of the country commanded the forces composed of northwesterners. Noting that men from the northwest were either privates or subordinate officers, he posed this question: "Is the Northwest only fit to raise corn for the army and to fatten the earth with the blood and bodies of her fallen children?"[5] McClernand hoped that Lincoln would rectify the alleged oversight.

The general struck another theme in this letter to Logan — Union strategy. McClernand suggested that another military department should be created to include the Mississippi River valley. He proposed, "If we are to have a new Department, it should be made soon. In my judgment the best interest of the service and the country demand it. What pretext can there be for subordinating the great and transcendent interests of the Mississippi river and valley to a <u>quasi</u> foreign pro consulate?"[6] In addition to the creation of this new department McClernand hinted that a man from the northwest should command it. And though he did not specifically request command of the proposed department, it was apparent that he wanted it. It also seems apparent that, given the general's nature, he wished Logan to recommend and support him for the command. Although Logan reported back to McClernand that he had "on all occasions been pressing the necessity of a separate Dept. at Cairo," nothing ever came of the proposal.[7]

Throughout the war a controversy raged between regular army officers and politicians-turned-soldier. McClernand first addressed this issue when he wrote to Logan in January 1862. He was a political general himself, writing to a politician turned officer, and he claimed to perceive a "professional, military jealousy of citizen generals." This was apparently a warning to Logan,

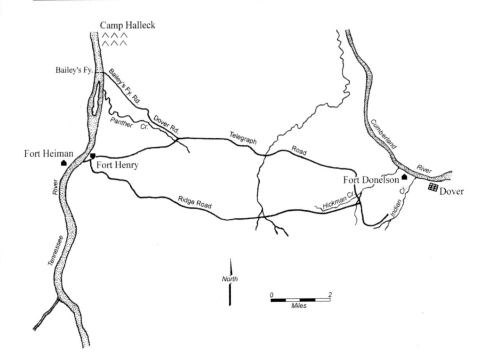

Fort Henry and Fort Donelson, 1862 (map by Julie Barnes Smith).

cautioning him about what to expect upon his return to the field. While alleging to have felt the influence of the jealousy, McClernand asserted he would avoid all controversy of this nature. However, if a quarrel did arise over the conduct of citizen generals he believed he had nothing to fear. In fact, McClernand prematurely credited these citizen generals with playing a large role in the successful prosecution of the war. "Mark the prediction!" he claimed.[8]

At long last, two months after Belmont, the troops at Cairo moved out on a large reconnaissance mission. With 5,192 men of all arms (3,992 infantry, 1,061 cavalry, and 139 artillery), McClernand led the expedition under Grant's command.[9] The object of the expedition was to make demonstrations into western Kentucky, toward Columbus and Mayfield, to keep the Confederates there from reinforcing the rebel army at Bowling Green. McClernand also believed the purpose of the campaign was to confuse the enemy about the Federal intentions. Were they attacking Columbus, destroying the railroads around Columbus, or attacking Camp Beauregard (at Feliciana on the New Orleans and Ohio Railroad, just north of the Kentucky-Tennessee line)?[10] The mission would allow the Federal Army of the Ohio, under General Don Carlos Buell, to face the Confederates at Bowling Green with relatively equal numbers.

The cavalry left Cairo on January 9 and camped that night at Fort Holt, just across the Ohio River from Cairo. The next day the infantry boarded transports and sailed down the Mississippi to Fort Jefferson, where it met the cavalry. Fort Jefferson was located about halfway between Cairo and Columbus where the Mississippi River met Mayfield Creek. From there reconnaissance missions were made to Blandville, Elliott's Mill, Milburn, and toward Columbus. There was hard marching every day over difficult roads covered with sleet. The cavalry got to within a mile and a half of Columbus, drove in the pickets there and took some prisoners. McClernand, learning more about combined operations, also ordered W.D. Porter, commanding the gunboat squadron, to make demonstrations toward Columbus, further confusing the Confederates.[11] The general reported that the rebels at Columbus had "collected around camp fires within their intrenchments, and indisposed to take the field." He believed that a well-planned attack could take Columbus.[12]

The expedition returned to Cairo on January 21, having succeeded in its purpose. No Confederate reinforcements left the area, which allowed Union General George H. Thomas to defeat the Confederate forces under Generals George B. Crittenden and Felix Zollicoffer at Mill Springs (or Logan's Crossroads), on the Cumberland River in East Tennessee, on January 19. McClernand also learned from a prisoner that the expedition caused much confusion for the rebels in the area. The man told his captors that the Federal demonstration had "excited much alarm, and induced the enemy to call in his forces at Jackson, Beauregard, New Madrid, and other places; two Mississippi regiments, according to the report, having burned up their tents before their flight."[13]

The positive accomplishments of the operation increased McClernand's desire for more active campaigns. In his report to General Henry W. Halleck — since November 9, 1861, the new department commander — McClernand urgently recommended "a renewed advance of our forces."[14] McClernand also expressed the same sentiment to Lincoln when the general reported the mission to the president. After a detailed account of the expedition, McClernand proposed an independent campaign under his command. "If you will give me 25,000 men and the co-operation of the gunboats, I will take Columbus," he pleaded. He also told Lincoln the men were disappointed at not being allowed to march upon Columbus. Claiming to be tired of delays and inaction, the general suggested a plan: "We should fight and push forward, and push forward and fight again."[15] With so much inactivity in other theaters, Lincoln must have welcomed a general who wanted to fight.

The general also instructed the president on the diplomatic ramifications of inactivity: "Will Europe wait much longer?" he inquired. European recognition would hurt American finances, McClernand claimed, perhaps hoping an economic plea might get him his independent command.[16] Whatever the justification — military, diplomatic, or economic — McClernand wanted an independent assignment. He was not particularly concerned what method worked or how he might receive this favor from Lincoln — he just wanted it.

McClernand was not alone in wanting to take the offensive. Grant had similar ideas. Grant believed the proper line of operations for his Union army was up the Tennessee and Cumberland rivers, which he believed would force the enemy completely out of Kentucky.[17] On January 28 he formally requested permission from Halleck to begin a campaign against Fort Henry, on the Tennessee River: "With permission, I will take Fort Henry, on the Tennessee, and establish and hold a large camp there." Andrew H. Foote, commanding the navy at Cairo, supported Grant's plan. Two days later Halleck gave his permission and the campaign up the Tennessee River began.[18]

This was an excellent proposal as the Confederates were not prepared for a move against either Fort Henry or Fort Donelson on the Cumberland River. Conditions at both forts were inexcusably weak since Confederate commanders neglected these river defenses. In early January both places were manned by a total of 4,600 men, 2,000 unarmed. Both rebel commanders in the area, Johnston and Polk, were warned of the forts' feeble conditions, but did nothing to strengthen them.[19] The terrain surrounding Fort Henry was virtually indefensible. An artillerist sent to the fort in September 1861 made an alarming discovery — during an average February, the rise of the Tennessee River would put the fort under two feet of water. This was communicated to Confederate authorities, but nothing was done. The fort was in imminent danger.[20]

Grant's forces were placed in two divisions, one commanded by McClernand, the other under General C.F. Smith's command. McClernand's division was composed of three brigades, under Colonels Richard J. Oglesby, W.H.L. Wallace, and William R. Morrison. All units — infantry, cavalry, and artillery — were made up of Illinois men. The general's staff included Major Mason Brayman, assistant adjutant general; Captain Adolph Schwartz, chief of staff; Captain James Dunlap, assistant quartermaster and aide; and Captain Warren Stewart, Lieutenants Henry C. Freeman, William H. Heath, and E.S. Jones, all aides.[21] The officers and men were ready to go.

The Fort Henry assault was to be three pronged. McClernand's division would advance from the east side of the Tennessee River, marching around the inundated Panther Creek. Smith's division would take Fort Heiman, located on commanding ground on the west bank of the Tennessee. And thirdly the gunboats were to hammer the fort from the river.

The movement began on February 2 when McClernand's First Division sailed up the Ohio River from Cairo to Paducah. There he met with Grant, who instructed McClernand to continue, allowing the two gunboats to precede the transports. The First Division turned into the muddy Tennessee River and disembarked at about 4:30 A.M. on February 4 at the Itra Landing, eight miles north of Fort Henry, on the east side of the river. After landing, McClernand sent aides to select the best campground and sent a cavalry detachment to reconnoiter towards the fort. The general himself rode out to scout the approaches to the intended target. Grant came to the landing site and met with McClernand when he returned from the scouting trip and ordered the First Division to reembark and land again closer to the rebel garrison. The second landing was accomplished in short order and the men disembarked at Bailey's Ferry, four miles from Fort Henry. That afternoon the division set up camp, which McClernand dubbed "Camp Halleck."[22]

Once established McClernand sent a cavalry detachment to scout the area between the camp and Fort Henry and later that evening the general and his staff made a reconnaissance. In addition, the general procured the services of a scout/spy, Charles Carpenter, a member of a unit called the Jessie Scouts.[23] He sent two regiments of infantry and a battery of artillery to guard the road leading from Panther Creek to the fort. The creek fed into the Tennessee River and was inundated at that time of year. That night, the fourth, the fires from Camp Halleck must have warned the Confederates in Fort Henry of the impending attack.[24]

The next day McClernand ordered Colonel Oglesby to reconnoiter in force the land between the camp and the fort. Oglesby discovered that, although artillery could travel on the roads, some of the creek crossings were impassable from recent rains. The force got to within a mile of the fort before coming in contact with enemy soldiers; there was a short skirmish and the Confederates withdrew.[25] In his report to Grant, McClernand stated that Fort Henry was being reinforced by steamers on the river. He suggested a plan for the gunboats to run past the fort during the night and sink the transports carrying the Confederate reinforcements. Rain and darkness would provide adequate cover for the naval flotilla. Once that was done the army and navy would converge on the unprotected fort.[26]

During the evening of February 5 General Grant sent out orders for the next day's movement, instructing the First Division to move out at 11:00 A.M. Gunboats would move at the same time, and Grant hoped the attack by both army and navy would come off simultaneously. He did not take into consideration the muddy condition of the roads, but Foote did and the admiral predicted the navy would take the fort without the army. McClernand directed his brigade commanders to prepare their men to march with two days' cooked rations in their haversacks and forty rounds of ammunition in their cartridge boxes. He concluded by admonishing them to "be active and energetic!"[27] An engineer from department headquarters, Lieutenant Colonel James B. McPherson, was sent to guide McClernand's men toward Fort Henry.

The First Division took the road from Bailey's Ferry to the Telegraph Road, which connected Fort Henry with Fort Donelson, twelve miles away. While trudging through the mud McClernand and his command watched for rebel reinforcements to Fort Henry and escapees from it. Once they reached the Telegraph Road, Fort Henry would be effectively cut off and its surrender a foregone conclusion.

The distance between Camp Halleck and Fort Henry was eight miles overland, four by the river. McClernand started his division toward the fort at 11:00 A.M. with nine companies of cavalry in the lead. Behind the horsemen were five regiments of infantry and two batteries of artillery, all part of the First Brigade. Colonel Wallace's Second Brigade was next in line with four infantry regiments and two batteries of artillery. The Third Brigade followed, and one company of cavalry served as the rearguard. The recent rains made marching difficult and slow, and the roads were described as being "reduced to the consistency of soft porridge."[28]

After marching through the mud for two hours the First Division had advanced all of four miles. Besides the bad condition of the road, several streams were too swollen to cross, so bridges had to be constructed. At about 1:00 P.M. the First Division heard firing from the gunboats and, hoping to cut off any retreat, hurried the movement to the fort. Two hours after the firing started McClernand received a report that the enemy was evacuating Fort Henry. He then ordered his cavalry to ride ahead and cut off the withdrawal or vigorously pursue any retreating Confederates.[29]

While the cavalry pursued the withdrawal the infantry marched on toward Fort Henry, reaching it about 3:30. The 18th Illinois, part of the First Brigade, was the first of McClernand's command to enter the fort, and they found that the garrison had already surrendered to Foote and the navy. Confederate general Lloyd Tilghman gave up the fort, having sent all but some 80 artillerymen to Fort Donelson. The cavalry pursuit netted 38 prisoners, six pieces of artillery with carriages, one caisson, and a large number of small arms.[30]

The capture of Fort Henry was a virtually bloodless victory. The navy suffered 2 killed and 37 wounded, while the army sustained almost no casualties. General McClernand reported losses only in animals and property from the march, none to combat. The First Division spent the night of the 6th in Fort Henry rummaging through the stores the Confederates had left. Logan's 31st Illinois donned gray uniforms they found while their own dried out. The fort's capture also meant taking possession of everything in it, which included 17 pieces of artillery in addition to the six pieces McClernand's cavalry took.[31]

The next day McClernand took it upon himself to honor Commodore Foote by renaming Fort Henry as Fort Foote.[32] He also sent a party to reconnoiter the land between Forts Henry and Donelson. These scouts advanced to within a mile of Fort Donelson, where they learned that the rebels from Fort Henry had fallen back to Donelson. A prisoner taken on the reconnaissance mission reported that reinforcements numbering about 15,000 men were moving toward the Cumberland River fort. McClernand questioned the truth of that report, as a prudent officer should. The general also reported that the guns at the fort were positioned to command the land approaches. McClernand suggested an attack by the gunboats simultaneous to a land assault.[33] For the next several days McClernand's cavalry scouted the area between the two forts, preparing for an advance on Fort Donelson.

McClernand did not lose a chance to inform Lincoln of the victory won at Fort Henry. Two days after the surrender he recounted the movements of his division and the fleet. He emphasized that his division was the first to enter the fort, and that his men likewise performed the pursuit of the retreating rebels. He also reported on the fort's new name and subsequent reconnaissance missions toward Fort Donelson. Not surprisingly, the general omitted any mention of Grant in his report to the president. He called the capture of Fort Henry "perhaps the most complete victory achieved during the war," and it sounded like he was taking credit for it.[34]

Like most other men in the Federal army, McClernand had his sights set on Fort Donelson. After several reconnaissance missions toward the fort the general sent Grant a plan for attacking it, a remarkable proposal that illustrated McClernand's narrow-minded focus on his own command. His First Division would take two different roads toward Fort Donelson. Arriving at the fort his men would form into a line of battle with his First and Second brigades forming the flanks, which would rest on creeks that were not fordable. If the Third Brigade did not fit into this line it would form the reserve while the artillery would occupy a high ridge that commanded the fort. The gunboats would cooperate with the infantry assault.[35]

In both general and specific terms it was not a bad plan. Unfordable creeks covered both of the flanks so they could not be turned. He made provisions for a reserve unit. The artillery was placed in a good position on high ground. And McClernand planned on the cooperation of the navy so the fort would receive fire from two sides. The only factor he did not properly consider was numbers. He reported to Grant that Fort Donelson was being reinforced by some 15,000 men (although he discounted the report), yet he believed he could take it with only one division. He was probably deceived by the ease with which Fort Henry had been captured. Because McClernand did not have a West Point education or military experience, he clearly did not understand the strategy of investing a fortress. With few exceptions (like Fort Henry) the attacking army must have superior numbers. The plan also displayed the general's preoccupation with his own division while not considering the rest of the army. He wanted all of the glory and accolades for himself and his division.

With attention focused squarely on Fort Donelson, Grant held a council of war to determine his subordinate officers' opinions on a movement toward the target. It was an interesting and diverse group of officers. Grant was in charge, but he was a soft spoken leader who did not habitually hold formal councils. Also in attendance was newly promoted Brigadier General Lew Wallace, who recorded the discussions at the meeting. Grant's two division commanders, McClernand and C.F. Smith, were also present. Smith was a regular army officer who had taught Grant at West Point. Now Grant's subordinate, Smith simply advocated an immediate advance upon Fort Donelson. McClernand, who had been described by Wallace as "brave, industrious, methodical, and of unquestioned cleverness," spoke next. He had prepared a rather lengthy plan that he read for the officers. It seemed to be a duplicate of the plan he had sent to Grant two days before. It featured his division, of course, with it in the van of the advance to the fort. Wallace recorded that Grant seemed disgusted with McClernand's presentation and quickly ended the meeting, apparently having already decided to move. One of Grant's biographers noted that the general thereafter dispensed with the "charade" of holding councils of war.[36]

Grant then made dispositions for the movement to the Cumberland River fort and sent them to his division commanders. The advance was to begin on February 12 with McClernand's First Division in the lead. It was to take two different roads, the Telegraph Road and the Ridge Road, toward Donelson with the Second Division, under General Smith, following.[37] The Telegraph Road was the more direct, about 12 miles to Fort Donelson, while the Ridge Road was a circuitous route, located a mile south of the Telegraph Road, and about 14 miles to the fort.[38]

McClernand directed his brigades to camp the night of February 11 about three miles from Fort Henry on the roads they were to take on the march the next day. Colonel Oglesby's First Brigade, which consisted of the 8th, 18th, 29th, 30th, and 31st Illinois regiments, two batteries of artillery, and four companies of cavalry, was to move on the Ridge Road. The Second Brigade, commanded by Colonel W.H.L. Wallace, would take the Telegraph Road. It included the 11th, 20th, 45th, and 48th Illinois Regiments, two batteries of artillery, and the 4th Illinois Cavalry. The Third Brigade, under Colonel Morrison, would follow the First Brigade on the Ridge Road. Intended to be the division's reserve, it comprised the 17th and 49th Illinois regiments. Two other regiments attached to the Third Brigade, the 32nd and 43rd Illinois, were ordered to remain at Fort Henry. The march was to commence "at an early hour" on February 12 and stop when within two miles of Fort Donelson.[39]

McClernand's First Division started its march on the 12th at 8:00 A.M. and got within two miles of the fort before noon. Confederate pickets contested the Federals' arrival, but were easily beaten back. McClernand placed the division on the right of the Union line, covering the left side of the rebel fort. When Grant arrived at 2:00 P.M. he placed the Second Division on the left of the line and directed General McClernand to move his men farther to the right. This was to prevent an escape from Donelson through Dover, a small river town two miles east of the fort. The First Brigade of the First Division was placed on the extreme right of the line covering the army's flank and the Second Brigade was to the left of the First Brigade. To the left of the Second Brigade was the Third Brigade, which connected to the Second Division and anchored the center of the entire Federal line.[40]

With the First and Second divisions in place Grant had approximately 15,000 men. Still on the way were 10,000 men in transports and 2,500 troops yet to arrive from Fort Henry. Until these men arrived Grant could do little since the Confederates had approximately 17,500 men inside Donelson, commanded by generals John B. Floyd, Gideon Pillow, and Simon B. Buckner, in order of seniority.

Outnumbered as he was, the Federal commander did not want a general engagement, so the remainder of February 12 was used getting into proper position and scouting the Confederate defensive line. When the 13th dawned McClernand continued to reconnoiter the right side of the Yankee line. During the morning some rebel batteries opened fire into the First Division. Because Grant ordered his officers to avoid a general engagement McClernand did not return fire immediately. After an hour and a half the Confederate cannonade stopped. McClernand then directed his artillery to open fire, an exchange he believed to be within Grant's order against a general engagement. What ensued was a relatively harmless exchange of artillery fire confined to the right side of McClernand's line, where the First Brigade was located.[41]

Shortly before noon the Confederates opened fire with artillery on the Second Brigade's position. This also was relatively harmless, more annoying than destructive. However, McClernand determined to silence the batteries and ordered the 17th, 49th, and 48th Illinois regiments to attack them. The 17th was part of the Second Brigade while the 48th and 49th constituted the Third Brigade. This assault was against orders and Grant recorded that the attack was made "without orders or authority."[42] The attackers advanced to within 50 paces of the enemy breastworks uncontested. Still undisciplined and inexperienced, the men opened fire without orders. The rebels returned fire and an hour-long firefight ensued.[43]

The Federal charge was subjected to a crossfire from both Confederate artillery and infantry. McClernand ordered the 45th Illinois, part of the Second Brigade, to support the assault. At this point the general believed that a diversionary movement on the left or bombardment by the gunboats would have rendered his attack successful. The assault progressed to the edge of the rebel works before the Federal line withdrew from the heavy Confederate fire. The number of casualties sustained in this senseless charge was 128. The unauthorized costly affair accomplished nothing, but McClernand praised it, probably because his First Division was involved, and exaggerated its significance: "Considering the difficulties attending this attack ... the brave and steady advance of the assailants may be justly regarded as one of the most brilliant and striking incidents of the four days' siege, gloriously terminating in the fall of Fort Donelson."[44]

The assault had ended, but the artillery exchange from both sides did not, and it continued well into the afternoon. The barrage was confined to the right side of McClernand's line, and he termed it "experimental." The artillery fire was continued to determine its effectiveness upon the fort at long range. It was apparently effective since percussion shells were fired into Donelson and were seen exploding within the fort, scattering Confederates and damaging buildings inside the fortress.[45]

By the time night fell on the 13th McClernand's men had been under artillery fire most of the day. At nightfall the weather turned bitterly cold and it began to snow and sleet. The men were unprepared for this since many had discarded their overcoats during the previous day's march to Donelson. Tents and camp equipment were likewise left behind. Because of the proximity of the opposing forces, campfires were not allowed, causing a most uncomfortable night. The men spent the evening shivering while Union and Confederate pickets exchanged shots. Yet spirits were high and the men had "one universal wish to meet the enemy, to carry the fort, and to end the suffering."[46]

On February 14 the gunboats took their turn at trying to reduce Fort Donelson, attempting a repeat of their victory a week earlier at Fort Henry. At about 3:00 P.M. Flag Officer Andrew H. Foote attacked the fort with four ironclad and two wooden gunboats. The vessels advanced to within 400 yards of Donelson during the attack, which lasted about an hour and a quarter. In this blaze of artillery fire Foote's flagship, the *St. Louis*, was hit 59 times and disabled by a shot to its wheel. Another ironclad, the *Louisville*, was likewise crippled by a direct hit to its tiller ropes. The rebels hit the other ships (the *Carondolet* and the *Pittsburgh* were the other two ironclads, and the *Tyler* and

Conestoga were the two wooden gunboats) many times, inflicting tremendous damage. The attack failed and the navy suffered 54 killed and wounded. Foote claimed that if he could have continued for another 15 minutes he would have captured the fort.[47]

Meanwhile, the army was busy as it watched and listened to the barrage of fire from the river, the noise from which one soldier called "terrific."[48] On McClernand's front the day was spent extending the line and reconnoitering the flank. There was one possible escape route for the Confederates and it was through McClernand's line. Just two miles east of the fort was Dover, and on from there was a road, Charlotte (or Forge) Road, that led southward toward Charlotte and then on to Nashville. That road had to be blocked, but McClernand's flank stopped about 300–400 yards short. If he simply extended the line it would be so thin as to be vulnerable to a Confederate attack. Luckily, General Lew Wallace arrived from Fort Henry with troops, designated the Third Division, and they were placed between the First and Second divisions. This allowed McClernand to stretch his line farther toward the road. And the gunboats unloaded the long awaited 10,000 men, bringing Grant's force to about 27,000.

McClernand knew that if the rebels attempted a breakout it would be on his side of the line. That was precisely what Confederate commanders planned during the night of February 14. Generals Floyd, Pillow, and Buckner made preparations for an assault against the Federal right to occur early in the morning of the 15th. The Union army spent another cold sleepless night.

The morning of February 15 Grant went on board the flagship to confer with Foote and while he was away he left none of his subordinates in overall command of the field. One of Grant's biographers claimed this was because the general had no confidence in any of his division or brigade commanders. Regardless of the reason, Grant was away and nobody else had control of the battlefield.[49]

The Confederate onslaught started about 6:00 A.M. in an attempt to open the Charlotte Road. Colonel John McArthur's brigade, part of the Second Division, held the extreme right flank of the army and bore the brunt of the opening barrage. To the left of McArthur was Colonel Oglesby's brigade and next in line was Colonel W.H.L. Wallace's brigade. When the battle began McArthur and Oglesby formed their men to oppose the Confederate attack. Seeing early that he would need reinforcements, McClernand sent a request to General Lew Wallace, whose Third Division was in position next to the First Division. Wallace passed this request to Grant and sent a brigade to aid McClernand. Colonel Charles Cruft brought up his brigade, consisting of three regiments, and took a position behind Oglesby's men as a reserve.[50]

The fight raged for two hours without word from Grant. By 8:00 A.M.

the right wing of the Federal line was in trouble. The Confederates concentrated their attack on one point in the Federal line, and the Yankee supply of ammunition did not keep up with the demands of the battle. This forced McArthur's men to withdraw, exposing Oglesby's brigade to a flanking fire. The entire right of the Union line was bending back, and some men were running from the battlefield. Another message was sent to Grant's headquarters. Two of Grant's staff officers, captains William S. Hillyer and John Rawlins, mounted their horses and dashed off. Hillyer went to contact Grant while Rawlins inspected the battlefield.

The withdrawal of McArthur's and Oglesby's brigades exposed McClernand's Second Brigade, under Colonel Wallace, to a flanking fire. McClernand told Wallace to hold steady and maintain his position "at all hazards" until more reinforcements arrived. Wallace decided he could not hold his line and ordered a withdrawal to form a new line of battle. The entire First and Second Brigades were in full retreat, intent on re-forming their lines.[51]

By noon McArthur's, Oglesby's, and Wallace's brigades had withdrawn about 400 yards, where they received supplies and ammunition and re-formed their line at a right angle with the old line. General Lew Wallace sent another brigade, under Colonel John A. Thayer, to stop the rebel attack. The Confederates' road of escape had been clearly open for over an hour, but they suffered from weak leadership and did not take advantage of their opportunity. Finally, at about 1:30 P.M. Grant arrived and took control of the battlefield.[52]

He found McClernand and Wallace in conference, and McClernand, apparently unhappy with Grant, muttered, "This army wants a head." Grant caught the remark and answered, "It seems so."[53] The three quickly decided to retake the lost positions on the right and to close the Charlotte Road. McClernand prepared his division while Grant went to the left wing to order General Smith's Second Division to attack. Confronted with this new assault, the rebels would have to weaken their force in front of McClernand. While Smith's advance started, Grant sent one of his staff, Colonel J.D. Webster, to inform McClernand to push forward. This was accomplished and the First Division reoccupied its former position as the Confederates retreated back into Fort Donelson.[54]

The Federal army held the battlefield after an all day battle. McClernand's division spent the night of February 15 in line of battle having suffered 1,502 casualties.[55] While preparing to resume the attack the next day McClernand learned of the fort's surrender. Jubilation reigned as the Federal army captured yet another rebel fort in the Confederate heartland.

McClernand wasted no time in claiming his division's place in winning the twin victories at Henry and Donelson. On February 17, the day after the surrender, he issued his congratulatory order for the capture of the two forts.

In it he announced the accomplishments of the First Division and proclaimed, "The death-knell of rebellion is sounded." While that claim was premature McClernand rightly stated, "An army has been annihilated, and the way to Nashville and Memphis is opened." He concluded by applauding his men with these words: "It will be your claim to a place in the affection of your countrymen and upon a blazoned page in history." This was a typical document for the general since it gushed with praise for his division and neglected all other parts of the army.[56]

As in the past McClernand also attempted to give a name to the battle and he wrote to the president. The general suggested to Grant that the battles of February 13–16 be called "The Battle of the Cumberland," if they had not already been named.[57] Wasting no time in reporting to Lincoln, on the 18th McClernand briefly described the capture of Donelson and enclosed a copy of his congratulatory order. He reported only on the First Division and did not mention that Grant was present. In words that smacked of insubordination he claimed that the high casualties in his division was a result of not being properly supported. McClernand ended with some sound strategic advice for the army: "We should now push on to Memphis and Nashville."[58]

At some time during the war a break occurred between McClernand and Grant, and some historians date this break from the Fort Henry campaign. One suggestion was that the problem stemmed from the Itra Landing debarkation on February 4, but that seems unlikely.[59] Grant probably started to grow annoyed and suspicious of McClernand after his congratulatory order after Belmont. This weariness probably increased during the council of war before the advance to Fort Donelson when Grant was visibly disturbed. Also, McClernand's habit of writing directly to Lincoln certainly wore thin. There was probably not one single incident that led directly to the break, but rather an accumulation of events.

Yet another historian has recognized that McClernand's "political agenda began to surface" during the campaign and rebuked the general because his battle reports concentrated entirely upon his own division. One must consider the purpose of battle reports — to detail the actions of one's units — so McClernand's after action reports must, by their very nature, concentrate on his command.[60] McClernand deserves censure for writing directly to Lincoln, circumventing the normal channels for official correspondence. These letters, whether informational, operational, or requesting an independent command, should have gone through the district or department headquarters or both before (if ever) reaching President Lincoln.

McClernand was obviously not an experienced commander and had much to learn about leading men and about military protocol. The Henry-Donelson campaign was only his second active military engagement. He was first a politician, and to think he would not use his contacts for advancement was perhaps naïve. That does not excuse his actions, but McClernand was just learning the art of war. He soon got his chance to demonstrate what he learned from the Twin Rivers Campaign. The army moved from Donelson up the Tennessee River deep into the Confederate heartland. There, in northern Mississippi, was an important railroad center at Corinth, where the Mobile & Ohio and Memphis & Charleston railroads converged. Just north of Corinth on the Tennessee River was a river landing called Pittsburg.

7

Into the Confederate Heartland

The twin victories at Fort Henry and Fort Donelson gave the Union cause a much-needed lift. The two forts made up the center of a Confederate defensive line that stretched from Columbus, Kentucky, to Knoxville, Tennessee, and their loss literally ripped the guts out of General Albert S. Johnston's defensive strategy. It would enable Grant's army to advance farther south and position itself between General Polk at Columbus and Johnston at Bowling Green. This accomplished, the Federal army would have interior lines and could flank either enemy force. The capture of the forts combined with the Yankee victory at Mill Springs/Logan's Crossroads in January forced the entire right of the rebel line to reel in defeat. Only Johnston himself at Bowling Green withdrew from the right unscathed. He took his men to Nashville, then to Corinth, Mississippi, where he joined with Polk's force and 10,000 men from Florida under General Braxton Bragg.

Grant recognized the opportunity to continue the campaign. It was a good time to take advantage of Tennessee's vulnerability as the Confederates were abandoning it. Grant proposed to move up the Cumberland River and take Clarksville, then Nashville, and believed he could take the former by February 21 and the latter by March 1.[1] In this move, which began in early March, McClernand commanded the First Division, composed of three brigades. The First Brigade included the 8th, 29th, 30th, and 31st Illinois regiments, Dresser's Battery, and Dollins, O'Harnett's, and Carmichael's cavalry. The Second Brigade consisted of the 11th, 18th, 20th, and 45th Illinois regiments, the 1st Battalion of the 4th Illinois Cavalry, and Taylor's Battery. The Third Brigade was made up of the 17th, 43rd, 49th, and 52nd Illinois regiments and McAllister's and Schwartz's batteries. The strength of the First Division was 7,028.[2]

The Federal plan called for Grant's army to join General Don Carlos Buell's Army of the Ohio and move deep into Tennessee and fight Johnston's rebels. In preparation for this move Grant, McClernand, and Colonel W.H.L. Wallace visited Clarksville on February 20.[3] While Buell's lead column occupied the important city of Nashville on February 24, McClernand was in bed with what he called a "painful and severe sickness."[4] He recovered enough to visit Nashville on February 27 with Grant and Wallace and while Grant conferred with Buell, McClernand and Wallace visited President James K. Polk's widow. This was a pleasant experience for McClernand because he had held President Polk in high esteem.[5]

While at Nashville McClernand again wrote Lincoln, this time complaining about how he had been treated. He stated that little information could get to the president about him through official channels, so the general had to write directly to Lincoln. He briefly recounted how his division was the first into both forts Henry and Donelson and to Clarksville. McClernand

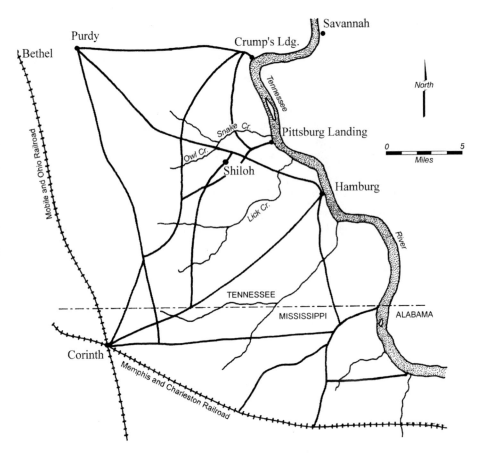

Shiloh, 1862 (map by Julie Barnes Smith).

claimed that at Donelson his First Division suffered over 1,500 casualties and the rest of the army less than 280. The gist of the correspondence was that he was not receiving the proper recognition, especially from Lincoln. This the general blamed on Lincoln's lack of information: "If you were acquainted with all the facts I think you would conclude that you had not done me justice." This may have been in response to Grant's promotion to major general while McClernand was yet a brigadier.[6]

The movement of Grant's army up the Tennessee River toward Savannah began in early March 1862 without its commanding general. Grant's absence was a result of the jealousy of the department commander, General Henry W. Halleck, who was envious of Grant's success at forts Henry and Donelson and tried to take the credit himself for those victories. Halleck claimed Grant did not report to him promptly and had lost contact with the department commander. Halleck also reported to General-in-Chief George B. McClellan in Washington that Grant had taken up his former bad habit — and was drinking again. For those reasons — Grant's alleged drinking and losing communication with Halleck — he was removed from command. Brigadier General C.F. Smith was placed in charge of the army and led its advance up the Tennessee while Grant waited at Fort Henry.

This presented a problem to John McClernand. When the army arrived at Metal Landing, Tennessee, on March 5 McClernand complained that he outranked Smith. He apparently did not know that Grant had been removed because he lodged a complaint with his commander: "I rank him as a brigadier and cannot recognize his superiority without self-degradation, which no human power can constrain me to do."[7] After stewing about it for some time McClernand fired off a letter to Smith stating that he received and recognized orders from General Grant only.[8] As for this ranking controversy, Smith's brigadier's commission dated from August 31, 1861 while McClernand's was offered on August 7, 1861 to date from May 17.[9] Technically, McClernand did indeed outrank Smith. This controversy may have been moot, as Grant used Sherman as the "'informal' camp commander" in Grant's absence.[10]

While this wrangling over rank was going on both McClernand and Smith were recommended for promotion. Illinois congressman Elihu B. Washburne made the recommendations to President Lincoln on March 1 and two days later the president sent a list of promotions to secretary of war Edwin M. Stanton.[11] In short order the Senate confirmed the promotions, and McClernand's major general's commission was dated March 21, 1862.[12] This was the benefit McClernand reaped from the successful campaigns against forts Henry and Donelson.

The confusion over rank between McClernand and Smith underscored the importance of Grant's absence. In response to the commanding general's removal, McClernand and several other officers penned a letter for Grant to use as he wished. "We have heard with deep regret of your having been deposed from your authority as Commander in the field of the forces in this district," it began. Offering thanks, respect, and gratitude, the officers continued: "As our Commander at Belmont and Forts Henry and Donelson, besides in numerous more skirmishes, you were successful. Under your lead the flag of the Union has been carried from the interior further towards the seaboard than by any other hands. You have slain more of the enemy, taken more prisoners and trophies, lost more men in battle and regained more territory to the Union than any other leader.... We place this spontaneous tribute at your disposal for such use as you may think proper to make of it."[13] In addition to this letter, Grant's officers ordered a ceremonial sword for their ousted commander. These actions were significant for several reasons. The letter and sword provided moral support for Grant just when he needed it most and McClernand's backing of Grant also provided powerful political support at a crucial time. When Grant was finally restored to command McClernand wrote to congratulate him on his "restoration to the functions incident to your rank and command. I hope soon to see you with us."[14] Considering the strained nature of their relations, it was an honorable act for McClernand to sustain his commander.

While Grant was being reinstated the Federal advance up the Tennessee continued. McClernand moved his division to Savannah, a small town on the east side of the Tennessee River, about 25 miles from Corinth, Mississippi. McClernand was ordered to occupy Savannah on March 14 and this was quickly accomplished.[15] When Grant returned to command he found his five divisions widely dispersed: at Pittsburg Landing were the divisions of Generals William T. Sherman and Stephen A. Hurlbut; General Lew Wallace's division was at Crump's Landing, located on the west bank of the Tennessee six miles from Pittsburg; and at Savannah were McClernand's and Smith's divisions. On March 20 McClernand moved his troops to Pittsburg Landing as Grant concentrated four of his five divisions there, leaving Lew Wallace at Crump's Landing.[16] General Benjamin M. Prentiss' division shortly joined Grant's army at Pittsburg Landing.

While his army was in position at Pittsburg Landing Grant maintained his headquarters at Savannah, and with Grant away the argument over rank between Smith and McClernand flared up again. On March 26 McClernand fired a message to Smith that he received orders only from Grant. Smith referred the letter to Grant with the notation that he "shall not notice this communication of Genl. McClernand, awaiting Genl. Grant's decision."[17] This forced Grant to issue Special Order No. 36, which named Smith the senior officer and in command at Pittsburg Landing until Grant arrived.[18] Even that did not satisfy McClernand. The next day he complained to Grant that as a brigadier he outranked Smith, and he wanted to be advised as to how Smith became his senior. McClernand wrote that "no earthly power" could make him recognize Smith's seniority unless promotion put Smith ahead of McClernand. Although claiming to respect Smith as a "gallant, experienced, and skillful commander," McClernand stated he would follow orders from him as if they originated from Grant.[19] The commanding general referred the question to General Halleck, who in turn passed it up to secretary of war Stanton. The secretary replied to Halleck, who sent a telegram to Grant on April 5: "The rank of Maj Genls is Grant Buell Pope McClernand CF Smith Wallace."[20] Grant solved the problem for the immediate future by moving his headquarters to Pittsburg Landing. The disagreement between the generals became moot when Smith injured his leg and died on April 25, 1862. Nevertheless the bickering among generals over seniority, common during the war, could only harm the cooperation of divisions and effectiveness of the army.

As if on cue, McClernand took the opportunity of a lull in the fighting to inform President Lincoln on the circumstances in the army. He sent a copy of his report on the capture of Fort Donelson, a move probably intended to show what part his division took in reducing the garrison. Since the general mentioned only himself and his troops in this report, he perhaps wanted to create the impression that his division did the great majority, if not all, of the fighting, and therefore deserved all the credit. He also passed along a copy of his correspondence with General Smith as it related to the rank and seniority question. He may have hoped to persuade Lincoln to intercede on his behalf and announce that McClernand outranked Smith. Finally, McClernand again requested an independent command "in an active and contested field," and if that requested were granted he would try to reward Lincoln's confidence with success. Once again the Illinois general circumvented the chain of command and corresponded directly with the president.[21]

While McClernand and Smith engaged in useless backbiting and McClernand complained to Lincoln, three armies prepared for battle. Grant's divisions, now called the Army of the Tennessee, were concentrated at Pittsburg Landing with designs to move on Corinth. The other Federal army, General Buell's Army of the Ohio, had occupied and left Nashville to join Grant.[22] The two armies combined would put about 68,000 men in the field (48,000 under Grant and 20,000 under Buell).[23] Once these two armies joined, department commander Halleck intended to take over and lead the advance on Corinth. Opposing this array of men was the Confederate Army of Tennessee under General Albert S. Johnston. The rebel government had also sent General P.G.T. Beauregard from Virginia to serve as Johnston's second-in-command. This Confederate army numbered about 42,000 men.

While awaiting the arrival of Buell, Grant's five divisions were spread over an area about two miles long. Sherman's division was on the right, near Owl Creek, which fed into Snake Creek and into the Tennessee. McClernand's division was on Sherman's left behind a small log building, Shiloh Church. Next to McClernand was the division of General Prentiss, and on the extreme left was one of Sherman's brigades under General David Stuart. The Federal left was on Lick Creek, which also ran into the Tennessee River. The divisions of Hurlbut and Smith (Smith's division was commanded by W.H.L. Wallace) were positioned as a reserve. As the army was positioned between Owl and Lick creeks, Grant's army was relatively safe from a turning movement. Any Confederate attack could come only through the three-mile gap between Owl and Lick creeks. Since Grant expected to advance he did not order his army to entrench, which left the troops unprotected against a possible frontal assault.

About a week before the attack took place McClernand got a hint that there were Confederate troops in the area. A man who lived in the vicinity reported to the general's headquarters that there was southern cavalry in the area. On April 1, McClernand held a review of his division and three butternut-clad men watched from a nearby rooftop. McClernand passed these warnings on to Sherman and Grant and suggested that both divisions send out a cavalry detachment to investigate.[24]

Early in the morning of April 6 the Confederate army under Johnston attacked the unsuspecting Union army. When the battle began Grant was at his headquarters in Savannah, but he hurried to Pittsburg Landing and the scene of the fighting, arriving at 9:00 A.M. The Confederates had assaulted Sherman's line and he requested support from McClernand. The Illinoisan responded, sending three regiments to help defend the area between the two divisions. A large force of rebels passed Sherman's left and made a full-scale attack on McClernand's front.[25]

By 9:00 A.M. the battle was two hours old, the entire Federal line was engaged, and McClernand had lost nine field officers (two colonels, two lieutenant colonels, and five majors).[26] Sherman's troops had received the brunt of the initial attack and had withdrawn, abandoning their original line. On the left of McClernand's line, his Third Brigade was forming to move to support Sherman when the Illinois general noticed a large force in his front bearing the American flag. McClernand believed these men were deceptive Confederates, but most likely they were elements of General Prentiss' division. At this point McClernand and Sherman re-formed and stabilized their lines about a half mile behind the original line and closer to Pittsburg Landing.[27]

At this juncture, about 10:30 A.M., the Confederates made a concentrated attack on McClernand's whole line. A furious assault followed and for about the next four hours Yankee and rebel troops surged and withdrew. The

First Division was in the midst of some of the worst fighting, with its commander "acting in perfect concert" with Sherman, commanding the Fifth Division.[28] An hour later, at about 11:30 A.M., McClernand and Sherman started a counter stroke, the initial Federal offensive of the day. The Confederates were unprepared for this assault and they broke. McClernand caused more confusion in the enemy ranks by ordering a bayonet charge. The Illinois general and several staff officers ran up and down the line urging the men forward, literally yelling, "Forward!"[29]

By 2:00 P.M. McClernand's division had withdrawn and re-formed its line five times and was low on ammunition. The division's ordnance officer brought up more ammunition which was distributed among the troops. This done, McClernand noticed a large enemy force gathering to his left, evidently preparing to turn his flank. Upon consultation with Sherman, the First Division commander ordered yet another withdrawal, the sixth of the day.[30]

Meanwhile the Confederates vented their full fury on the left of the Union line, where General Prentiss and his division put up a determined defense. At a place variously called the Sunken Road and the Hornets' Nest, Prentiss repulsed rebel attacks all morning and afternoon. Troops on both sides of his division had withdrawn, leaving Prentiss vulnerable on three sides. Late in the afternoon, only after the Confederates brought up 62 pieces of artillery, Prentiss and his division finally surrendered. The hard fighting of these men allowed the rest of the army to re-form its lines and bring up fresh troops.

McClernand's First Division established its sixth line and awaited the ensuing assault. The new line was formed, along with Sherman's division, with the right covering the bridge by which Lew Wallace's division was expected to arrive any minute. The rebel cavalry carried out the next attack and when the horsemen got within 30 paces of the Federal line McClernand gave the order to fire. One volley was enough to cause the cavalrymen to retreat in disorder. While this cavalry attack was repulsed the enemy concentrated its infantry for a final assault on the First Division. To defend against this attack McClernand ordered the left of his line to fall back and form an obtuse angle with the center. In this charge the Confederates abandoned their flanking maneuvers and assaulted the center of the First Division. McClernand's men poured a terrific fire into the rebel line, which was led by Louisiana Zouaves. They wavered then turned and fled the field when McClernand's division counterattacked.[31]

Despite this repulse, the right of the Federal line collapsed. Men streamed to the rear to be under the protection of the gunboats on the Tennessee River. Those not fleeing to the landing were withdrawn in good order to re-form the line for the expected fight the next day. Because of the great ferocity of the battle there was considerable mixing of commands; there was little organizational unity within divisions. The conflict on April 6 lasted ten hours, and Grant recalled that the hardest fighting of the day was that in front of McClernand's and Sherman's divisions.[32] After intense fighting the two armies spent a sleepless, wet night straightening their lines and preparing to resume the battle the next morning. In preparing for the resumption of hostilities the Union army was fortunate to have a large number of fresh troops unengaged on the 6th. General Lew Wallace's division arrived from Crump's Landing and was placed on the extreme right, next to Sherman's division. General Buell's Army of the Ohio came up and took its place in the Union line. The general arrangement of troops for the renewal of battle the next day was Grant's army on the right and Buell's on the left.

Because of the great mixing of commands during the fighting on April 6, Grant ordered McClernand to take command of all detached and fragmented units around his line in addition to his division. Grant also ordered a general movement for the morning of April 7.[33] At daylight the Union advance started with skirmishers in front of the main line. The First Division began its movements only to be annoyed by an enemy battery. McClernand immediately called up artillery of his own, McAllister's Battery, to silence the rebel guns, which it did. The First Division continued its advance and recaptured its lost camp.

An enemy force confronted McClernand's division on its left. A fierce exchange ensued, which McClernand called "one of the severest conflicts" of the two days' fighting at Shiloh. The rebels fell back, but not for long, as they received reinforcements. Luckily for McClernand he also received support from the Louisville Legion, part of General Lovell Rousseau's brigade from Buell's army. This unit poured a withering fire into the Confederates, broke their center, and forced them to retire in disorder.[34]

The advance continued until a messenger from Sherman arrived and informed McClernand of a large enemy force on his left. Again the Illinoisan brought up artillery and blasted the rebels out of that position. Here he conferred with General Alexander McCook, who was commanding a brigade in Buell's army, and who agreed to pursue the enemy McClernand's artillery just dislodged. The First Division engaged the Confederates in its front and drove them back.

The Confederate army made one last stand in front of McClernand's division. Here the general again ordered McAllister's Battery to silence some annoying rebel guns. Without artillery the enemy could not withstand the Union assault and broke for the rear. This essentially ended the second day of fighting, which lasted from 7:00 A.M. until 4:00 P.M. The Confederates were driven back a distance of approximately three miles, but the victorious Federal army organized no vigorous pursuit. When McClernand returned to his tent after the battle, he counted 27 bullet holes in it and found a dead Confederate with his head resting on the general's desk.[35]

The Battle of Shiloh was the fiercest of the war to that time. McClernand's division started with 7,028 men and suffered 1,861 casualties, just over a 26 percent casualty rate.[36] The First Division captured vast stores, including 3,460 small arms, three 6-pounder guns, two carriages, thirteen 6-pounder caissons, and various types of artillery ammunition.[37] The conduct of McClernand and his division was generally good. The only instance of questionable behavior came at the end of the first day after the last Confederate assault was repulsed and some elements of his command retreated to the safety of the gunboats at the landing. McClernand himself never shirked responsibility, often conferring with Sherman and acting in unison with him. In his official report the Fifth Division commander, in fact, complimented McClernand and his division on their conduct during the battle.

McClernand wasted little time in reporting the battle to the president, and as in previous notes his command took center stage. He remarked that his division "as usual, has borne or shared in bearing the brunt." The general briefly summarized his division's activity in the two-day battle and called it "a great mistake" that no pursuit was organized. He suggested that the Confederates would concentrate their efforts in the western theater, bringing in reinforcements from Virginia. McClernand may have done this to strengthen his previous requests for an independent command. He also remembered to thank Lincoln for his promotion in March, which he hoped to "reward by acceptable service." The general's service was acceptable, but his politicking was not.[38]

The Illinois general kept up a steady stream of correspondence to Grant on a variety of topics. Four days after the battle McClernand suggested strategic maneuvers to his commanding general. As he advised Lincoln, McClernand intimated that the Confederates were concentrating troops for a decisive campaign in the west, abandoning Virginia. In view of this information, he recommended either vigorously pursuing the enemy or entrenching and reinforcing their position.[39] Perhaps in response to allegations of discipline problems during the battle, McClernand also broached that subject and specifically asked if a fine was an appropriate punishment to ensure proper discipline. The general himself believed that fines were appropriate for minor offenses, since the court-martial process was inconvenient.[40]

Grant was roundly criticized after the battle for several alleged errors of conduct and tactics. On his conduct, the rumor spread that Grant was drunk during the engagement and that was the reason his army was surprised on April 6. Department commander Halleck apparently believed the allegation and planned to go to Pittsburg Landing to take personal command of the army. Halleck's assumption of command was probably more a result of his jealousy of Grant's success than the rumors that Grant was drunk on April 6. Grant was also widely censured for not digging entrenchments at Pittsburg. Because he planned to move forward on Corinth there was no reason to dig trenches. Nevertheless, upon Halleck's arrival at Pittsburg Landing Grant was removed from command for those transgressions.

Halleck thoroughly reorganized the forces under his command. Buell remained at the head of the Army of the Ohio, but Grant was replaced by General George H. Thomas. Grant was named second-in-command, a useless and unimportant position since he commanded no troops. Halleck called up General John Pope's Army of the Mississippi, which had just captured Island Number 10 on the Mississippi River. When Pope's army arrived on April 21 Halleck had assembled a massive force over 100,000 strong.

In this reorganization McClernand received a new assignment. On April 30 Halleck ordered him to take command of the Reserve Corps, composed of his former First Division, Lew Wallace's division, and one division from Buell's army under General Thomas Crittenden.[41] From an organization position this was a promotion — from commanding one division to leading a corps of three divisions. However, the Reserve Corps rarely saw action so there was little chance for McClernand to distinguish himself in battle.

Halleck planned to advance upon Corinth and occupy it. As a proponent of the Henri Jomini–inspired strategy of maneuver, Halleck wanted to take Corinth without a general engagement. He wanted to keep his forces in close contact so they could support each other, a reaction to the dispersed arrangement of Grant's army just before Shiloh.[42] Halleck ordered all men to carry 100 rounds of ammunition at all times, despite his admonition to subordinates not to bring on a general engagement. His march to Corinth was to be a slow and careful movement, devoid of any risk or danger.

In the early stages of this movement McClernand's Reserve Corps was ordered to investigate numerous enemy threats to the army. From the Shiloh battlefield his cavalry inspected all possible approaches through Owl Creek and kept them under watch. Crossing Owl Creek was a road that led to Purdy, a town about 15 miles west of Pittsburg Landing. Responding to numerous reports of enemy forces gathering at Purdy, McClernand had his horsemen scout the town and roads leading into it.[43] Lew Wallace's division occupied Purdy on May 3.

The first part of the movement was tedious. The army advanced a short distance and entrenched, then it did the same thing the next day. Halleck was determined not to get caught without trenches as Grant had at Shiloh. Lew Wallace recalled the snail-like pace of the advance: "I was notified to move a mile beyond General Sherman in my front, halt the division, and throw up breastworks. Then somebody else passed McClernand a mile and halted, and threw up breastworks. And so it continued a mile a day."[44] By May 15 McClernand's reserve was guarding the entire right flank of the army. Stationed at Locust Hill, his corps was stretched along a line 16 miles long. His corps, minus one entire division assigned elsewhere, was positioned along Owl and Lick Creeks all the way back to Pittsburg Landing. Scouting along this line was difficult since McClernand possessed only 359 cavalrymen.[45]

The slow pace, which Grant described as "a siege from the start to the close," continued and Lew Wallace reported that disgust with the progress of the movement and Halleck's order not to bring on a fight was "very general."[46] By May 21 part of McClernand's reserve under General John A. Logan was within three miles of Corinth and there assumed a fortified position. At this location on the right of the Union line McClernand's men took on the double assignment of an advance and the reserve. A week later McClernand passed information to Grant that he gleaned from an army doctor who had just left Memphis. While there the physician learned from colleagues that the Confederate force at Corinth numbered 146,000 men. The true strength of the rebel army was closer to 70,000 men, one-fourth of whom were listed as sick. Although he refused to comment on the report, McClernand did state that he believed the enemy would show itself in large force at Corinth.[47] On May 28 McClernand's troops moved closer to Corinth and skirmished with enemy pickets about two miles from the town.[48]

On May 28 it was apparent to McClernand and Logan that the Confederates were evacuating Corinth, not reinforcing it as many Federal officers expected. Logan reported to his commander that some of his men had made this determination by putting their ears down on rails of the Mobile & Ohio Railroad and listening to the sounds of the trains. These men believed that empty trains came into Corinth and left loaded with rebel troops.[49] McClernand himself believed that Corinth was being evacuated simply because the Confederates allowed the Union army to approach so close without offering resistance. McClernand and Logan approached Grant with this information on the 28th. Grant took the report to Halleck, who dismissed it with an announcement that the Federal left was in imminent danger of attack.[50]

This attack never materialized and on May 30 the Union army occupied Corinth without firing a shot. The Confederates had been evacuating the town for several days, leaving "Quaker guns" to deceive the Federals. As Corinth was an important rail center this was a fine victory for General Halleck. However, since the rebel army was allowed to escape intact without being damaged in any way, the occupation of Corinth was a hollow victory. The evacuation eased pressure on the commanding general, and McClernand took the opportunity to complain to Halleck. He wrote that Halleck's reorganization of the army placed McClernand in a position of "*actual* inferiority, if not *practical* subordination" to officers inferior to him in rank. This was evident in the comparative size of commands — he had two small divisions while officers junior in rank commanded as many as five divisions (specifically General Thomas). To McClernand this was a personal humiliation. He claimed to bring these facts to Halleck "in no spirit of egotism or vainglory, but in justice." Considering his record in the war it seems likely that his ego and quest for glory were precisely what caused him to bring this matter to Halleck's attention.[51]

Halleck responded to McClernand a few days later and stated that the Illinois general was not put in a subordinate position. The commander stressed the importance of the reserve, that since it supported the left, center, and right of the Union line, its chances for combat were three to one. He explained that the reserve was supposed to be composed of four divisions, but the "exigencies of service in the field" made it necessary to reassign various units, "without regard to the seniority" of the officers involved. He intended no disrespect, Halleck continued, and he pointed out that McClernand's command had doubled since Halleck assumed control of the army. Halleck added that because of troop dispersions General Buell commanded but two divisions and General Thomas was essentially without a command. Despite McClernand's complaint Halleck made no adjustments in his command structure.[52]

Once Corinth was taken Halleck made provisions to occupy and control the surrounding area. On June 2 one of McClernand's divisions under General Lew Wallace was ordered to occupy Bolivar, Mississippi, about 30 miles south of Jackson, Tennessee. The next day McClernand joined him there with his other division.[53] McClernand then notified Wallace to send a portion of his division, to consist of one brigade of infantry, three companies of cavalry, and four pieces of artillery, to Jackson.[54] Wallace arrived on June 8 and set up camp under the command of General John A. Logan. McClernand, meanwhile, remained at Bethel, near Corinth, until mid–June when he moved his headquarters to Jackson.[55] His duties at Jackson were to watch for Confederate forays into the area and to repair railroad track damage by the enemy.

From Jackson McClernand took time out from post duties to again request an independent command from Lincoln. He stated that he had no complaint about his treatment by the president, but implied poor treatment from others. This was obviously a reference to Halleck's refusal to increase McClernand's command earlier in the month. The Illinois general asked for an independent field of action, and he specifically requested "Arkansas South of the Arkansas river, between Louisiana Texas and the Indian Nation." He wished that area to be a new department and pleaded with Lincoln to "let one volunteer officer try his capabilities." This was apparently a shot at professional soldiers, decrying the practical value of a West Point education. It seemed to be special pleading to prove that volunteer officers were just as competent and able as professionals.[56]

Although he requested a larger command from Lincoln, a few days later it was actually decreased. Special Orders No. 118, issued by Grant, dissolved the Reserve Corps. McClernand's command was to include "all troops occupying the country south of Union City and north of the Memphis and Charleston road."[57] Before he received this communication Halleck ordered him to take his troops to Grand Junction or La Grange (Grand Junction was located about 40 miles west of Corinth in Tennessee). McClernand did not make it to Grand Junction since he received new orders from Halleck. On June 30 Halleck ordered him to prepare his men to move to Washington, D.C., a result of General George B. McClellan's defeats in Virginia during the Peninsula campaign. McClernand probably rejoiced at this order because it moved him away from Halleck and closer to his benefactor in the White House. The joy was short-lived, however, since the orders were suspended the next day.[58]

McClernand then received Grant's order dissolving the Reserve Corps, on July 3, and from then on he kept his headquarters at Jackson. Grant and Halleck sent conflicting orders during the first part of July, and he was therefore unclear about his sphere of command and responsibilities. Because of this confusion McClernand threatened to resign: "My state of incertitude is most embarrassing. I will ask to be relieved unless my official relations & responsibilities shall be defined."[59] He stayed on at Jackson, but seemed uninterested in work there. McClernand had dispersed his troops to locations around Jackson for a variety of duties, and wanted to recruit men to bring his units to full strength. He requested permission from Grant to visit the governor of Illinois for this purpose "and many other subjects." It seemed as if he just wanted out of his situation under Halleck and Grant and a trip to Springfield might prove valuable in that regard.[60] The general wrote Illinois representative Elihu B. Washburne on July 9 and asked to be transferred to Virginia.[61] On July 16 the Illinois congressional delegation visited the War Department to request that McClernand and his troops be transferred to the James River. Secretary of war Stanton dodged this petition by telling them that Halleck commanded the army in the west, and he made all the decisions regarding those troops.[62] McClernand simply wanted out of Jackson and would do almost anything to accomplish that.

On July 11, 1862, Halleck was summoned to Washington, D.C., to serve as President Lincoln's general-in-chief. McClernand probably received this as good news, since he was uncomfortable serving under Halleck. He appeared to respond better when Grant was his immediate superior officer. McClernand did not receive permission to visit Governor Yates of Illinois, and after moving his headquarters to Bolivar he settled down to the mundane routine of garrison duty. His biggest challenge there came from Confederate raiders. In opposing these rebel cavalrymen McClernand seemed to lose his patience and vented his frustrations on subordinate officers, especially fellow Illinoisan John A. Logan.

Whether McClernand was simply frustrated at the enemy or unhappy with his standing in the army, his frustrations came to a head at the end of July, and Logan was the unfortunate recipient of McClernand's temper. Both generals were trying to fight off the rebels while at the same time complaining to Grant about each other. On July 28 and 29 McClernand and Logan sent numerous angry telegrams back and forth between each other and to Grant. This accomplished little except to destroy the relationship between two Illinois generals and political allies.[63]

Through mid–August McClernand continued the monotony of garrison duty and rebel chasing. On August 12 the general hit upon another possible solution to his disagreeable assignment. He wrote to Illinois governor Richard Yates and asked him to write the secretary of war to request McClernand's aid in recruiting troops in Illinois.[64] Yates made the request and within a week the orders came through.[65] On August 25 Grant telegraphed orders to McClernand: "by direction just received from Maj. Gen Halleck you will report Springfield Ills. and assist Governor Yates in the organization of volunteers...."[66] This was the break from the field that McClernand wanted, but this order could be a double-edged sword. While it certainly freed McClernand from his unhappy command assignment, recruiting duty did not provide much opportunity for glory or heroics. McClernand would have to create that opportunity for himself.

8

The Mississippi Expedition

For several months Major General John A. McClernand had chafed under the constraints of post duty at Jackson and Bolivar, Tennessee. Orders assigning him to recruiting duty in Springfield must have been a great relief to the general. Recruiting was not progressing well in the fall of 1862 for a variety of reasons, one of which was the nature of the conflict. As casualty lists grew longer fewer men were willing to join the army, and the antiwar Copperhead movement was picking up more supporters in the Midwest. This faction was most closely associated with the Democratic party and became a powerful opponent of the war. As a gifted speaker McClernand could help both Lincoln and Illinois governor Yates. The president could count on the general to bring Democratic support to the war effort, as he had done when the conflict started, while at the same time assisting the governor in filling his quota of recruits. This new assignment gave McClernand a respite from campaigning in the field and an opportunity for politicking.

McClernand's orders to report to Springfield were issued on August 25 and three days later he turned his command over to General Leonard F. Ross and headed home.[1] The general arrived in Springfield on August 30 and reported to Governor Yates on September 1 ready to "render every assistance."[2] The governor believed McClernand and his staff would be most useful instructing and training the new regiments then in camps throughout the state. He suggested McClernand's staff spend time at Camp Butler in Springfield, where there were four new regiments, and visiting new units in Jacksonville, Rockford, Shawneetown, and Carlinville among others.[3]

After settling in, McClernand proceeded to visit many Illinois cities in a sort of victory tour, making speeches supporting the war and probably inspecting whatever troops were available. In early September he went from Springfield to Jacksonville, where he visited with his former in-laws. At the

Dunlap House a crowd gathered, serenaded the general, and called for him. McClernand appeared on the balcony and made a speech in which he advocated "the principle of making this a 'war to the knife, and the knife to the hilt.'"[4] From Jacksonville the general went to Chicago. There McClernand addressed large crowds. He told them, "Any commander who relied wholly upon STRATEGY must fail. We want the right man to lead us; a man who will appoint a subordinate officer on account of his merits, and not because he is a graduate of a particular school." He also explained that "the way to *whip* an enemy was to *attack* him, at every possible point, and wherever an opportunity was given."[5] This was apparently a critique of Halleck's campaign against Corinth when he wished to avoid an engagement. McClernand also took the opportunity to show his displeasure of professional soldiers, claiming a volunteer general could perform just as well, if not better.

While McClernand continued to whip up support for the war all over Illinois, Governor Yates prepared to travel to Washington, D.C. Before leaving, Yates asked the general to accompany him and assist "in regard to matters affecting the organization of the new levies of troops in this State."[6] McClernand saw that here was an opportunity to ask for an independent command in person. McClernand knew that Lincoln was concerned about the Midwest states, particularly the opening of the Mississippi River and its effects on commerce. The general was also astute enough to combine two important factors into one proposal — his desire for an independent command and Lincoln's need to open the Mississippi River. McClernand was determined to get his independent command on this trip to Washington.

By September 25 McClernand was in the capital staying at Willard's Hotel; he had made contact with the secretary of the Treasury and former governor of Ohio, Salmon P. Chase. It is significant that McClernand chose to contact a cabinet member from the Midwest who might be sympathetic to his plan to reopen the Mississippi. Chase's secretary informed McClernand that Chase would meet with the president "in relation to your wishes."[7] It is not difficult to discern what the general wanted from Chase — he wished the secretary to approach Lincoln about an independent command for the Illinois general to reopen the Mississippi River. McClernand met Chase the next day, September 26, in Governor Yates' room, and made a "very favorable impression" upon the secretary. The general called on Chase at the Ohioan's office on the 27th, and the secretary recorded that his "favorable impression of last evening was strengthened."[8] McClernand had a plan for a campaign that he laid before Chase, hoping the secretary would convey it to Lincoln, especially since Chase liked the plan.

On September 27 Chase mentioned McClernand in a cabinet meeting, in which the president was reported to have assessed the general's abilities:

"Said he thought him brave and capable, but too desirous to be independent of every body else."[9] The president had assessed McClernand's personality perfectly. "At the instance of the President," the general later recalled, he presented the plan to Lincoln in writing the next day.[10] McClernand's plan had as its two primary goals "crushing the rebellion and reopening the Mississippi River." While the Mississippi was significant militarily McClernand emphasized its commercial importance. Opening it up would benefit the "overflowing granaries of the North West." The people of the Mississippi valley "are earnestly solicitous and painfully anxious upon the subject."[11]

McClernand's plan called for 60,000 men presumably under his command, although he never specified who would lead the expedition. The men were to board transports and, along with a number of gunboats, descend the Mississippi River. Reaching the Yazoo River the column would ascend it until arriving at the first available landing spot on the south bank. The men would disembark and march on Vicksburg, and with aid from the gunboats seize the fort. After fortifying the garrison the expedition would move to Jackson and then to Meridian, where the Southern Mississippi and Mobile & Ohio railroads met.[12]

The next immediate objective, wrote McClernand, would depend on the action of the Confederate army. The general believed the enemy army would march to either Montgomery or Mobile, and the Federal expedition should follow the rebels. This part of the plan indicated McClernand's understanding of the changing nature of warfare. By advocating the strategy of pursuing armies rather than places McClernand displayed advanced military thinking. The general rejected the place-oriented strategy described by Henri Jomini and employed by General Halleck in the recent Corinth campaign. Instead he preferred an army-oriented strategy, sometimes called the strategy of annihilation, as outlined by Carl von Clausewitz in his treatise On War.[13]

Regardless of where the enemy army went a depot should be established at Mobile, suggested McClernand, and from there the expedition would move to Opelika, Alabama, another important rail center. Taking that place would, according to the general, "...sever the southern communication, by rail, between the Revolted States east and west...." The next object was to be Rome, Georgia, "the site of one of the principal arsenals and manufactures of arms in the revolted States." This indicated progressive military thinking on the general's part, but imperfect intelligence. Columbus, Georgia, was more significant than Rome and it was closer to Opelika. The advent of "total war" determined that any or all industrial and manufacturing establishments be destroyed, effectively reducing the enemy's ability to make war, and possibly terminating the conflict sooner. McClernand believed that factories should be targets of the Federal army.[14]

After taking Rome the expedition would move on to Atlanta, one of the most important railroad centers in the South. Once Atlanta was captured the Union force would then move in cooperation with the eastern Federal army. This was the plan of operations McClernand proposed to Lincoln; a map accompanied the plan. There were two significant aspects of the general's proposal: (1) the opening of the Mississippi River; and (2) the method of warfare McClernand advocated to defeat the Confederacy. The opening of the river was essential to commerce in the American Midwest. As an Illinoisan, Lincoln was certainly sympathetic to the concerns of midwesterners. He was likely to support a plan to reopen the Mississippi, perhaps more so if the expedition was led by a man who could recruit the troops for the campaign. By suggesting that railroad centers as well as industrial establishments be destroyed, McClernand was advocating the progressive "total war" strategy. But perhaps the most interesting aspect of the general's plan was that its final objective, Atlanta, was similar to Sherman's in 1864. The first part of the plan was not particularly sound militarily. His proposal to take Vicksburg from the north, i.e., via the Yazoo, was not possible to accomplish, as Sherman discovered in December 1862 with the debacle at Chickasaw Bluffs. On the other hand, the latter part of McClernand's proposal outlined *in concept* how the war in the West was eventually won!

On September 30 McClernand met with Lincoln, and in this White House meeting Lincoln invited McClernand to join him on a trip to the Antietam battlefield. The general accepted the invitation and accompanied the president to Maryland from October to 1 October 4. There he visited not only the battlefield but he also met the Army of the Potomac commander, General George B. McClellan. On this trip McClernand had the opportunity to speak at length with both Lincoln and McClellan. He was able to do additional lobbying for his plan, and may have discussed it with McClellan. He also posed for photographs with the president and the chief of secret services, Allan Pinkerton.

McClernand seemed confident that the president and secretary of war would approve his plan. On October 7 Lincoln explained in a cabinet meeting that he wanted to organize an expedition to open the Mississippi and expected to give command to McClernand. According to Chase, Stanton was not opposed to the idea and the only obstacle for McClernand seemed to be General-in-Chief Halleck.[15] By October 9 the president had apparently decided that the expedition would indeed be organized under McClernand, although the general did not receive official notification until October 21. On the 9th Lincoln spoke with Admiral David D. Porter about taking Vicksburg and, after meeting with the president, Porter consulted McClernand about the plan. Porter's journal and the diary of secretary of the navy Gideon Welles

General McClernand (right) with President Lincoln (center) and Allan Pinkerton (left) near the Antietam battlefield, October 1862 (Library of Congress).

give conflicting accounts of Porter's reaction to McClernand's role in the campaign. Welles recorded at the time that Porter did not want to work with a West Pointer, and that he was "gratified" to learn that McClernand was to command the land forces. Porter concluded in his journal, which was written after the war, that McClernand was not fit to command the expedition.[16] Regardless of Porter's opinion the president had approved the Mississippi Expedition, and Lincoln also consulted with Stanton and Halleck, so those officials also knew the plan had been approved.[17]

General McClernand (right) with President Lincoln (center) and Allan Pinkerton (left) near the Antietam battlefield, October 1862 (Library of Congress).

When Porter visited McClernand on October 9 the general must have surmised that the plan neared approval. For the next several days he worked to organize the expedition, working on details such as how many men and supplies were needed. He believed that the campaign could be carried out with a large percentage of new recruits. McClernand suggested to secretary of war Stanton that as much as 75 percent of the expedition could be green, untried recruits. He requested the remaining 25 percent be taken from the Army of the Tennessee, and the general asked for specific regiments and officers from that army.[18] It seems clear that by October 15 the general's plan had received verbal approval, although he had not yet been given an official order. On that day he sent Stanton another plan for organizing the expedition, with the number of men and supplies needed, a document the secretary apparently requested. A copy was also sent to Halleck.[19]

There was still more scheming on McClernand's part. The plan had been approved, but a commander had not been named for the campaign. McClernand met with Lieutenant James H. Wilson, a Shawneetown acquaintance, who was in Washington looking for an assignment. Wilson was a witness in a court-martial at Pleasant Valley, near George B. McClellan's headquarters, and commuted between there and Washington. When McClernand met with Wilson the general asked the lieutenant to give McClellan a message: Lincoln was going to remove McClellan as commander of the Army of the Potomac for his inaction after Antietam. This McClernand apparently learned from his conversations with the president. Wilson took a map of the Mississippi Valley to McClellan, and on October 16 offered McClellan command of the expedition McClernand had planned.[20] Not certain of receiving the command himself, the Illinois general wanted McClellan to have it if he could not. Since McClellan outranked Grant, he would have command of the entire theater if he moved to the west. According to one of McClellan's biographers, the general was aware that he might be moving to the west "to take the supreme command there." McClellan apparently remarked to General Darius Couch, "I expect to be relieved from the Army of the Potomac, and to have a command in the West...."[21] Yet another intriguing possibility, perhaps one McClernand considered, was his commanding the Army of the Potomac if McClellan went to the west. That was not out of the realm of McClernand's thought process since he had previously requested a transfer to the James River.

Finally, after several weeks of not knowing his association with the expedition, Stanton summoned McClernand to his office in the War Department on October 21.[22] There McClernand was handed a confidential order signed by Lincoln and Stanton that authorized the general to raise troops, by volunteering or draft, in Indiana, Illinois, and Iowa. They were then to be forwarded to Memphis, Cairo, or some other place designated by the general-in-chief. Once sufficient troops were raised they would be organized for a campaign against Vicksburg under McClernand's command.[23] Lincoln also added a notation to the order stating that although the order was confidential McClernand was authorized to show it to governors or others to expedite the raising of troops. The president's endorsement essentially allowed McClernand to claim executive privilege in recruiting troops.[24]

McClernand finally had what he wanted — an independent command. Or so he thought. A close reading of the order shows that there were conditions on the expedition, and McClernand may not have been fully aware of the impact of those conditions. The order read, in part, "to the end that, when a sufficient force not required by the operations of General Grant's command shall be raised." This sentence allowed Grant to use the troops McClernand raised for his own purposes if he needed them. If Grant wanted those troops McClernand's independent command was all but eliminated. The last sentence in the order also qualified the general's independent status: "The forces so organized will remain subject to the designation of the general-in-chief, and be employed according to such exigencies as the service in his judgment may require."[25] This sentence subjected his recruits to Halleck's orders. The entire campaign, therefore, was at the mercy of two men who disliked John McClernand.

The whole process of requesting and granting command of the Mississippi Expedition by McClernand, Lincoln, Stanton, and others was politicking of the highest order. Both the president and the general possessed some power or gift that the other desired. Lincoln had the authority to give his fellow Illinoisan an independent command, something McClernand wanted badly. On the other hand, the general had the power to speak and raise troops for the war effort, especially among Democrats who were wavering in their support of the war. Governor Yates benefited from McClernand's presence in the state as Illinois was behind in meeting its quota of recruits and the general could bolster that effort. This episode displayed the political skill of the president. He probably granted McClernand the command not so much because he and the general were acquainted, but for what he could do for the administration. Once the new recruits were in the field McClernand could be removed or replaced or the troops transferred, and the blame placed on either Grant or Halleck. Or, because Lincoln certainly knew the enmity between these three men, he could simply step away and let Halleck and/or Grant remove or replace McClernand. Yet another possibility was McClernand taking some action that necessitated his replacement or removal by his superior officer. Either way Lincoln could survive such an ordeal unscathed and keep his relationship with McClernand intact.

Since much of the negotiating and planning for this campaign was done in secret, there was considerable speculation about McClernand's command. The *Chicago Tribune* announced that McClernand had been assigned "to a highly important command in the department of the Ohio." The Jacksonville newspaper, in the hometown of his in-laws, was also unaware of the general's destination: "Gen. McClernand is soon to be assigned to an important command, and wherever he may go we shall, doubtless, hear a good report from him." And after his command was announced, the *New York Times* asked, "McClernand's Army-What Will He Do with It?"[26]

With his orders in hand McClernand proceeded to the Midwest to recruit troops for his expedition. On October 23 he stopped in Indiana and met with Governor Oliver P. Morton, who enthusiastically supported the campaign. Morton was interested in opening the Mississippi River and had written to Lincoln about this concern. The governor immediately began to recruit troops for McClernand's expedition.[27] By October 25 the general was back in Springfield and had conferred with Governor Yates, who also responded with great enthusiasm for the campaign. Yates promised to raise the necessary troops as soon as possible for his friend. McClernand did not immediately visit Iowa; instead he wrote to Governor Samuel D. Kirkwood and explained what he expected from the Hawkeye State. The Illinoisan wrote that he was sending his assistant adjutant general, Major Walter B. Scates, to call on the governor personally to explain the arrangements and answer any questions.[28]

Throughout the recruiting process secretary of war Stanton kept in constant communication with McClernand, giving and promising support. Stanton seemed genuinely in favor of McClernand's succeeding. A week after the general left Washington the secretary wrote and encouraged McClernand: "Everything is favorable here for your expedition.... I hope you will exert yourself diligently so as to be on foot without delay."[29] On October 29, Stanton sent McClernand a confidential communication, again encouraging him: "Every confidence is reposed in your zeal and skill, and I long to see you in the field striking vigorous blows against the rebellion in its most vital point."[30] He informed the general that he had ordered Major General Nathaniel P. Banks to organize an expedition in Texas to create a diversion so the Confederates could not concentrate all of their forces against McClernand. The general also made certain other cabinet members were informed on the progress of the expedition. When McClernand did not write he asked friends to visit with cabinet officials.[31]

Secretary Stanton seemed to be the most supportive member of the administration, as all of his communications to McClernand were positive, sustaining the general's activities. If there were persons who McClernand had to fear, they were Halleck and Grant. From the beginning Halleck distrusted McClernand's competence as a commander, and he worked to prevent the Illinois general from ever taking command of the Mississippi Expedition. As quickly as McClernand sent troops forward Halleck had them sent to Grant. As early as October 30 Halleck instructed Illinois governor Yates to send new regiments directly to Grant: "It seems that General Grant is likely to be hard pressed by the enemy, and it is important that these troops be sent to him as rapidly as possible."[32] These were troops that McClernand needed for his own campaign. Though on the surface it may appear that Halleck was redirecting McClernand's troops to Grant, until McClernand was released for service in the field the only place to send these recruits was to Grant's army. Neither McClernand nor Stanton suspected that Halleck was redirecting McClernand's troops.

If Stanton was not suspicious of Halleck's activities, neither was the president. Lincoln played no role in thwarting McClernand's independent command, and in fact the president probably grew anxious for the campaign to begin. Lincoln always preferred generals who fought, and McClernand portrayed himself as a fighting general (and in his short Civil War service he was always ready to fight, although heretofore as a subordinate). In November 1862 Lincoln issued a memorandum that stated, in part, "The army, like the nation, has become demoralized by the idea that the war is to be ended, the nation united, and peace restored, by *strategy*, and not by hard desperate fighting."[33]

The process of raising and forwarding troops in Illinois, Indiana, and Iowa was progressing well. By November 10 McClernand reported to Stanton that he had sent a total of 20 infantry regiments forward to the front (12 from Illinois, 5 from Indiana, and 3 from Iowa). He expected to forward another 20 infantry units along with 6 cavalry regiments in a short time.[34] He also sent a copy of this report to Halleck. By the end of December when McClernand finally left Springfield to take command of his troops, he reported raising a total of 61 infantry regiments, 5 cavalry units, and 10 companies of artillery.[35] Despite McClernand portraying himself as a fine recruiter, many of those regiments were probably already being formed and the general simply forwarded them and took credit for raising them.

By the first part of November McClernand was more than a little suspicious that something was amiss with the Mississippi Expedition. In his November 10 communication with Stanton he broached his concerns that there might be a lengthy delay in starting his campaign. The general wrote that if "obstacles such as opposed you in the beginning or for other causes." the expedition must be delayed, McClernand wanted Stanton to "cut my supposed connection with it and order me to other duty in the field at once."[36] This shows McClernand's correct perception that there was opposition to his campaign. The reference to obstacles that opposed Stanton in the beginning seems to be a reference to the general-in-chief. The letter also demonstrates that McClernand simply wanted to fight. He also made sure to send a copy of this communication to Lincoln to ensure that the president was notified of all developments with the Mississippi Expedition.

By November 13 McClernand seemed to associate Grant with a plan to take control of the troops he was forwarding. On that day McClernand reported to Stanton that six Indiana regiments were being forwarded to Memphis, and he added an intriguing sentence: "I infer that General Grant claims the right to change their destination and to control all the troops sent to Columbus and Memphis."[37] What was McClernand thinking when he composed that line? Did he really believe that Grant would divert his troops and use them for his own campaign? Or did he think Grant was assembling the men in a different location in preparation for McClernand's taking command?

What McClernand did not know was that Halleck and Grant were already working to deprive him of his command. Halleck had previously instructed Illinois governor Yates to send all new regiments to Grant, and as early as November 3 the general-in-chief informed Grant that the troops were on the way to him. Halleck also expected to send another 20,000 troops to Grant in a short time.[38] A week later Grant questioned Halleck about an expedition being fitted out from Memphis, an obvious reference to McClernand's campaign. Grant also wanted to know the status of General Sherman: "Am I to have Sherman move subject to my order, or is he and his forces reserved for some special service?" The allusion to "some special service" is yet another reference to McClernand's expedition. Halleck was more blunt and to the point about the troops: "You have command of all troops sent to your department."[39]

Halleck's role in this scheme was much more questionable than Grant's. Stanton had officially informed the general-in-chief about McClernand's Mississippi Expedition, while Grant's information was based solely on rumors. Grant in fact wrote to Sherman about "the mysterious rumors of McClernand's command."[40] This indicated that Grant was in the dark officially about McClernand's expedition, but had heard vague rumors about it. Although not officially notified about the campaign, Grant was a willing participant in this act of collusion. In correspondence between Halleck and Grant, John McClernand's name was never used. They both adroitly avoided naming their adversary, as if they were pretending he did not exist or maybe that he would go away.

But McClernand would not go away and by late November his suspicions about the expedition grew. On the 20th he wired Governor Yates, then in Washington: "Please see the Secretary of War, and learn the status of the enterprise."[41] Yates contacted Stanton and assured the secretary that McClernand had sent all the available troops into the field, and he hoped Stanton would send the general forward soon.[42] McClernand asked Illinois senators Lyman Trumbull and Orville H. Browning to inquire on his behalf. Trumbull reported that he had spoken with Stanton and that the secretary regarded the expedition as important and that "nothing had been or should be done to embarrass it." Senator Browning visited Lincoln on the matter and reported back to the general that the president and secretary of war "are very anxious for you to have the command of the expedition, and intend to stand by you, and sustain and strengthen you. Go ahead — you are in no danger."[43] Lincoln and Stanton appeared to support the campaign fully.

Despite these reassurances McClernand despaired of ever taking command of the Mississippi Expedition; he was frantic, almost desperate. On December 1 the general requested the secretary of war to order him forward. A few days later, to make certain Stanton knew that he was waiting orders, he requested that General John M. Schofield join the expedition.[44] When orders were not forthcoming McClernand again asked to be sent forward, sending his request to both Stanton and Lincoln. After stating that he had already forwarded about 40,000 men, with more on the way, he implored the president, "May I not ask therefore to be sent forward immediately?" To Stanton he pleaded, "I am anxiously awaiting your order sending me forward for duty in connection with the Mississippi expedition."[45] Neither Lincoln nor Stanton immediately authorized McClernand to take the field; and since Halleck had issued the order for McClernand to report to Springfield in August 1862, the order for McClernand to return to field service must also originate from Halleck's office. Certainly neither Lincoln nor Stanton wanted to meddle in the general-in-chief's responsibilities without cause.

Did McClernand have cause to despair over his situation? Absolutely. For a month and a half he forwarded upwards of 40,000 men for his own independent command, and by mid–December it seemed that he would never lead his expedition. The obstacles to McClernand's command were the machinations of Halleck and Grant. These two men planned a campaign down the Mississippi River that would use the men McClernand forwarded. Grant gave command of this expedition to Sherman on December 8 and Halleck concurred the next day.[46] Grant ordered Sherman to travel to Memphis and take command of all troops there, which were McClernand's men. Grant wanted Sherman to take command of the troops as soon as he could so McClernand could not. Grant later justified these actions: "I feared that delay might bring McClernand, who was his [Sherman's] senior and who had authority from the President and Secretary of War to exercise that particular command, — and independently."[47] The trio of Halleck, Grant, and Sherman hoped to prevent McClernand from assuming command of the Mississippi Expedition. One of Grant's biographers admits that it "seemed almost more important for Grant and Sherman to deprive McClernand of Vicksburg than to take it from the Confederates."[48]

By mid–December McClernand's dismay reached its zenith. On December 15 he received a telegram from Stanton expressing surprise that Halleck had not sent orders: "I had supposed that you had received your orders from the General in Chief. I will see him & have the matter attended to without delay."[49] A frenzy of correspondence to friends and government officials followed this telegram. On the 16th McClernand contacted Halleck and Senator Browning. He literally begged the general-in-chief to order him forward, "in accordance with the order of the Secretary of War of the 21 of October, giving me command of the Mississippi Expedition."[50] The communication with Browning demonstrated McClernand's desperation to have the matter settled and, though his accusations were mostly accurate, the tone was angry. He wrote:

> I am satisfied that the President and Sec of War favor me as the commander of the Expedition, but I am persuaded the Genl in Chief is my enemy — personal enemy and senselessly so. My state of uncertitude is cruel. It is humiliating to the last degree. For Gods sake relieve me! Learn and let me know my fate! Whether the order of the Sec. of War made in the presence of the President, and notwithstanding the objection or at least hesitation of the Genl in Chief, is to be carried out, or am I to be superseded notwithstanding that order. Let me know!
>
> I think I understand the Genl in Chief as well as any man living. I think he designs to give the command of the Expedition to Sherman....[51]

McClernand repeated the final sentiment to a friend in Jacksonville, not knowing that Halleck and Grant had already given Sherman the command.[52]

McClernand contacted anybody and everybody conceivable to find out his status with the expedition. He wired Lincoln: "I believe I am superseded. Please advise me."[53] He sent a similar message to Stanton, who replied that the general had not been superseded and that Halleck was to issue the order to send McClernand to his command immediately. Even that did not force Halleck to order the general forward. Finally, on December 23, after so much time had elapsed and so much badgering on McClernand's part the secretary of war, not the general-in-chief, released the general from duties in Springfield to report to General Grant.[54]

The long wait was finally over. At last McClernand was going to get a chance to command an independent expedition. But the campaign was still under the watchful eye of Grant, who could withdraw McClernand's independent status at any time. McClernand's hard work finally bore fruit. All the general had to do was wage a successful campaign against the Confederates and he would be vindicated.

Before delving into McClernand's expedition, it is useful to examine and analyze how he practiced the art of political generalship during the first part of the war. When Fort Sumter was bombarded in April 1861 John McClernand had spent the previous one and one-half years in Congress trying to negotiate some compromise to prevent war. When he did not succeed he was willing to fight. What were McClernand's credentials to lead troops into battle? Militarily he had virtually none. His only prior military experience was in the Black Hawk War in 1832, during which he saw no combat and led no troops. McClernand's service lasted substantially less than the ninety days for which he enlisted and his most significant experience was when he served as divisional quartermaster and courier. His general's commission in 1861 was not, therefore, a result of his military experience, background, or education. It was purely political. As a Democrat he could serve as an example to all Illinois Democrats and rally them behind the stars and stripes. President Lincoln needed him to keep Illinois, and more specifically southern Illinois, loyal to the Union. Great military deeds were not expected from this politician in uniform, General John A. McClernand.

So what was expected of General McClernand, and where does the administration put this political general? The obvious place to station McClernand is where he would best serve Lincoln's political needs — southern Illinois — hence, the appointment to Cairo. McClernand was fortunate to be placed in the District of Southeast Missouri, with its headquarters at Cairo, because he was under the command of General Ulysses S. Grant. Though Grant had been out of the army for a few years before the war started, he had the necessary education, training, and experience to lead troops. This was the best situation for McClernand because he could learn the art of war from Grant. And McClernand had to learn quickly, as he commanded a brigade of four regiments. He did not have the luxury of starting at the bottom, leading a regiment for example, and working his way up after learning how to command troops.

McClernand's learning process, his training, was simply through experience. As he fought in one campaign after another he gained valuable experience in all aspects of commanding troops in war. He learned how to keep men occupied when they were not in actual combat, how to shield his troops from the enemy while on the march, how to arrange his troops during a battle, all of the lessons of war he learned as he fought. While this training regimen did not compare to a West Point education, McClernand recognized the necessity of learning as much as he could as quickly as he could.

McClernand was forced to learn quickly because General Grant, his immediate superior, was a fighter. The district commander wanted to move quickly and fight whenever the opportunity presented itself. The first opportunity was at Belmont in November 1861, the first Civil War combat for both Grant and McClernand. Because the number of men engaged was small and because this was early in the war, bravado can mask command deficiencies. The Federal frontal attack succeeded in capturing the rebel camp, but both generals lost control of their troops, who started looting. In addition,

McClernand led the men in cheers while the fighting raged and the enemy brought up reinforcements. This loss of control and McClernand's obvious politicking demonstrated that he had much to learn about warfare.

In succeeding campaigns, Fort Henry, Fort Donelson, and Shiloh, McClernand showed improvement in his command skills. His sphere of command was increased to a division and he competently led his men. In this divisional capacity McClernand seemed most effective and he was rewarded with promotion to major general. Leading a division McClernand's aggressive nature could be utilized effectively, under Grant's careful command. McClernand did not have the freedom to move and position his troops — Grant did this for him. His conduct in battle and on the march was exemplary, in part because he lacked the freedom a corps or army commander might have.

Even as a corps commander, during the Corinth and Vicksburg campaigns, McClernand was solid.[55] One reason was that the army commanders, Halleck and Grant, directly supervised him and his freedom to maneuver was limited. McClernand's 13th Corps was in the lead for most of the Vicksburg campaign, when he easily could have been relegated to rearguard duty. McClernand's service as a subordinate was solid, if unspectacular.

Through McClernand's prewar political career he learned one dubious lesson about successful generals — they often became presidents. He learned that firsthand in 1840 and 1848 when military heroes ran successful presidential campaigns (and he campaigned against both). McClernand learned through his experience that successful military careers led to more successful political careers. His ambition drove McClernand to learn how to command, and more important, how to be a successful general. The Illinois general also knew that aggressive, fighting generals win accolades. This was yet another reason to learn quickly and succeed quickly — accolades, fame, and glory. So in learning the art of war, glory and future political success — ambition — drove McClernand at least as much as preserving the Union.

So how does a political general with no military credentials succeed and win renown quickly? By commanding an army or department and winning decisive victories. This presented a problem for McClernand because he did not possess the independent status to win victories in his own right — he was relegated to serving under General Grant. If he could get this independent status McClernand believed he could prove he was a great general and win the accolades that he so justly deserved. Before McClernand had even been commissioned a general, and continuing throughout his Civil War service, he proposed the creation of separate military departments and devised many military plans. In all of these McClernand would exercise an independent command where he stood to gain all of the glory from successful campaigns.

Examining these proposals will demonstrate his ambition to become a great military commander and allow insight into his maturation as a strategist and tactician. These plans will show just how much McClernand learned about the art of war.

His first proposal came in April 1861 before the secessionists fired upon Fort Sumter. This plan, which had Texas as the central point in the war effort, was the work of an obvious amateur. McClernand shared his ideas with President Lincoln, who wisely took no action to even attempt to implement it.[56] The proposal showed McClernand's immature understanding of warfare, and it is important to note that it was presented before he entered the army. Once he had some experience his plans and proposals became more militarily feasible, if not politically so.

After entering the army McClernand's proposals for military operations, the creation of new departments, and requests for independent commands came fast and furious. Many were poorly conceived and badly timed while others were practicable, but all illustrated several facets of the general's personality and character. One hallmark of his Civil War service was the desire for an independent command. His ambition was so great that he seemed to have a difficult time taking orders from others. With an independent command McClernand could also claim the glory that naturally went with any successful campaign, which he undoubtedly believed he could ride to higher political offices. In obtaining this independent status McClernand had no problem intruding on the command sphere of others. In one remarkable proposal he requested a separate command that encroached on the authority of three departments.[57]

Shortly after the Battle of Belmont, McClernand asked the president to create a new department in Missouri and Kentucky.[58] The goal was to drive the Confederates from Columbus and Belmont. While the ends were admirable, the goal was far too limited for the creation of a separate department. Just two months later, in the same lull after Belmont, McClernand again proposed the creation of a new department along the Mississippi River and suggested a man from the northwest should command it, an obvious reference to himself.[59] These two proposals were badly timed coming on the heels of Belmont, and they would create the incongruity of a separate department within the sphere of other departments. Both were denied.

Yet another lull in fighting after the capture of Corinth led McClernand to request yet another independent command, this time in Arkansas.[60] The general did not outline what he hoped to accomplish or how it would fit into the Federal strategic picture, he simply wanted an independent command. This proposal was likewise denied, but a recognizable pattern emerged. McClernand could not win magnificent victories performing garrison duty;

he needed an active theater of operations. So regardless of the strategic value the request was made.

The most significant of McClernand's proposals was his plan to capture Vicksburg that he submitted to President Lincoln in September 1862.[61] It is the most important because it fit into Lincoln's overall strategy, it was workable, and it was granted. This plan was also important in assessing McClernand's understanding of strategy and tactics. By September 1862 McClernand had grasped the fundamentals of Civil War strategy. The plan advocated the strategy of pursuing enemy armies rather than places, which indicated McClernand's understanding of the changing nature of warfare. He rejected a place-oriented strategy and wished to implement an army-oriented strategy. In addition, McClernand proposed the destruction of all manufacturing and industrial establishments in the course of the campaign. This also demonstrated advanced strategic thinking and the recognition that warfare had changed. President Lincoln granted this plan and McClernand finally had his independent command.

As the pivotal year of 1863 opened, John A. McClernand had the opportunity to show what he had learned after two years as a subordinate officer. His command of the Mississippi Expedition was a test for himself and all political generals. His success could go a long way in removing some of the stigma of politicians as poor generals. If he failed he would only cement that opinion in many minds.

9

"We Have Disposed of This Tough Little Nut"

The Arkansas Post/Fort Hindman Campaign

December 23, 1862, was a memorable day for John McClernand. On that day secretary of war Edwin Stanton issued orders that released him from Springfield and sent him to fight the rebels. The general also got married, for the second time, on the 23rd to the younger sister of his first wife, who had died on May 8, 1861. His second wife, Minerva McClernand, was some 24 years younger than the general. The wedding took place in Jacksonville and among the hundreds in attendance was Governor Yates. Shortly after the wedding the new bridegroom left Springfield (accompanied by his new wife), boarded the *Express*, and headed south so the general could meet with General Grant.

On December 28, after a 22-hour trip from Cairo down the Mississippi River, McClernand expected to meet with Grant at the latter's Memphis headquarters. When Grant was not there McClernand left a note for his commander to which he attached several documents that he hoped would solidify his independent command. These documents were: (1) Stanton's confidential order of October 21 giving McClernand command of the Mississippi Expedition; (2) an order from Halleck giving Grant authority over McClernand's expedition; and (3) Stanton's order releasing the general from duty in Springfield. Although Grant and McClernand were antagonists, the latter perhaps attempted to mend fences with this note when he wrote, "I regret that the expectation that I would find you here is disappointed. I have much that I would like to communicate to you."[1] This seemed to indicate that McClernand was willing to cooperate with Grant in the campaign.

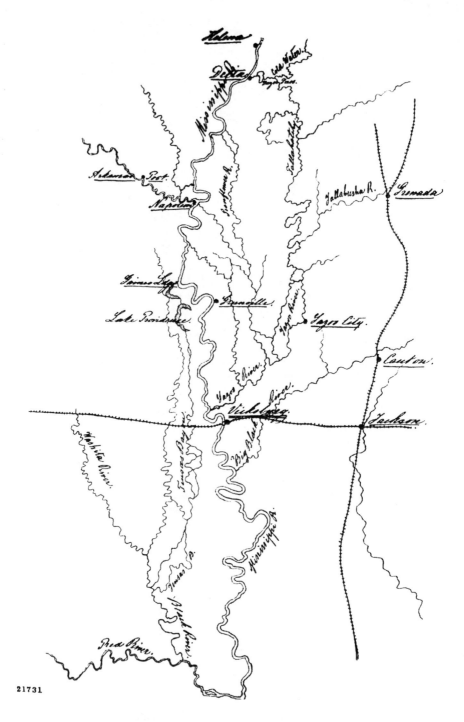

21731

Map of the Mississippi River area that General McClernand drew and included
in his February 14, 1863, letter to President Lincoln (Library of Congress).

Meanwhile McClernand sent two staff officers to find Grant, who was at Holly Springs, Mississippi, about 45 miles southeast of Memphis. They located Grant there that evening and were told that orders giving command of the expedition to McClernand were forwarded earlier that day (December 28). The general received those orders the next day. It should be noted that Grant sent the orders as a letter rather than a telegram. A letter would take more time to find McClernand, and by the time the Illinoisan received the letter, Grant or Sherman might have already captured Vicksburg.[2] Because there were no troops for McClernand to command he realized that there was a scheme to prevent him from leading the campaign. He spelled it out to Stanton that "either through the intention of the General-in-Chief or a strange occurrence of accidents, the authority of the President and yourself, as evidenced by your acts, has been set at naught, and I have been deprived of the command that had been committed to me."[3] McClernand blamed Halleck for this, apparently overlooking Grant's role.

At Memphis McClernand boarded the steamer *Tigress* for the remainder of the trip. Safely on board he found time to compose a note to President Lincoln, advising him that Confederate officials in Grenada, Mississippi, wanted the "restoration of peace." These officials were willing to accept peace "on any terms that the people of the North West may be willing to honor and justice to dictate." McClernand did not state his opinion on the reliability of these officials, except to say he received the information from a "gentleman of the first respectability." At the end of this communication McClernand took another shot at the person or persons keeping him from his command: "Either accident or intention has conspired to thwart the authority of yourself and the Secretary of War and to betray me, but with your support I shall not despair of overcoming both."[4] Lincoln must have tired of hearing the same refrain from McClernand time and time again. It was a testament to the president's patience that he did not rebuke McClernand.

Leaving Memphis, McClernand and his staff of 49 went to Helena, Arkansas, approximately 50 miles south of Memphis on the Mississippi. There on December 30 he met with General Willis A. Gorman, who commanded the District of Eastern Arkansas. Conferring with Gorman, the Illinois general suggested the importance of taking a rebel fortress, Fort Hindman (or Arkansas Post) on the Arkansas River.[5] The fort was relatively new, construction having been completed in November 1862, and was located on the Arkansas River 117 miles below Little Rock and about 105 miles north of Vicksburg. The fort's significance lay in its disruption of commerce. A few days before McClernand's meeting with Gorman an unarmed Federal steamer, *Blue Wing*, loaded with military stores, was forced to surrender to Confederate artillery fire from the Arkansas shore and was taken to

Fort Hindman. This helped convince McClernand to capture Arkansas Post.

With a definite plan McClernand continued south to find his command. He reached Milliken's Bend, 15 miles above Vicksburg, on December 31 and by January 2, 1863, his entourage reached the mouth of the Yazoo River, which was just north of Vicksburg. McClernand met with General Sherman, who had just returned from his disastrous repulse at Chickasaw Bayou on December 29, the campaign Halleck and Grant gave him with McClernand's troops. Sherman graciously turned over command to McClernand, his superior, and updated the new commander on his troops' condition. Both men agreed that nothing could be accomplished on the Yazoo River and the force should move to Milliken's Bend.[6]

McClernand's opinion of Sherman was positive. The two generals had cooperated well at Shiloh, and McClernand considered Sherman a "brave and meritorious officer." McClernand did not blame him for the defeat at Chickasaw Bayou, but credited him for "good purposes, which unfortunately failed in execution."[7] Though Sherman may have had some reservations about McClernand and his ability, the hatred he held for the Illinoisan later was not yet openly evident.

Still aboard the steamer *Tigress* on January 4, 1863, and having arrived at Milliken's Bend, McClernand issued General Order No. 1, by which he assumed command of the Mississippi Expedition. He divided his forces into two army corps to be commanded by generals Sherman and George W. Morgan, Sherman commanding the Second Corps and Morgan the First. McClernand styled his force the Army of the Mississippi, proclaiming his independence from Grant's Army of the Tennessee.[8] Again Sherman graciously accepted his subordination to McClernand and urged his troops to "give him the same hearty support and cheerful obedience they have hitherto given me."[9]

During the evening of the 4th McClernand, Sherman, and Admiral David D. Porter, who commanded the Mississippi naval fleet, met onboard Porter's flagship, *Black Hawk,* to discuss strategy. This council of war proved to be an intriguing meeting. Both Sherman and Porter became vehement anti–McClernand officers, and their sentiments began to show in the postwar accounts of this planning session. McClernand had already made tentative plans to reduce Arkansas Post, which he discussed with General Gorman in Helena almost a week before, on December 30. But Porter claimed that Sherman originated the plan and passed it on to McClernand at their first meeting on January 2. In all probability both men recognized the necessity of attacking Arkansas Post at about the same time.[10] Sherman reported that at this January 4 meeting McClernand had no definite plan, but "spoke in general terms of opening the navigation of the Mississippi, 'cutting his way to the sea,' etc., etc., but the *modus operandi* was not so clear." In fact, Sherman recalled that McClernand made "various objections" to attacking Arkansas Post.[11] This simply was not the case.

In examining Sherman and his memoirs one must consider that they were written years after the events and may not be accurate on all counts. One of Sherman's biographers, John F. Marszalek, implies (but does not outright state) that Sherman suffered from selective memory, that he did not pay attention to details when writing his memoirs, and that he "tried to make himself look good in his memoirs." Historian Albert Castel has suggested that Sherman wrote "deliberate falsehoods" in his memoirs. Whatever the explanation, historians must be extremely careful when consulting Sherman's memoirs, and in this instance Sherman's recollections were not accurate.[12]

Both Porter and Sherman agreed in their postwar accounts of this meeting that the admiral was particularly curt and nasty toward McClernand. Sherman and the admiral retired to another chamber in the ship and the general apparently attempted to calm Porter. The admiral recalled that he agreed to cooperate with the army on this expedition only if Sherman was in command. According to Porter, McClernand agreed to this condition, which was unlikely. Considering all the trouble he had in getting this command, McClernand was not likely to forfeit his authority over the expedition. In the end all three agreed that the correct course was to attack Arkansas Post.[13]

Despite Porter's memory and his later hatred for the Illinois general, McClernand retained command of the assault on the rebel fortress. The next day, January 5, McClernand issued orders for the operation and sent them to Sherman, Morgan, and Porter. The expedition would move down the Mississippi until it met the White River, and then continue up that river. From there the flotilla would sail up to the Arkansas River, which ran into the White River. At a suitable place on the east bank of the river, below the fort, the troops would then disembark. The First Corps, under General Morgan, would form the left wing and Sherman's Second Corps the right wing. Sherman's troops would march behind the fort until they reached the Arkansas River, forming the right of the Federal line, above the fort. Morgan's men would establish the left of the line, also linking up with the Arkansas, below the fort. Sherman and Morgan would then connect, effectively encircling the rebel fortress.[14]

Construction on Arkansas Post had been completed in November 1862. It formed a hollow square, 190 feet on each side with a bastion at each corner, surrounded by a ditch 20 feet wide and 8 feet deep. It was on a bluff 25 feet above the Arkansas River, 50 miles from the river's mouth. General Thomas J. Churchill commanded about 5,000 Confederates inside the fort.

Artillery firepower consisted of four 10-pounder Parrott rifles, four 6-pounder smoothbores, and three 9-inch Columbiads.[15]

As the movement on Arkansas Post began, McClernand took time out to inform Lincoln of his opinion of Halleck, a vicious attack upon the general-in-chief, probably the result of months of pent-up frustrations. "At whatever personal cost" to himself, McClernand charged Halleck with "wilful contempt of superior authority, and with utter incompetency." He criticized Halleck's handling of the Corinth campaign and suggested that he "curtailed the success of our arms at Fort Henry" by not coordinating the movements of the army and navy. The Illinoisan continued the onslaught: "Since he assumed the functions of General-in-Chief, scarcely anything but disaster has marked the experience of our arms." He followed with a litany of Union setbacks. The general queried, "How can the country be saved in its dire extremity, with such a Chief at the head of our armies!" He then answered his own question by suggesting that Lincoln remove Halleck: "In removing him, you will remove an anomaly in the organization of the command of our armies — an anomaly incompatible with its unity and responsibility." And it was obvious that McClernand was speaking of himself when he stated that Halleck was "personally hostile to very many, if not all, of our officers who are not West Point graduates, or who do not belong to the class of his instruments." This was a blistering attack on General-in-Chief Halleck, which did not endear McClernand to many in the administration. The general was burning his bridges, setting up his own demise.[16]

Lincoln was not the only recipient of McClernand's barrage of accusations against Halleck. To others he blamed the delays in his taking command of the Mississippi Expedition on Halleck and called the delays "criminal." He even went so far as to imply that the general-in-chief wanted him killed. In traveling from Cairo he reported that "if it had been the purpose to expose me to the hazzard [sic] of being shot at, if not shot, during my passage down the river, a more feasible plan could not have been devised." This exposure was the result of McClernand not having a military escort. The general put his belief in a higher authority, suggesting that "Providence will be kinder to me than the Genl. In Chief." Did McClernand recognize the dangers of his speaking out against Halleck? He did, suggesting that "it may be that my official ruin will follow as the consequence of my boldness to superior officers."[17]

In conducting the campaign McClernand was determined to keep Grant informed of his movements, perhaps because he knew Grant opposed his commanding the expedition. Sensing opposition to his plan to take the rebel fort, McClernand even offered a set of justifications for attacking Arkansas Post. Free navigation of the Mississippi River was an important reason to take the Confederate outpost, as evidenced by the recent capture of the *Blue Wing*. A victory would help morale, which McClernand believed decreased after the defeat at Chickasaw Bayou. A campaign against Arkansas Post would serve as a diversion to help General Samuel R. Curtis, who commanded the Department of the Missouri. After the Arkansas Post expedition, McClernand wished to continue an active campaign, he explained to Grant. He wanted to turn his attention to the area on the Mississippi River around Vicksburg, specifically Monroe and New Carthage, both on the Louisiana side. This would serve to isolate Vicksburg, thought McClernand, softening it up for an attack.[18]

Meanwhile, the campaign was underway. McClernand's command numbered approximately 32,000 men, an amalgamation of Illinois, Indiana, Iowa, Ohio, Wisconsin, Kentucky, and Missouri troops. The naval flotilla was made up of the ironclads *DeKalb Louisville* and *Cincinnati*, the ram

General John A. McClernand in his major general's uniform, 1862 or 1863 (Library of Congress).

Monarch, gunboats *Tyler* and *Black Hawk* (the flagship), and tinclads *Rattler* and *Glide*. In addition, the squadron included various transports and steamers such as the *Romeo Juliet Forest Rose Marmora Signal* and *Lexington*. The *Red Rover* and *Torrence* were to stay behind, at the mouth of the White River. McClernand himself remained on the steamer *Tigress*.[19]

The expedition reached the mouth of the White River on January 8, and from there the troops sailed to a cut-off that led to the Arkansas River. Sailing up that river, McClernand believed he had succeeded in tricking the rebels, at least until he was within 30 miles of the fort. At about 5:00 P.M. on January 9 the flotilla landed at Notrib's farm, which was approximately three miles from Arkansas Post. There the soldiers disembarked, a task that lasted until noon the next day.[20]

On the morning of January 10 McClernand and a staff member, Lieutenant Colonel Adolph Schwartz, reconnoitered the approaches to the fort.

They got to within a mile and a half of Fort Hindman and saw that the Confederates had abandoned a line of rifle pits. McClernand communicated his discovery to Sherman, whose troops had started marching at 11:00 A.M. The Second Corps, led by local guides, marched a circuitous route behind the fort to approach the Arkansas River above the bastion. General Frederick Steele, commanding Sherman's First Division, led the corps' march. After trudging through two miles of swamp, the column halted to determine the next line of march. McClernand came up and informed Sherman that seven more miles of swampland lay ahead, and he ordered him to countermarch. The troops turned around and followed the route of Sherman's other division, led by General David Stuart, a route closer to the river. This took all day and the men were not yet in position when the moon rose.[21]

Meanwhile Morgan's two divisions, commanded by Generals Andrew J. Smith and Peter J. Osterhaus, were themselves getting into position, guided by one of McClernand's staff officers. This column did not have to march through swampland, so there was less difficulty getting into proper position. As the afternoon of January 10 turned into night McClernand requested Admiral Porter's gunboats to fire into the fort to distract the rebels while the ground troops took their positions. The admiral did this for about an hour, until nightfall. The troops then spent a cold night without tents or fires, waiting for the next day's fight.[22]

When the sun rose on January 11 McClernand's army was ready for the attack, with Sherman's corps on the right and Morgan's on the left. The plan was for the gunboats to open fire on the fort, followed by the infantry assault. The naval bombardment began at about 1:00 P.M., and shortly thereafter the artillery opened up from both sides of the Federal line. By 1:30 the fort was sufficiently softened up and the infantry assault began.[23] As Federal troops advanced upon the fort the heavily outnumbered Confederates poured a destructive fire into the blue columns. Porter's gunboats, continuing to rain fire into the rebels, passed by the fort and opened a reverse fire. By 3:30 P.M. the Union attackers were within 100 yards of the fort, and artillery fire from within it had ceased. As the Yankee assault bore down it was obvious that further resistance was futile and at 4:30 P.M. the white flags of surrender appeared.[24]

Having planned the assault McClernand left its execution to his corps commanders. He hung back close to the river to supervise the general direction of the attack. He even had a staff member climb a tree to report on the progress of the battle. With the surrender the Illinois general won his greatest military victory. He then assigned command of the fort to General Morgan and responsibility for prisoners and all other matters to Sherman.[25] McClernand dashed off a note of congratulations to Admiral Porter for the "efficient and brilliant part taken by you...." The naval commander sent similar congratulations to McClernand: "I congratulate you that we have disposed of this tough little nut.... I only wish there was another of the same kind to attack on the morrow."[26]

The capture of Arkansas Post was an important Union victory. McClernand's expedition netted seven enemy flags, almost 5,000 prisoners, many artillery pieces, gun carriages, thousands of small arms, and a great deal of ammunition.[27] Additionally, the Federal army recaptured the stores the Confederates had taken from the *Blue Wing.* McClernand sent the prisoners to St. Louis for exchange and had the fort destroyed, but not before he had a piece of a rebel cannon sent to Illinois governor Yates as a prize of war.[28] Federal casualties numbered 134 killed, 898 wounded, and 29 missing.[29]

The victorious general immediately notified Grant of the fort's capture. McClernand gave Admiral Porter his due recognition, stating that he had "efficiently and brilliantly co-operated in accomplishing this complete success."[30] As was his custom after a battle, McClernand issued a congratulatory order to the troops. Issued the day after the surrender it was vintage John McClernand: "SOLDIERS OF THE ARMY OF THE MISSISSIPPI: I congratulate you.... With ranks thinned by former battles and disease you have waded and cut your way through miles of swamps and timber in advancing to the attack." The general continued: "[A] success so complete in itself has not hitherto been achieved during the war." McClernand closed the order by urging the troops to more victories: "Win for the Army of the Mississippi an imperishable renown. Surmount all obstacles, and relying on the God of Battles wrest from destiny and danger the homage of still more expressive acknowledgements of your unconquerable constancy and valor."[31] The general was certainly ecstatic over the triumph, and saw it in terms of personal success. After the surrender he was alleged to have boasted, "Glorious! glorious! my star is ever in the ascent!"[32]

The Federal victory at Arkansas Post was perhaps more significant than even McClernand imagined. Though General William S. Rosecrans' Army of the Cumberland had just defeated the Confederates at Stones River, Union military successes were scarce. General Ambrose Burnside's Army of the Potomac met defeat at Fredericksburg and Sherman had been repulsed at Chickasaw Bayou. Grant's campaign against Vicksburg had stalled. Union morale was low and McClernand's victory helped rejuvenate the Federal army.

After the surrender McClernand began to plan his next moves. When he informed General Curtis, who commanded the Department of the Missouri, of the victory he announced that his next target was Little Rock, water level on the Arkansas River permitting.[33] A few days later Curtis suggested that McClernand raid Arkadelphia, located 70–80 miles southwest of Little

Rock at the head of the Washita River. Curtis described it as "the great store-house and arsenal of the rebels in the west."[34] It was a place McClernand certainly considered in determining his next move.

Others were determining the general's next move for him. The opposition of Generals Halleck and Grant to McClernand's expedition was obvious from the beginning. These two men, who had failed to prevent McClernand's campaign months earlier, were at work once again. Even as McClernand's Army of the Mississippi was locked in mortal combat Grant was attempting to take his command from him, explaining to Halleck that McClernand was on "a wild goose-chase."[35] At the same time, Grant informed McClernand that he did not approve of his "move on the Post of Arkansas.... It will lead to the loss of men without a result." He then ordered McClernand to "immediately proceed" to Milliken's Bend and await further orders.[36]

Halleck wasted no time in responding to Grant. On January 12 he authorized Grant to remove McClernand from command of the expedition and take over himself or give it to the next in rank.[37] The next in rank was Sherman, whom both Halleck and Grant had wanted to command the expedition in the first place. Grant wrote out an order removing McClernand, but for some reason never sent it. For the immediate future McClernand's command was safe.[38]

Since mail travel was slow, Grant had not yet received McClernand's January 8 communication that explained his plans and justifications for taking Arkansas Post or the note announcing the victory on the 11th. Grant apparently did get those communications before he sent the removal order he wrote on January 12, which might explain why the order was not sent. For whatever reason, by January 13 Grant seemed to have had a change of heart. Grant wrote to McClernand on the 13th in a much calmer tone and informed his subordinate that he had forwarded his dispatch announcing the victory on to Washington. In this subdued tone Grant suggested that McClernand return to Milliken's Bend to prepare to move against Vicksburg. It was not an order, but a suggestion.[39]

McClernand's response to Grant was typical — he sent out a stream of letters protesting his treatment. The general first complained that he had anticipated Grant's approval of the successful campaign, not his condemnation. McClernand seemed to interpret Grant's January 13 note as a reprimand. He believed he would have been guilty of a "great crime" had he remained idle and inactive at Milliken's Bend. Instead he moved against Arkansas Post, reduced and destroyed it, yet still was censured by Grant.[40]

McClernand was still suspicious of Grant's intentions when he addressed Lincoln the same day. The general was blunt and to the point: "I believe my success here is gall and wormwood to the clique of West Pointers who have been persecuting me for months." He pled with Lincoln: "Do not let me be clandestinely destroyed, or, what is worse, dishonored, without a hearing. The very moment you think I am an impediment to the public service, upon the slightest intimation of it my resignation will be forwarded."[41] McClernand again went directly to the president, circumventing the chain of command.

The Illinois general could soon add Sherman to the list of officers who wanted him removed as soon as possible. From Arkansas Post the troops moved to Napoleon, Arkansas, and from there to Milliken's Bend. At Napoleon Sherman took the liberty of skipping the chain of command and wrote to Grant directly. In this "semi-official" communication, he explained to Grant the importance of reducing Arkansas Post. Sherman was under the correct impression that Grant did not approve of the operation, and in addition to defending the campaign he lobbied Grant to take command of the expedition personally. Sherman did not trust McClernand's abilities as a military commander: "I only fear McClernand may attempt impossibilities."[42]

With Sherman firmly in the anti–McClernand camp (along with Halleck, Grant, and later Porter and McPherson) the Illinois general stood little chance of keeping his command. As the expedition moved from Napoleon to Milliken's Bend on January 18, Grant was coming from Memphis to meet with McClernand, Sherman, and Admiral Porter. During the visit, which took place on January 19, Grant concluded that there was "not sufficient confidence felt in General McClernand as a commander, either by the Army or Navy, to insure his success." Grant decided to take personal charge and he reported to Halleck that it was a matter he did not seek out, but rather was "forced" upon him.[43] With Grant commanding in person, McClernand's independent status would be eliminated. Grant's visit was the beginning of the end of McClernand's independent command.

In the middle of this crisis Lincoln addressed McClernand's accusations against Halleck. In a typical Lincoln letter he informed the general that he had "too many family controversies, (so to speak) already on my hands, to voluntarily, or so long as I can avoid it, take up another." The president knew that McClernand would lose a power struggle against the general-in-chief, and he wanted McClernand to concentrate on "the better work"— the war. Although Lincoln expressed his appreciation for the general's "brilliant and valuable" victory at Arkansas Post, McClernand must have been disillusioned that the president avoided the issue of Halleck.[44]

McClernand's removal from command of the Mississippi Expedition was a foregone conclusion by the end of January. As early as the 22nd Grant assumed command of all Union troops in Arkansas, which included those under McClernand. As part of Special Orders No. 22, Grant assigned certain troops to the 13th Army Corps, to be commanded by General McClernand.[45] This signified that Grant considered McClernand's sphere of command to be only the 13th Corps. Also, when Grant corresponded with McClernand he addressed his notes to the commander of the 13th Corps, not to the commander of the Mississippi Expedition. Grant started this practice toward the end of January, another indication that McClernand's independent status was essentially gone.

Though Grant had not yet officially and formally relieved McClernand from his command, he did so in a short time, and it was a brash complaint from McClernand that led to his removal. He wrote to Grant about a minor problem over the camp location of an Indiana regiment. After explaining the problem, McClernand blistered Grant for issuing orders directly to corps commanders without going through him first: "I understand that orders are being issued directly from your headquarters directly to army corps commanders, and not through me." Since McClernand had authority from the president and secretary of war to command the expedition, he believed that he should issue all orders. McClernand was evidently unaware that Grant considered his sphere of command reduced to only the 13th Corps. McClernand suggested the matter be immediately referred to Washington, "and one or the other, or both of us, relieved." Truer words were never written than when he concluded that "two Generals cannot command this army."[46] A separate, independent command within another general's department was an irregularity that could not last long, and what McClernand did not understand was that he would be the one relieved or demoted. Besides, because of the conditions of McClernand's October 21, 1862, order, Grant was well within his rights to take over command of the expedition.

Receipt of this letter forced Grant to remove McClernand from command of the Mississippi Expedition, his association with the president notwithstanding. Grant did understand that because of political considerations he could not send McClernand home, so he assigned him to command the 13th Army Corps.[47] Though McClernand vigorously protested his removal, he accepted it "for the purpose of avoiding a conflict of authority in the presence of the enemy."[48] He requested that all correspondence concerning his removal be sent to Washington for evaluation by authorities there, probably hoping that Lincoln would reinstate him. That did not happen. The president was willing to leave matters as they stood without his interference.

So it was finally done. What Halleck and Grant had been trying to do since November 1862 was carried out in January 1863. McClernand was removed and Grant had overall command of the campaign against Vicksburg. What, if anything, did McClernand accomplish in his short tenure with an independent command? He demonstrated the ability to plan a campaign and successfully carry it out. His overwhelming superiority of numbers probably rendered the Arkansas Post campaign a foregone conclusion, but reduction of the fort was his crowning military success. His capture of the fortress was not inconsequential. Freer navigation of the Mississippi and a morale boost for the Union army were the most important military results of the expedition. Though Vicksburg was supposed to be his primary target, McClernand believed he was still operating within the spirit of his orders from the president and secretary of war when he attacked Arkansas Post. Grant apparently thought Vicksburg was to be McClernand's first priority, and that he should not have gone on his "wild goose-chase" in Arkansas. The final, and perhaps most lasting, result of this campaign was the solidification of an anti–McClernand bloc among the officers in the Army of the Tennessee and the navy. McClernand had a talent for alienating high ranking officers, and it was prominent in this campaign. It was a skill that would haunt him a few months later, but for the immediate future his attention was focused on helping capture another Confederate fortress — Vicksburg.

10

"Warriors Stripped for the Conflict"
Vicksburg and Removal

As the war continued into 1863 one of the important Union objectives remained the opening of the Mississippi River. Besides splitting the Confederacy in half, control of the Mississippi would open it up for commercial purposes, and the destruction of Arkansas Post was a small step toward that objective. The greatest obstacle to opening the river was the great Confederate fortress at Vicksburg.

The rebel bastion at Vicksburg was located on the east side of the Mississippi on a 200 foot bluff overlooking the river. From the river this bluff was unscalable. The city was situated on one of the river's most extreme hairpin curves, which made running past it hazardous. Any ship was forced to slow down while navigating the bend, making it an easy target for Confederate artillerists. The fortress was surrounded by the 250-mile long, 60-mile wide Mississippi-Yazoo alluvial delta. This was the region between the two rivers on the east side of the Mississippi, extending from Vicksburg northward to Memphis. It consisted of many rivers, swamps, bayous, and thick forests, which rendered it virtually impassable to an invading army. The west side of the Mississippi was also cut up with swamps and bayous, forming yet another difficult obstacle to invasion. The best way to assault Vicksburg was from the southeast, avoiding the delta. The only invasion route from the north side of the fort was up the Yazoo River, which ran into the Mississippi a few miles north of Vicksburg; but there invaders were confronted with enemy fortifications at Chickasaw Bayou. Topography was the principal problem facing any Federal army attempting to capture Vicksburg.

While McClernand was in Washington in the autumn of 1862 politicking for an independent command to take Vicksburg, Grant was formulating his own plans to take the town. He proposed a two-pronged attack, one column under his command and the other under Sherman's. Grant gathered his troops at Grand Junction, Tennessee, just north of the Mississippi-Tennessee border. From there he would take the Mississippi Central Railroad south through Holly Springs, Oxford, and on to Grenada, Mississippi. He planned to rebuild the railroad along this route and stockpile stores at a supply depot at Holly Springs. Simultaneously Sherman would take troops already at Memphis, forwarded by McClernand, up the Yazoo for a movement on Vicksburg. Grant's plan was for his column to draw the Confederate troops out of Vicksburg while Sherman captured the fortified city and trapped the troops between the two Federal forces.

Grant and Sherman did not anticipate an intrusion by the Confederate cavalry. Rebel generals Earl Van Dorn and Nathan B. Forrest disrupted Grant's plans. Before Grant reached Oxford, Forrest destroyed about fifty miles of railroad and telegraph lines behind the Federal army, cutting off Grant's lines of communication and transportation. Van Dorn, with another cavalry force, rode to Holly Springs and destroyed the supply depot there. By the time Grant reached Grenada he was deep into enemy territory without supplies or communications, and he was forced to turn back. Because his line of communications was cut, Grant could not inform Sherman of his withdrawal, leaving Sherman to confront the Confederates by himself, which he did unsuccessfully on December 29 at Chickasaw Bayou. The embattled Sherman took his troops to Milliken's Bend, just above Vicksburg, where he turned them over to McClernand in early January.

Even though Grant's first attempt to take Vicksburg failed he did not give up. Because the swamps and bayous dominated the area surrounding the town, the river would be the dominant feature of the campaign. Grant had to find a way past the fortress city while at the same time avoiding the rebel artillery inside it, so he commenced digging a series of canals, hoping to elude Vicksburg, none of which succeeded. In addition to bypassing the town, Grant hoped the canal digging would keep the soldiers busy during the winter months while they were not fighting. By late March Grant finally decided that the canals would not work, so he devised another plan. Since bypassing Vicksburg had failed, the general wanted to try to run gunboats, transports, and supply ships past the town. Once south of Vicksburg he could transport the army, which was to march by the fort on the west side, across the river to dry ground.

Meanwhile, McClernand was growing restless with the inactivity. General Orders No. 13, relieving him from command of the Mississippi Expedition, assigned him to garrison the post at Helena, Arkansas. There the general

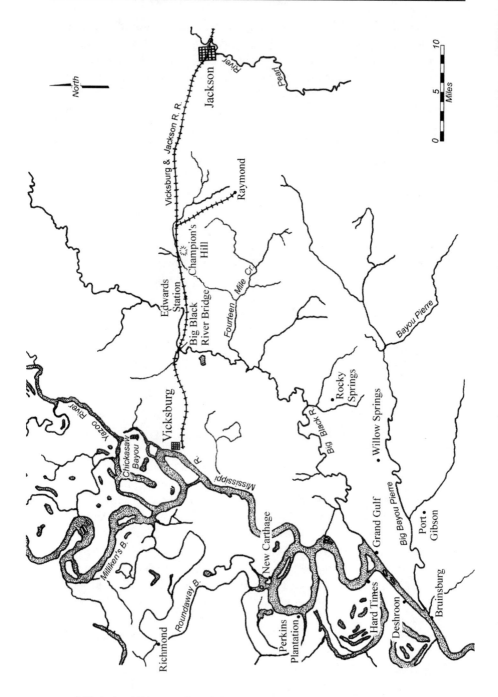

Mississippi River and Vicksburg, 1863 (map by Julie Barnes Smith).

and his corps were responsible for holding the west bank of the Mississippi River south of Helena. They were also part of Grant's expedition to take Vicksburg and were to cooperate with his movements.[1]

Though he had been demoted to corps command, the Illinois general wanted an active campaign and requested permission from Grant to attack both Arkadelphia and Little Rock. He described Arkadelphia as "an extensive depot of rebel stores," and said he believed the capture of those two places would "consummate the expedition begun in the reduction of the Post of Arkansas." From there McClernand expected to cooperate with General Nathaniel P. Banks, who was moving against Port Hudson, a Confederate fort on the Mississippi River in Louisiana about 110 miles south of Vicksburg. With Port Hudson reduced, Grant, Banks, and McClernand could then turn their combined attention to Vicksburg.[2]

This proposal illustrated several tendencies on McClernand's part. The first was his desire for an active campaign — he wanted to fight. Throughout the war McClernand demonstrated a willingness to fight at any place, regardless of the propriety of the movement. He was a fighting general and fighting was, after all, how one attained fame, glory, and renown. Second, it showed his wish to be free from Grant's control. The proposed movement to Arkadelphia and Little Rock would be independent of Grant, and McClernand could garner all of the glory after the victories. Third, the plan showed his meddlesome nature. He would ostensibly have an independent command within several different departments, circumventing the authority of those department commanders. McClernand would be encroaching upon the authority of Grant (Department of the Tennessee), Banks (Department of the Gulf), and Curtis (Department of the Missouri). And lastly, that McClernand sent a copy of this proposal to Lincoln demonstrated another disturbing, yet common habit.[3]

Later in February McClernand renewed his proposal to invade Arkansas while he reassembled his staff. On February 15 he asked permission to take 20,000 men and invade Arkansas, a request General Grant denied, stating that all troops in the vicinity of Vicksburg must be used for the campaign against the fortress.[4] McClernand renewed his proposal to Grant on February 28, again without success.[5] The initial rejection, however, did not prevent him from offering his insights about the military situation to an authority over Grant's head — Lincoln. The general made essentially the same proposition to Lincoln that he made to Grant: "If it should be deemed advisable to postpone the movement against Vicksburg for a time, the forces here might be turned against the enemy in Arkansas."[6] Again McClernand attempted to separate himself from Grant and squeeze out an independent command. The general also advised the president that the best way to take Vicksburg was by siege.

McClernand prevailed upon Illinois governor Yates to help him. Once more he suggested that an effort be made to conquer for good the west side of the Mississippi River. He asked the governor to "urge the President" to allow him to do that, declaring that he would have "wrested Arkansas and Louisiana by this time from the rebellion but for a blind order restraining me." He claimed that the destiny of the northwest depended upon Union control of the west bank of the Mississippi River.[7] Once again McClernand attempted to use his influence and political contacts to promote himself and his position in the war.

As the Army of the Tennessee floundered in the mud digging canals, McClernand continued to beg for activity and schemed for a command. "Time is passing and the republic is dying of <u>inertia</u>. The fall and winter have passed, and the spring is now passing, and nothing decisive has been done in this quarter," the general complained to Governor Yates from his headquarters at Milliken's Bend. He wanted the governor to ask President Lincoln to send a "competent commander" for the department. "For our country's sake do," he admonished Yates. McClernand also prevailed upon the governor, not surprisingly, to work for an independent command or department for him. The general wanted to operate in Arkansas, northern Louisiana, and eastern Texas, essentially along the western side of the Mississippi River. McClernand wanted to fight rather than dig canals, and felt he was not being given that opportunity. "My situation is intolerable," he claimed.[8]

McClernand was also willing to participate in a common Grant-bashing scheme if the result was a separate independent command for himself. That scheme was, of course, Grant's alleged drinking problem. In a letter to Lincoln in March 1863 McClernand reported that Grant had been "gloriously drunk" on March 13 and sick in bed all the next day. This note was delivered personally to the president by Captain William J. Kountz, who could "furnish the name of the officers of high standing to substantiate" the charge.[9] The significance of this accusation was that if Grant was either removed or injured (and hence unable to command) because of a drinking binge, McClernand, as the next ranking officer, would command the army. McClernand outranked all other officers in the Army of the Tennessee, so if anything happened to Grant command of the army would go to McClernand.

Was the accusation accurate or did McClernand invent this story to get Grant removed? While this seemed like one of McClernand's schemes to get a command, there may be a kernel of truth to the charge. On June 6, 1863, John Rawlins, Grant's assistant adjutant general, wrote a letter to Grant in which he referred to a pledge Grant made to him "last March that you would drink no more during the war."[10] Was this pledge in March in response to a binge? If so, there may have been some truth to McClernand's accusation.

According to Charles A. Dana, a War Department observer and Grant supporter, these drinking binges ordinarily took place during a lull in the fighting, and by March 13 the army's activity consisted of attempting to dig canals in the Mississippi mud.[11] Regardless of the accuracy of the report, McClernand employed extreme measures to get Grant removed so he could command the army.

Grant retained command of the army and on March 23 he ordered it to concentrate at Milliken's Bend for a movement south, since the general had decided to abandon the digging of canals. Once the army was assembled Grant planned to march along the west bank of the Mississippi River to some place south of Vicksburg. Once there the naval fleet would attempt to sail past Vicksburg, a dangerous task considering the configuration of the river and the town's location on one of the Mississippi's hairpin curves. Admiral Porter warned Grant that once the vessels ran past Vicksburg they could not return. Sailing against the river's current would put the vessels at the mercy of the Confederate batteries far too long.[12] If successful the navy would then transport the army across the river and Grant's blue-clad troops could attack the fort from the only place geographically possible.

The Army of the Tennessee was organized into three corps — McClernand's 13th, the 15th under Sherman, and the 17th, commanded by General James B. McPherson. The 13th Corps was divided into four divisions, each with two brigades. McClernand's four division commanders were Brigadier Generals Peter J. Osterhaus (9th Division), Andrew J. Smith (10th Division), Alvin P. Hovey (12th Division), and Eugene A. Carr (14th Division). The 13th Corps included 40 regiments of infantry from throughout the Midwest, 6 companies of cavalry, and 9 batteries of artillery.[13]

McClernand's 13th Corps started from Milliken's Bend on March 29 at the head of the entire army.[14] Grant wanted McClernand leading the march because he supported Grant's proposed campaign, while Sherman did not.[15] Because the winter of 1862–1863 was unusually wet many of the roads were still flooded in late March, which made the expedition difficult, not to mention presenting many opportunities for ambushes. In addition, the movement would threaten the Vicksburg, Shreveport, & Texas Railroad, so McClernand could expect stiff Confederate resistance. By 2:00 P.M. on March 30 part of General Osterhaus' division reached the head of Roundaway Bayou, opposite Richmond, about 12 miles from Milliken's Bend. A small force of rebels was dispersed from Richmond. By the evening of April 3 Osterhaus' entire division arrived at Richmond after a 200-foot long bridge was built over the bayou. Accompanied by Osterhaus, General McClernand made a reconnaissance down Roundaway Bayou toward New Carthage on April 3. They discovered that the area between Roundaway Bayou and Bayou Vidal was inundated (only the roofs of the buildings were above water), which meant the entire expanse from Richmond to New Carthage was flooded. Within a half mile of New Carthage the two generals were fired on and were forced to turn back.[16]

Having occupied Richmond and scouted to New Carthage, the latter place was the next destination. On April 6 a flatboat set sail on Roundaway Bayou toward New Carthage armed with a mountain howitzer and a small party of 54 men under the direction of General Osterhaus. These troops drove the Confederates out of New Carthage, which was then occupied by parts of the 13th Corps. The general's men constructed scows, yawls, and other small craft from materials obtained from a local sawmill and transported troops and supplies to New Carthage. For the next week to ten days the remainder of the army advanced on New Carthage. McPherson's 17th Corps arrived after McClernand's 13th, and Sherman's 15th Corps brought up the rear. Sherman's men provided a distraction to the enemy, as they feinted toward Vicksburg from the north, and following this movement Sherman's corps marched to join the rest of the army. From New Carthage the next objectives were the Perkins plantation and Hard Times, Louisiana, just across the Mississippi River from Grand Gulf, Mississippi.[17]

Marching through the flooded bayous was a tortuous, tiresome task. One notable accomplishment during this movement was the bridges the Engineering Corps built. McClernand's men constructed four bridges over the bayous, two of them over 600 feet in length, for a total of 2,000 feet of bridging.[18] An easier way to move the troops and provisions had to be found. McClernand claimed to have suggested to Grant the idea of "forwarding steam transports and gunboats from their moorings above Vicksburg below to Carthage."[19] Running past the batteries at Vicksburg was a dangerous proposition. Ships would have to navigate the hairpin curve slowly at the town, which would make them easy targets for the Confederate artillery. Grant was willing to take the risk. During the evening of April 16–17 Admiral David D. Porter ran the batteries with a fleet of gunboats, supply barges, and transports. The barges carried the camp equipment for McClernand's corps.[20] This maneuver was so successful that five more transports repeated the feat during the night of April 22–23 (one was sunk). The importance of these movements cannot be overstated. In addition to the obvious transportation and supply advantages, the gunboats significantly increased Federal firepower.

With the navy present south of Vicksburg, the gunboats and transports could cooperate in further movements. The goal was to secure a landing on the east bank of the Mississippi and eliminate the Confederate batteries there. Grant's initial choice was Warrenton, which was about 17 river miles above Ione, the proposed staging location, and less than ten miles from Vicksburg.

The trip from Ione to Warrenton would take about three hours. After determining that Confederate troops from Vicksburg could reach Warrenton before Federal forces landed, Grant changed his mind. On April 18 Grant conferred with McClernand at Pointe Clear, approximately 30 miles south of Milliken's Bend, and suggested Grand Gulf as a potential landing point. At this meeting McClernand asked Grant for more shipping to transport his corps across the river. Grant agreed, and additional vessels ran past the Vicksburg batteries during the night of April 22–23.[21]

After Grant chose Grand Gulf on April 20, McClernand began to move his corps southward to locate a staging area closer to Grand Gulf. The initial choice was the Perkins Plantation, but it could handle only two divisions at a time, far too small for what was needed. Just south of the Perkins Plantation was a more suitable location, Hard Times, which was large enough to accommodate two entire Federal corps. While his troops made their way to Hard Times, McClernand, along with one of his division commanders, General Osterhaus, boarded the gunboat *General Price* on April 23 to scout Grand Gulf. McClernand determined the rebel positions to be "very strong." On April 26 he met with Governor Yates, who was visiting the army.[22] By April 28 the majority of McClernand's corps was concentrated at Hard Times and remained there that night preparing for an assault on Grand Gulf the next day.[23]

The plan was for the naval gunboats to silence the enemy batteries at Grand Gulf and the infantry, McClernand's 13th Corps, to quickly disembark and "carry the works by storm."[24] At 8:00 A.M. on April 29 Admiral Porter began the bombardment with eight gunboats, while McClernand's men huddled on the transports waiting to effect a landing. The battle lasted some five hours and one of McClernand's staff described it as "the most magnificent scene I ever saw."[25] Porter's gunboats could not silence the batteries, so the flotilla withdrew at about 1:00 P.M. With this plan thwarted, McClernand's infantry disembarked on the west side of the river at Hard Times to locate another place for a landing.

The next day, after disembarking, the 13th Corps marched south along the river to the Disharoon plantation, a point below Grand Gulf. That evening, April 29, the fleet ran past the batteries at Grand Gulf, repeating its performance earlier in the month. Safely beyond the guns at Grand Gulf, the transports could begin crossing the infantry to the east side of the river without distractions. For the landing Grant chose Bruinsburg, about five miles downstream from the Disharoon plantation and ten miles below Grand Gulf. The 13th Corps crossed on April 30. The entire corps disembarked before noon and halted only long enough to distribute three days' rations, which were to last five days. Unfortunately, it took four hours to distribute the rations because the supply wagons were left at Hard Times and had to be transported across the river.[26] McClernand's troops marched out about 4:00 P.M. to fight the rebels.

The landing at Bruinsburg was effected without rebel opposition largely for two reasons. Sherman's 15th Corps was still feinting north of Vicksburg, which attracted a great deal of attention, and secondly, Colonel Benjamin H. Grierson, commanding 1,700 cavalrymen, attracted attention of his own. Starting at La Grange, Tennessee, on April 17, Grierson disappeared, causing havoc and confusion among the Confederates until he reappeared in Baton Rouge, Louisiana, on May 2. His command destroyed property, wrecked railroad communications, repeatedly fought rebel cavalry, and generally caused disorder among the Confederates who could not locate him. Grierson's raid through Mississippi diverted Confederate attention away from Grant's movements.

Once McClernand's corps landed at Bruinsburg its objective was to capture Grand Gulf, which was to be Grant's base.[27] From Grand Gulf, Port Gibson was the destination, as roads led from there to Vicksburg and Jackson, the capital of Mississippi. A road led directly from Bruinsburg to Port Gibson, and Bayou Pierre, a navigable stream, bisected the road. Once McClernand's 13th Corps, 19,000 strong, landed, the rebels abandoned Grand Gulf and moved toward Port Gibson. Hoping to capture the bridges over Bayou Pierre before the retreating Confederates destroyed them, McClernand ordered a forced march during the evening of April 30–May 1.[28] The night march may also have been an effort to make up for the lost four hours at Bruinsburg.

General Carr's division led the advance, and at 1:00 A.M. on May 1 the first contact was made with the enemy, about 12 miles from Bruinsburg and 4 miles from Port Gibson. This contact was brief and consisted of light infantry and artillery fire. Carr returned fire for about two hours, after which the Confederates withdrew. Following this short fight the entire corps rested until daylight. At dawn on May 1 McClernand discovered that the road leading to Port Gibson diverged into two. On the left was the Bruinsburg Road and the Shaifer Road was on the right. The distance between them was no more than two miles at any place and the land between the roads was cut up with forests, hills, and ravines. The two roads ran into Rodney Road, which led into Port Gibson.

Osterhaus' division was positioned on the Bruinsburg Road and was to be a distraction from the principal attack, which would be on the right. Generals Carr and Hovey were positioned on the Shaifer Road and constituted the main attacking force. General Smith's division was the reserve. A brigade from General John A. Logan's division from McPherson's 17th Corps supported Osterhaus. The battle began about 5:30 A.M. on May 1 as Osterhaus moved his men forward on the left. As the engagement raged on that side McClernand, who spent the day on the right, ordered Carr to advance at 6:15 A.M. This was the main attack. Soon after Carr was engaged, Hovey's division joined the fight on the right.[29]

The Confederates put up a stubborn resistance. At about 10:00 A.M. after several hours of hard fighting Hovey ordered a charge and, with Carr following suit, forced the rebels to withdraw and form a second line of defense. This withdrawal has been compared to a dam breaking.[30] In this charge Hovey's division captured many prisoners as well as artillery pieces, caissons, flags, and ammunition. Loud shouts resonated through the troops when Grant and McClernand appeared on the battlefield together accompanied by Illinois governor Richard Yates. Both Yates and McClernand delivered short congratulatory speeches to the troops before McClernand ordered Carr and Hovey to push the attack vigorously.[31] At this point the Confederates massed a force on the extreme Federal right hoping to turn the flank. To thwart this attempt McClernand brought up part of General Smith's division, which was in reserve. Together with massed artillery on the right the rebel flank attack was stopped.[32]

As night approached the Confederates defending Port Gibson abandoned the field to McClernand and his men. The battle lasted all day and cost 826 casualties in the 13th Corps.[33] McClernand called the engagement "one of the most admirably and successfully fought battles." His troops captured 580 prisoners, 2 flags, 2 artillery pieces, 3 caissons, and a large amount of small arms and ammunition.[34] The most important result of this clash was that the Federal bridgehead was secure and the army had broken out and was able to pursue the retreating Confederates.[35] McClernand's corps fought the battle with little help from the rest of the army, a point the general noted in his traditional battle report to Lincoln.[36] The general commended the rank and file for their effort in this battle. The men of the 13th Corps were without wagons, tents, cooking utensils, and ambulances and McClernand described his troops as "literally, warriors stripped for the conflict."[37]

An interesting occurrence took place during the battle that demonstrated the severity of the split between Grant and McClernand. During the engagement two of Grant's staff officers, Lieutenant Colonels John A. Rawlins and James H. Wilson, assistant adjutant general and inspector general respectively, asked Grant to reconcile with McClernand. Rawlins and Wilson believed the time was right for a *rapprochement* between the two generals. They wanted Grant to ride over to McClernand and "thank him for his good conduct and brilliant success." Much to their surprise Grant refused. Not only did Grant reject this idea but, as Wilson remembered, he was determined "to keep a close watch and a steady hand over his self-constituted rival. From that day forth Grant not only maintained the most formal attitude toward McClernand, but, so far as practicable, refrained from meeting him in person or giving written orders." There continued to be a great deal of friction between McClernand and Grant throughout the Vicksburg Campaign.[38]

On May 2 the Federal army occupied Port Gibson after the rebels evacuated it and burned the bridges over Bayou Pierre. By the next day Union forces occupied Grand Gulf. At this time only McClernand's and McPherson's corps were on the east side of the Mississippi, as Sherman's 15th Corps did not cross over until May 6. The Federal line of march was in a north-northeasterly direction. The army marched from Port Gibson and Grand Gulf to the Big Black River, and there turned in an easterly direction. This was done because Confederate General Joseph E. Johnston was at Jackson, about 40 miles east of Vicksburg, with a force of about 6,000 entrenched troops. Grant proposed to march on Jackson to prevent Johnston from joining with the force at Vicksburg, under General John C. Pemberton. It could be dangerous if both Johnston and Pemberton moved out to attack Grant, catching the Federal army between the two Confederate forces.

The Yankees moved much too quickly to get trapped. Grant decided to cut loose from his supply lines, so the only obstacle to the march was the enemy. A foraging party from General Hovey's division returned to camp on May 4 with an excellent haul—180,000 pounds of ham and other meat.[39] An excellent road ran from Grand Gulf to Edwards Station along the east bank of the Big Black River. The river was an obstacle to the Confederate army; it was large enough to protect the Federal left flank as it marched northeast. After the army rested from May 3 to May 6 the 13th Corps marched along the Big Black River through Willow Springs, Rocky Springs, Five Mile Creek, and on May 12 Fourteen Mile Creek.[40] At Fourteen Mile Creek McClernand's troops fought a small skirmish and suffered only light casualties. During the evening of May 12 Grant ordered McClernand to take his corps toward Edwards Station, on the Vicksburg & Jackson Railroad. From its position on Fourteen Mile Creek, the 13th Corps marched to Raymond, where General McPherson's corps had fought an engagement earlier that day. While McClernand occupied Raymond, Sherman and McPherson moved on Jackson to confront Johnston.[41]

As the 15th and 17th Corps moved on Jackson, McClernand's troops were ordered to positions in support of Sherman and McPherson. Osterhaus' division was at Raymond, Hovey's at Clinton, Carr's at Mississippi Springs, and Smith's, along with General Blair's division of Sherman's corps, at New Auburn.[42] Sherman and McPherson attacked Johnston on May 14 and sent the Confederates reeling in retreat. On May 15 McClernand began to move his divisions in a northwesterly direction to Bolton Station after Grant received a report that the rebel troops in Jackson and Vicksburg were trying to unite. The occupation of Bolton Station would block such an attempt. McClernand's troops marched at dawn on May 15 and arrived at Bolton Station about 9:00 A.M.

Grant's objectives to prevent a junction of Johnston and Pemberton and to drive Pemberton back into Vicksburg seemed to be succeeding. During the evening of May 15 Grant ordered McClernand to march his corps from Bolton Station to Edwards Station, "feeling the enemy" without starting a general engagement. There were three roads that connected the two places and they converged three miles from Edwards Station. At 5:00 A.M. on May 16 General Smith's division moved on the southernmost of the three roads, Raymond Road, along with Blair's division of Sherman's corps. At 6:00 A.M. Osterhaus marched his division on the center road, Middle Road, with Carr's division in support. General Hovey took the northernmost road, Jackson Road, also at 6:00 A.M., with Logan's division of McPherson's corps. McClernand himself went with Osterhaus and Carr in the center.[43]

The Confederates occupied a height that was variously called Midway Hill or Champion's Hill, about three miles east of Edwards Station. Midway Hill was used because the hill was about halfway between Jackson and Vicksburg. Champion's Hill was the more common name and was derived from the name of the owner of the land. The hill was about 60–70 feet high and the Vicksburg and Clinton Road ran over its crest. To the south (or left from the position of the approaching Federal army) the terrain was severely broken, cut up with ravines, hills, and tangled woods. It was virtually impossible to pass through except as skirmishers, which meant an invading army would have a difficult time. This land ends at a narrow creek. On the opposite side of the creek (the north side of the hill) the terrain was more accessible to an attacking force. Open and undulating fields dominated this terrain, which was the primary site of the impending clash.[44]

McClernand's 13th Corps, along with portions of both Sherman's and McPherson's corps, took up the line of march toward Champion's Hill early on May 16. In the approach to the heights, Smith and Blair (the latter from Sherman's corps) were on the left on Raymond Road, which completely circumvented Champion's Hill. Osterhaus and Carr were in the center on Middle Road, which skirted the hill. Hovey, Logan, and Crocker (the latter two from McPherson's corps) were on the right on Jackson Road, and they headed directly for Champion's Hill and the bulk of the Confederate force. McClernand accompanied the center column, while McPherson and Grant rode with the right.

Early on the 16th McClernand rode to McPherson's camp and the two conferred on strategy. McClernand suggested that if the 17th Corps was not needed for support McPherson should place it on the flank and rear to cut off the rebels' line of retreat. McClernand believed that this was his fight alone, and McPherson and Sherman were there simply to support the 13th Corps. When discussing McPherson's place on the battlefield McClernand used the phrase "in the event I should beat the enemy."[45] The Illinois general treated this battle as his own.

By 6:00 A.M. the entire 13th Corps was marching toward Champion's Hill. Smith's division, on the left, encountered rebel skirmishers at about 7:30 A.M., and shortly thereafter artillery fire, which he silenced with his own guns. Osterhaus, in the center, also faced skirmishers and artillery. Since the terrain in his front was rugged, Osterhaus took only one battery of artillery with him. The one cavalry regiment Osterhaus had was withdrawn because of the rough nature of the ground. This regiment, the Third Illinois Cavalry, was later used to connect Osterhaus' line with Smith's. The left and center of the Federal line faced minimal opposition, the main obstacle to their advance being the terrain.[46]

Most of the fighting took place on the right of the Federal line, where Hovey's division was joined by Logan's and Crocker's divisions of McPherson's corps. By 10:30 A.M. Hovey had thrown out skirmishers and Logan had taken a position on the flank at a right angle to Hovey's men. Crocker's division served as a reserve to Hovey and Logan. As the skirmishers pressed forward the rest of the troops followed and by 11:00 the battle had started in earnest. For 600 yards up the slope of the hill Hovey's and Logan's men advanced against a withering Confederate fire. The Yankees drove the rebels back for an hour, capturing many prisoners and artillery pieces.[47]

The Confederates regrouped under cover of the woods on the hill and forced Hovey's men to fall back. Hovey requested aid from Grant, who sent a brigade and two additional regiments from Crocker's division. The fresh troops arrived in good order, but could not prevent a further withdrawal by Hovey's men. By 2:30 P.M. Hovey and Crocker made a stand at the brow of the hill and beat back the rebel advance. Hovey brought his artillery forward, which he had not yet utilized because of the irregularity of the lines. Because he believed he could distinguish the positions of the two armies, Hovey unlimbered the heavy guns and placed them between his men and Logan's troops. This move effectively enfiladed the Confederate line and forced it to retreat.[48]

Cheers from the Federal line told the artillery's success, and an infantry advance followed. Hovey's and Crocker's divisions moved forward and drove the Confederates before them, and ultimately off of the hill. By 3:00 P.M. the battle was over. The artillery barrage, along with a bayonet charge by Logan's division on Hovey's right, decided the engagement. The Federal right fought this battle almost by itself, a fact borne out by the casualty figures.

Total casualties in McClernand's 13th Corps numbered 1,363, of which 1,202 were in Hovey's division. Logan's division suffered 407 casualties.[49]

McClernand's role in this battle was minor. He was in the center throughout the engagement and not in the thick of the fight as he surely must have wanted. Grant roundly criticized McClernand, especially in his postwar memoirs, for not moving his troops fast enough to the front, thereby allowing the Confederates to escape. As one Grant biographer has pointed out, part of the blame for this lay with Grant, because early messages to McClernand ordered him to be cautious. In addition, the nature of the terrain made it difficult for Grant to communicate with McClernand.[50] Although the enemy force immediately in McClernand's front was relatively small, he was moving over difficult terrain. Probably because he was Grant's hated rival and Grant became the war's hero, McClernand has usually been assigned the blame for not capturing a large part of the Confederate army at Champion's Hill. Where McClernand does deserve criticism is in the immediate aftermath of the battle. He was assigned the responsibility of pursuing the retreating rebels with the largely fresh troops under his immediate command and McClernand moved far too cautiously, allowing the Confederate forces to escape.[51]

General Carr's division pursued the retreating rebels, reaching Edwards Station, three miles west of Champion's Hill, at 8:00 P.M. Osterhaus' division joined him there. At Edwards Station Carr discovered that the Confederates had set fire to their supplies to prevent the Federal army from capturing them; Carr's men doused the flames and saved a large amount of artillery ammunition and about 90,000 rounds of infantry ammunition.[52] Early on May 17 Grant's army moved out of Edwards Station close on the heels of the retreating Confederates. McClernand's corps was again in the lead, with Osterhaus and Carr in front. Realizing perhaps that he had missed an opportunity on May 16, McClernand had his forces marching by 3:30 A.M. on May 17. After marching several miles west, the Federal army discovered General Pemberton's troops at the Big Black River, entrenched on both sides. One more battle was imminent before the Federals reached Vicksburg.

Confederates on the east side of the Big Black River (facing the Union army) had their left and right flanks on the river, creating a semicircle with their line. Carr and Osterhaus prepared their troops for the assault, Carr on the right and Osterhaus on the left. After a short skirmish General Smith's division came up and McClernand posted it on the left where Confederates appeared to be massing a large number of men. Before the rebels could mount an attack, a brigade of Carr's division discovered it could move to an advantageous position on the right flank without being detected. Under cover of the riverbank this brigade, under General Michael K. Lawler, charged the Confederates and drove them across the Big Black River in great confusion.[53]

This battle was fought entirely by segments of the 13th Corps, which suffered 273 casualties and captured a large amount of enemy stores. McClernand's men took about 1,500 prisoners, the same number of small arms, 18 artillery pieces, and 5 battle flags.[54] This was the rebels' last stand before Vicksburg. They burned the bridge over Big Black and retreated to their great fortress on the Mississippi River. Though not a battle on the scale of Champion's Hill, McClernand did not pass up an opportunity to trumpet the accomplishments of his troops. "All this was the work of two divisions of my corps unsupported by any other force," he explained to Lincoln in a characteristic report.[55]

Since the Confederates had burned the lone bridge over the Big Black new ones had to be constructed. Troops from the Engineering Corps spent the evening of May 17 building three bridges, one each by McClernand's, Sherman's, and McPherson's men. The 13th Corps bridge builders faced pesky rebel snipers throughout the day and evening of May 17, but the sniper fire ceased about midnight and the bridge was completed. After crossing early on May 18 McClernand's 13th Corps marched toward Vicksburg on the Jackson and Vicksburg road with Smith's division in the advance, followed by Osterhaus and Carr. By nightfall the army was about two miles from Vicksburg, within sight of the extensive fortifications around the city.

On May 19 the army completed its march to Vicksburg and established a line with McClernand on the left, McPherson in the center, and Sherman on the right. The corps commanders were to get their troops as close to the enemy's works as possible and prepare for an assault at 2:00 P.M. that day. By that time McClernand had his corps within 800 yards of the rebel fortifications, Smith's division on the right, Osterhaus on the left, and Carr's in reserve. The attack was carried out at the appointed time, but the Confederate works were too strong. The 13th Corps advanced to within 500 yards of the enemy, but was driven back. Osterhaus' division got to within 350 yards of the enemy before being repulsed by a storm of rebel lead and steel.[56]

The May 19 attack gained virtually nothing. Grant had hoped to subdue Vicksburg's defenders while they were still demoralized by their recent defeats, but his only accomplishment was a closer position to the Confederate entrenchments.[57] With this setback the Yankees began a siege of Vicksburg. For the next two days more reconnaissance missions were made to determine the best place for another assault. They revealed few weak spots in the Confederate line. More men were added to the Federal siege, as one brigade of Hovey's division was brought forward from the Big Black River. This strengthened McClernand's sector none too soon, as Grant planned one more assault to defeat the river fortress.

On the evening of May 21 Grant ordered his three corps commanders to assault the Confederate lines at 10:00 A.M. the next day. Bayonets were to be fixed and no shots were to be fired until the attackers reached the rebel outer works. Some time before 10:00 McClernand began an artillery bombardment with about 39 guns. At precisely five minutes before 10:00 the bugles in the 13th Corps sounded the order to charge and the final assault on Vicksburg had begun.[58]

Against the murderous fire from the entrenched rebels the brave Yankee soldiers charged. Two brigades of Carr's division rushed forward and succeeded in planting their flags upon the outer works of the Confederate fortifications. Two brigades of Smith's division repeated this feat. Many enemy soldiers defending those two areas were captured and sent to the rear. The struggle at those two points was particularly bloody; at one spot a dozen men leaped into a Confederate fort within the entrenchments and only one came out alive. The Chicago Mercantile Artillery was reported to have taken one of its fieldpieces close to the rebel works and double-shot it with ammunition. The ensuing discharge wrought great death and destruction to all Confederates in its path.[59]

The Yankee onslaught on McClernand's front lasted all day. At about noon McClernand believed that the Confederates were massing their forces to stop his progress, and that with assistance he could break through the enemy line, so he requested from Grant either a diversion on the right or reinforcements. Since the conflict on the right and center, Sherman's and McPherson's corps respectively, had by then stopped, McClernand was fighting on the left alone.[60] If the right and center of the Federal line had stopped fighting, that would certainly have allowed rebels the opportunity to mass troops on the Union left. Grant did not believe McClernand's report that his corps could break through the Confederate line. The army commander ordered McClernand to look elsewhere for reinforcement, while Sherman argued that Grant had to renew the fighting on the right.[61] Grant finally ordered both Sherman and McPherson to renew their attacks and sent General Quimby's division from McPherson's corps to McClernand. The renewed attacks and additional troops did not succeed, since the enemy works were too strong to be taken by assault. Nevertheless, McClernand's corps continued to fight until about 8:00 P.M., when the troops withdrew to safety.[62]

With this defeat Grant settled down to take Vicksburg by siege, which was exactly how McClernand had suggested it should be taken back in February.[63] The May 22 assault was costly — McClernand's 13th Corps suffered 1,487 casualties.[64] Grant, in ordering the assaults of May 19 and 22, hoped to catch the rebels demoralized and vulnerable. That obviously did not happen, since the Confederates fought stubbornly from behind formidable entrenchments. Now the boring, mundane work of besieging Vicksburg began.

Almost immediately after the May 22 assault McClernand heard a series of rumors that blamed him for the failure of the attack. He was aware of these rumors by the time he wrote to Governor Yates on May 28 and President Lincoln on May 29. The general confronted Grant with them on June 4: "It is reported among other things, as I understand, that I attacked the enemy's works on the 22nd ulto. without authority; again, that I attacked too late; again, that I am responsible for our failure and losses; again, that I am arrested and being sent North; again, that my command is turned over to another officer; and again that you have, personally, assumed command of it."[65] McClernand flatly denied the charges. The complaints that he attacked without authority and too late were simply absurd. The 13th Corps buglers signaled charge five minutes early, so his troops attacked in a timely manner. The suggestions that he had been arrested and removed from his command were likewise without merit.

The accusation that McClernand was responsible for losses in the army deserves some attention. All commanders bear some responsibility for losses in their command. The charge against McClernand was that the army suffered more casualties (Grant claimed 50 percent more) from his request for a renewed attack or reinforcements. In the general's defense, however, his 13th Corps was the only Union force that did not quit fighting. While Sherman's and McPherson's corps withdrew to safety early, McClernand's troops continued to fight against the strongly fortified enemy. And while it is true that McClernand's request caused additional casualties in the other corps, had the 15th and 17th corps fought as long as the 13th they would have suffered the same losses, perhaps more. While McClernand has been universally censured for his action on May 22, he cannot be accused of quitting a fight early.

Perhaps in response to these rumors, on May 30 McClernand issued General Orders No. 72 — another congratulatory order. It traced every step of the Vicksburg Campaign to that time, from Milliken's Bend to the May 22 assault. Though written specifically to glorify the accomplishments of the 13th Corps, McClernand did in fact acknowledge the participation of McPherson's corps at Port Gibson and Champion's Hill. It was a recapitulation and glorification of the successes of the 13th Corps; in other words it was vintage John McClernand.[66]

The problem with this congratulatory order was that it seemed to imply that Sherman and McPherson did not fight up to their abilities on May 22. McClernand suggested that any success on that day was achieved solely by the 13th Corps. After writing the order McClernand made what turned out to be a fatal error — he sent the order to the newspapers without first sending it through his superior's headquarters. After the publication of the order both Sherman and McPherson complained bitterly to Grant. They suggested that the order was written not for the men of the 13th Corps, but rather for political gain — that it was directed at McClernand's political constituents in Illinois. Sherman also reminded Grant that official orders were prohibited from being published, and that the author of such should be dismissed.[67]

After learning from McClernand that the order published in the newspapers was a correct copy, Grant issued Special Orders No. 164, which relieved McClernand from command of the 13th Corps. The general was to proceed to any point in Illinois and report to army headquarters in Washington, by letter, for orders.[68] McClernand traveled to Illinois, and upon reaching Cairo he wired Lincoln: "I have been relieved for an omission of my Adjutant. Hear me."[69] General Sherman, one of the architects of McClernand's removal, was ecstatic and wrote that his removal "was a relief to the whole Army."[70]

During the Vicksburg campaign General McClernand succeeded in antagonizing even his hometown acquaintance Lieutenant Colonel James H. Wilson, Grant's inspector general. Wilson was from Shawneetown. McClernand had served under his father in the Black Hawk War, and McClernand attempted on several occasions early in the war to have Wilson assigned to his staff. Wilson delivered a message to McClernand from Grant shortly after the May 22 assault on Vicksburg. The general cursed the message, which Wilson took as a verbal assault on himself and he threatened to "pull you off that horse and beat the boots off of you." McClernand apologized by explaining that he was "simply expressing my intense vehemence on the subject matter, sir, and I beg your pardon."[71] It was Wilson who was given the duty, one he probably relished after this confrontation, of delivering McClernand's removal order. In typical fashion, McClernand believed the order would bring down Grant, as he exclaimed, "By God, sir, we are *both* relieved!"[72]

But he was wrong. McClernand's service with the Army of the Tennessee was over and though he protested his removal, it was to no avail. McClernand had succeeded in antagonizing Grant, Sherman, and McPherson, and no amount of protesting to Lincoln could reverse his removal. The desire to rid the army of an unwanted political general had finally succeeded. What Halleck and Grant could not do in the fall and winter of 1862, Grant, Sherman, and McPherson accomplished in June 1863. But it was not without significant assistance from McClernand himself. If the general had learned to bridle his thirst for glory he might have been a participant in the July 4 surrender of Vicksburg.

11

Recriminations, Red River, Resignation

Major General John A. McClernand had been removed as commander of the 13th Army Corps, Army of the Tennessee. "Having been appointed by the President to the command of that corps," he informed General Grant, he could "justly challenge" his superior's authority to relieve him.[1] McClernand did not accept his loss of command without protest. Even before McClernand arrived in Springfield both he and Grant were explaining their positions and actions to Washington. It would be a nasty affair.

Grant struck first, notifying Halleck on June 19 that he found it necessary to relieve McClernand. His reason was McClernand's congratulatory order that Grant claimed was "calculated to create dissention and ill-feeling in the army." The commanding general also informed Halleck that he should have "relieved him long since for general unfitness for his position."[2] Grant had wanted to relieve General McClernand long before he did and the congratulatory order was simply the final straw, and to Grant a justifiable cause for dismissal.

From Cairo McClernand began his assault on the removal order and Grant's motive for relieving him. He first sent Lincoln a telegram on June 23 announcing that he had been relieved. The same day he penned a rather lengthy explanation of the episode, which was personally delivered to the president by a Major Rives. In this letter McClernand sent a copy of his congratulatory order and informed Lincoln that he stood by everything in it. The general claimed that his statements in the order would withstand "the fullest and most conclusive proof." He also alleged that "partizans [*sic*], intent only on exalting their chief, continued to misrepresent and falsify a portion of them to my prejudice." Because of this prejudice the general told Lincoln he was forced to confront Grant with the rumors then circulating in the army, which he did with his June 4 note. These partisans McClernand referenced were undoubtedly Sherman and McPherson.[3]

Having briefed Lincoln on the events leading up to his dismissal, McClernand then examined the reasons for Grant's actions. If he was removed because his adjutant did not send a copy of the congratulatory order to his commander, then all Grant could do was arrest and try the offending general, claimed McClernand. Besides, he continued, "It is a fine point upon which to hinge so cruel and unauthorized an act." If the order was the immediate reason for his removal, "what then was the motive to so extraordinary an act?" he rhetorically asked the president. McClernand firmly believed "personal hostility" was the motive: "I answer personal hostility — hostility originating in the fact that you, in the first instance, assigned me to the command of the Miss. River Expedition — hostility, inflamed by the contrast made by my subsequent success to the previous failures and disasters, and in West Point prejudices. Even my expedition, resulting in the reduction of Arkansas Post, was disapproved by him. This I believe to be the motive."[4]

In light of those facts the exiled general invited an investigation, believing he would be vindicated. McClernand wanted an investigation not only of his own actions, but also those of Grant from Belmont to Vicksburg. This, he believed, would bear out that his conduct at Belmont, Fort Henry, Fort Donelson, Port Gibson, Champion's Hill, Big Black River, and the Vicksburg assaults was above reproach. He led the advance in those campaigns and gained the only measure of success at Vicksburg on May 22, he said, and reminded the president that he planned and successfully captured Arkansas Post. He also emphasized that at Vicksburg "Genl. Grant planned the assault and is alone responsible," hoping to portray himself as the model soldier and Grant as something less. McClernand's final request was that Lincoln reinstate him to command of the 13th Corps at least until Vicksburg fell.[5]

McClernand did not stop with Lincoln, but inundated Washington with his pleas. After arriving in Springfield on June 26 he laid out his case to both Stanton and Halleck, but the general-in-chief was not sympathetic. Halleck had disliked McClernand since the Corinth campaign and had authorized Grant to remove him as early as January 1863. Stanton had been supportive of McClernand's efforts since the fall of 1862, so appealing to him might be more fertile ground for sympathy and possible reinstatement.[6]

The general ostensibly contacted the general-in-chief for orders but he also forwarded several documents to Halleck that he believed were relevant to his situation. He sent his June 4 letter to Grant along with all of the correspondence between himself and Grant concerning his removal. McClernand requested that he be reinstated to command of the 13th Corps until

Vicksburg fell. To Stanton McClernand made the same pleas he made to Lincoln; he reviewed the entire campaign and suggested that Grant removed him because of "<u>personal</u> hostility." He asked the secretary of war, as he had the president, to investigate "Genl. Grant's and my conduct as officers from the battle of Belmont to the assault of the 22nd upon Vicksburg, inclusive." Lastly, McClernand asked Stanton to reinstate him.[7]

Officials in Washington were also deluged with correspondence concerning McClernand. Governor Yates suggested to Lincoln on June 30 that the general have command of Western troops in Pennsylvania, an obvious reference to the Army of the Potomac's recent troubles.[8] Because he had not received any replies to his inquiries, in July McClernand asked secretary of the Interior John P. Usher for any information in regard to his situation.[9] Again, no reply and no satisfaction. Perhaps trying to elicit a response from the president through political news, McClernand wrote Lincoln about the draft in Illinois and a meeting in Springfield in which people were "hurrahing for Jeff. Davis and the ashes of Stonewall Jackson."[10] When that got no reply the general resigned his commission to Halleck, who did not accept it.[11]

Through August the flow of correspondence to Washington officials reached tidal wave proportions. In early August the general appealed to Lincoln that, if the rumors of a court-martial were true, he be dealt with honorably.[12] Three days later Governor Yates again pleaded with Lincoln to give McClernand some command. In a showing of support for the Prairie State general Yates had Illinois secretary of state O.M. Hatch and Illinois state auditor J.K. Dubois sign the letter, which was then hand delivered to the president by William G. Greene, a mutual friend.[13]

Finally, a week later, Lincoln responded to his exiled general in Springfield with a typical Lincoln letter, soothing and to the point. The president wrote it after inquiring of Stanton if there were any charges filed against McClernand. There were none. "I doubt whether your present position is more painful to you than to myself," Lincoln comforted the general. He informed McClernand that no charges had been filed against him, and expressed gratitude for the general's "patriotic stand" early in this "life-and-death struggle." As to the matter at hand, the president took the position that he could not intervene in the clash between the two generals because it would only magnify the rift: "Better leave it where the law of the case has placed it. For me to force you back upon Gen. Grant would be forcing him to resign." In response to McClernand's many requests for a command, the president had none to give.[14]

As consoling as Lincoln's words may have been, they did not solve McClernand's immediate problems — he still had no command and his reputation had been tarnished without cause (or so he believed). He continued to present his side of the story to anybody in a position of authority and again expressed his desire for an investigation or a court of inquiry into both his and Grant's conduct. He also complained that while he was dismissed Sherman and McPherson were promoted. Stanton informed the general that a court of inquiry would take officers out of the field and therefore it could not be done.[15]

McClernand's final effort, also in vain, was an official statement he sent to both Lincoln and Halleck. Reading much like an attorney's legal brief, he disputed, almost line by line, Grant's official report of the Vicksburg campaign. McClernand enclosed numerous statements from officers in the 13th Corps to support all of his claims concerning his conduct, activities, and successes during the Vicksburg campaign, especially the May 22 assault. Once the proper officials in Washington reviewed the statement the general proposed publishing it. Since he was denied a court of inquiry, publication was his only avenue to clear his name.[16]

The general's friends continued to work on his behalf. Illinois Senator Lyman Trumbull spoke with Lincoln about McClernand, but got no satisfaction.[17] John F. Cowan, Salmon P. Chase's secretary, corresponded with McClernand on various topics and in December 1863 Cowan informed the general that he probably would not get another command and suggested that he come to the East to give political speeches. If McClernand would come to the East, Cowan claimed that he could organize meetings in a few days.[18] Three weeks later Cowan again suggested McClernand travel to the East, this time for a different reason. Cowan informed the general that General Benjamin Butler was interested in meeting with him if McClernand could come to Philadelphia or Baltimore. Perhaps Butler could provide a command for McClernand.[19] Again, in mid–February, Cowan wrote McClernand of Butler's disappointment that he had not visited. Butler "wants to see you very much," he explained, but McClernand never made it to the East to visit Butler.[20]

The Illinois general had gotten no satisfaction from his many pleas to Washington except for the offer to meet with General Butler. He was not reinstated or given another command, his resignation was not accepted, and his requests for a court of inquiry or investigation were turned down. McClernand was a general without a command. While he waited for some action on his requests McClernand got involved in Illinois politics. He gave numerous speeches throughout the state, many in support of the war effort, an honorable act considering his standing in the conflict at the time. In these speeches he retraced the steps of the 13th Corps. He was well received in most places, and in Springfield he was given a "salute of thirty-four guns."[21] By January 1864 McClernand had waited long enough — he again tendered his resignation to both President Lincoln and secretary of war Stanton. He claimed that he was not allowed to fight or defend himself against the charges of Grant, therefore he should not hold his commission.[22]

Finally, after six months of writing to anybody who would listen, McClernand was reinstated to command of his 13th Corps, which was part of General Nathaniel Banks' Department of the Gulf in Louisiana. The Illinoisan was ordered to report to Banks in New Orleans.[23] It was probably comforting to know that Grant was in Tennessee and not associated with this assignment. General Banks' Red River campaign was one of President Lincoln's few strategic blunders in the war. Banks was initially to capture Mobile, but was diverted by the administration's desire for a campaign up the Red River. There were several objectives for this expedition: (1) By capturing Shreveport, Louisiana, the administration could expand its control over the state; (2) To seize a large amount of cotton reported to be stored along the Red River; (3) Having a presence in Texas and Louisiana might discourage the French in Mexico from invading those states; and (4) Control of Louisiana would make the reconstruction process easy and swift there.

McClernand's role in the Red River campaign was small and relatively insignificant. Before he left Springfield he invited Governor Yates to visit the troops in the Department of the Gulf. Yates, along with several other Illinois officials, had already written to Banks to describe McClernand's impressive character: "In General McClernand you will find a sagacious Statesman, discreet, tried & true; and undaunted, energetic and valuable laborer in your efforts in the Department of the Gulf."[24] McClernand reported to Banks on February 15 and assumed command of his corps on February 23 in New Orleans. His first order of business when reunited with his old corps was to issue, not surprisingly, a congratulatory order. "I will never cease to admire your heroism and applaud your virtues," the general announced. After praising the troops for their part in the May 19 and 22 assaults upon Vicksburg, McClernand made an assault of his own — on the authorities who had prevented him from taking part in the July 4 surrender of Vicksburg. "My nonparticipation in that memorable event was involuntary and constrained, and is deeply deplored on my part," he proclaimed. All that aside, he called for new heroics: "Comrades, new fields of duty and peril are before us. Let us hasten to make them historic with the valor and success of American arms."[25]

Though McClernand remained in New Orleans his troops were scattered along the Gulf coast of Texas. Detachments were stationed in Brownsville, Point Isabel, Corpus Christi Bay, and Matagorda Bay. His responsibility was control over military affairs on the Texas frontier, and to do that McClernand requested permission to recruit troops in Texas, white and black. His duties were mostly carried out in defensive operations, something that

was not his best suit. On March 6 the
general left New Orleans and on the
10th assumed personal command over
the Texas coast and frontier, with his
headquarters at Pass Cavallo, in the
Matagorda Islands.[26]

The first order of business was to
organize a staff and McClernand used
many of the same officers who had previously served in that capacity, including Walter B. Scates, Adolph Schwartz,
and Henry C. Warmoth, among others.[27] Though much of his time was
taken up in constructing defensive
works, McClernand took time out to
propose offensive military operations
to Banks. Shortly after assuming command in the field he suggested that
while the Confederates' attention was
on the Red River, the 13th Corps could
concentrate for an expedition into
Texas. McClernand believed that he
could capture Galveston, Houston,
and the mouth of the Brazos River.

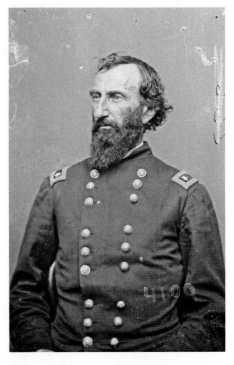

General John A. McClernand, 1862 or
1863 (Library of Congress).

This would allow, he thought, "the speedy overthrow of the rebel power
throughout Texas."[28] Later in April he proposed to concentrate his 13th Corps,
and with additional troops from the 16th, 17th, and 19th corps, he could
launch a successful campaign.[29] Even in the far reaches of the Department of
the Gulf McClernand still wanted to lead independent expeditions.

While in Texas the Illinois general also did some politicking, something
at which he was quite skilled. He corresponded with Juan N. Cortina, governor and commandant of the Mexican state of Tamaulipas. McClernand
requested that Cortina close the Mexican borders, especially along the Rio
Grande River, to Confederates. If the rebels and their property were allowed
into Mexico, that might "lead to the disturbance of the friendly relations"
between the two countries, the general asserted.[30] The general felt comfortable writing to the governor because, four days before, Cortina had reviewed
McClernand's troops and the two shared "a splendid dinner" that the Illinoisan
put on for Governor Cortina in Brownsville.[31] The general reported to Banks
that Governor Cortina was cooperative and all but declared war upon the
rebels.[32]

By the time McClernand reported to Banks on April 8, the department commander was distracted by the Confederates. On his way to Shreveport, Banks fought and lost the Battle of Sabine Crossroads, near Mansfield, Louisiana. Banks had wandered too far inland from the Red River and his troops were strung out too thin to be effective. The Federal army withdrew to Pleasant Hill, where it fought another battle on April 9, which was tactically a Union victory since the Confederates abandoned the battlefield. These conflicts forced Banks to order McClernand back to department headquarters in New Orleans, where he was to prepare to take the field with the 13th Corps.[33]

McClernand arrived in New Orleans on April 21 and made preparations to advance into the field. Sailing up the Red River the general and his troops, which consisted of six regiments of infantry and one battery of artillery, a total of 2,762 men, reached Alexandria on April 26.[34] The general never advanced beyond Alexandria. During the first part of May McClernand got ill with malaria, which forced him to stay in bed for quite some time.[35] His condition did not improve and on May 6 he was forced to turn his command over to General Michael K. Lawler. McClernand only got worse, and on May 12 he was described as "too feeble at present to attempt any business whatever."[36] A week later the general was too weak to even write a report to Banks and was too ill to continue the campaign so he took a leave of absence to Illinois to recover.[37]

Although he was recuperating at home and not actively campaigning McClernand kept up with the war effort. By July he felt well enough to devise yet another plan by which he could have an independent command. To Lincoln and Stanton the general proposed the creation of a separate department that would encompass the "Mississippi River from St. Louis to New Orleans." He believed his old 13th Corps could man this new department, or in the event it was unavailable, he could recruit fresh troops. He believed this department could be defended with 41,025 men, of which 30,690 would be infantry, 1,078 light artillery, 1,738 heavy artillery, 1,249 engineers, and 6,270 cavalry. This arrangement, McClernand argued, would free veteran troops for combat duty. The Illinois general, as he had done in the past, declared his desire to fight, and promised that he would "earnestly endeavor to meet every just expectation as commander of the proposed Department, if I should be assigned to its command."[38]

McClernand received no reply to this proposal so he tendered his resignation to Adjutant General Lorenzo Thomas. The only response was an indefinite extension of his leave of absence, which effectively ended McClernand's Civil War service. Six months later, on November 23, 1864, McClernand again offered his resignation to General Lorenzo Thomas. This time it was accepted.[39] He never again saw action on the battlefield.

The general had been very active in the Civil War, having served in many significant campaigns. From Belmont to Vicksburg McClernand performed his duty loyally and energetically. It ended too quickly for him, and he was robbed of the joy and satisfaction that goes with participating in the final surrender. This was not how McClernand envisioned his military service ending. Instead of returning home as the conquering hero (a role reserved for his rival, Ulysses S. Grant), McClernand came home in an ambulance, sick. His Civil War ended in a whimper, not a full-scale star-spangled blaze of glory that would take him to the White House. That too, was Grant's destiny, not McClernand's.

12

The Politics of Command

When appointing officers and granting commissions for generalships President Lincoln considered many exigencies, including political persuasion and influence. He had to consider how an individual could help the administration and the war effort. If a man supported the war but was associated with the political opposition he was a valuable tool and might merit a general's commission, regardless of past military experience. John A. McClernand was one of those individuals. Though he possessed almost no military experience he was valuable because of his affiliation with the opposition Democratic party. He was important because he could speak in favor of the war and recruit volunteers from among those who might otherwise oppose the conflict.[1]

McClernand was a political general who owed his commission to his prewar politics and his association with Lincoln. As he was a politician-turned-general many professional soldiers scorned him, as they did most political generals. Politicians in uniform did not have good reputations as first-rate fighters; the stereotype was of a bungling, incompetent officer, and for many this was accurate. There were, however, some citizen generals who were capable and competent leaders. Though McClernand had his faults, he was not incompetent.

McClernand's best quality as a general officer was his willingness to fight — he would fight the enemy anywhere, anyplace, anytime. The Illinoisan was bold and aggressive, necessary traits in commanders, especially early in the war when the president had few fighting generals. One of Grant's biographers wrote that McClernand was "the only general who wanted to fight when Grant did not."[2] This was a considerable testimony to McClernand's readiness to fight (even when it might not have been prudent), since Grant had a deserved reputation as a fighting general. McClernand despised the strategy of maneuver as evidenced by his frustrations during the Corinth campaign. He simply would not dodge a battle — he knew that fighting was the only way to end the war and gain recognition for himself in the process.

The general's understanding of warfare progressed as he gained experience. This was evident by the military plans of operation he proposed. His first plan, made before he ever took the field, displayed the thinking of an amateur. Believing Texas was the central point in the war effort, he completely ignored the importance of the Mississippi River. The plan was never implemented.[3] McClernand's next significant proposal was his plan to subdue Vicksburg, which he presented to President Lincoln in the fall of 1862. This proposal showed that he understood how warfare had changed and progressed. One example of his understanding was the general's suggestion that the invading Union army pursue the enemy's army instead of capturing specific locations. He also proposed that the Federal army destroy any and all industrial and manufacturing establishments along its line of march. This suggestion showed that he recognized the importance of destroying the enemy's ability to make war.[4]

The Arkansas Post campaign illustrated that in addition to devising military plans the general was capable of carrying them out. Although McClernand's detractors credit Sherman with proposing the movement on Arkansas Post, it seems clear that McClernand had decided to attack the fort before he met with Sherman. And the campaign demonstrated that the Illinoisan could competently lead an independent expedition, at least on a small scale.

McClernand the politician-turned-general was a relatively competent commander, ably leading his brigade at Belmont and his division at Fort Henry, Fort Donelson, and Shiloh. McClernand was at his best when in the thick of the fight. Brave in battle, he cooperated well with superiors and other commanders; Sherman even complimented him on his conduct at Shiloh. However, after receiving command of a corps he seemed to be blinded by glory. Wishing to be a war hero the general clamored for more authority, but when entrusted with an enlarged command his effectiveness decreased. This diminished ability was primarily a result of his constant scheming for larger commands. McClernand's attention was distracted by attempts to obtain independent commands, so his effectiveness deteriorated; his political maneuvering seemed to take precedence over fighting. The politician in McClernand took control and largely dominated the soldier in him.

While he recognized that fighting would win accolades, the general believed that politicking was the way to get a larger command. He did not understand or realize that good, hard fighting won not only larger commands, but also respect. McClernand's politicking alienated many important army and navy officers as well as high ranking administration officials. These men recognized only the politician in the man and never respected his fighting ability. His constant railing against a West Point clique won him no friends. He was never able to separate the political from the military, and that got him in trouble.

One naval officer McClernand antagonized, and who hated him intensely, was Admiral David D. Porter, commander of the Mississippi Fleet. Porter first met the general in October 1862 while McClernand was in Washington. The admiral was visiting the capital, where he received command of the Mississippi flotilla. He was to cooperate with the army in taking Vicksburg and Lincoln suggested that he meet McClernand, who was slated to command the army's expedition down the river. Porter later recalled that his first impression of McClernand was not favorable, and this bad feeling continued as Porter prepared for the campaign against Arkansas Post in January 1863. Before McClernand joined his troops Porter remembered notifying Grant that a "hybrid general" was given a separate command within Grant's department. Despite this apparent dislike for McClernand, the two officers cooperated well in reducing Arkansas Post. But Porter still hated the Illinois general and in his memoirs referred to McClernand along with Generals Banks and Butler as "the three greatest charlatans in this or any other country."[5]

The source of the admiral's hostility toward McClernand is not difficult to discern. Porter became a Grant supporter during the Vicksburg campaign, and for that reason he came to oppose McClernand. One must also remember that the admiral wrote his journal after the war ended, an account that may not be wholly reliable. Porter's diatribe against McClernand in his journal could be interpreted as a postwar bashing of a Grant rival.

McClernand's opponents in the army were almost too numerous to count. Almost to a man the antipathy toward the Illinoisan was a result of his political maneuverings and ambition, and John A. Logan was a fine example. Logan and McClernand were both Illinois Democratic politicians before the war and both worked for the nomination of Stephen A. Douglas in the 1860 presidential campaign. Both were political generals, and on at least one occasion McClernand warned Logan about the jealousies of the West Point officers toward "citizen generals."[6] The source of Logan's dislike of his fellow Illinois Democratic politician-turned-general, according to his biographer, was the "political-military rivalry" between the two men.[7] Logan's wife even warned her husband that McClernand would "never do you justice" as long as Logan was under McClernand's command.[8] The hatred Logan felt toward McClernand increased as the war progressed.

The case of William T. Sherman was remarkably similar to that of Admiral David D. Porter. Initially Sherman worked well with McClernand, especially at Shiloh where they first fought together. During the battle the two generals' divisions fought side by side on the right of the Federal line.

Sherman reported that he and McClernand fought "in perfect concert," and the Illinoisan responded "promptly and energetically" to his request for reinforcements.[9] He also wrote of the two generals consulting on the battlefield. This cooperation faded as Sherman and Grant became friends. One of Sherman's biographers suggested that McClernand's behavior drew Grant and Sherman closer, that he was "the means of uniting Grant and Sherman in stronger bonds of friendship."[10]

When McClernand superseded Sherman in January 1863 to command the Mississippi Expedition, the latter was driven firmly into the Grant camp. Sherman explained his feelings to his brother John: "Mr. Lincoln intended to insult me and the military profession by putting McClernand over me, and I would have quietly folded up my things and gone to St. Louis, only I know in times like these all must submit to insult and infamy if necessary." He continued: "I never dreamed of so severe a test of my patriotism as being superseded by McClernand."[11] Even after McClernand was removed Sherman's bad feelings for him lingered, as when he wrote to John Rawlins of McClernand being "ingeniously disposed of by being sent to command in Texas."[12] After the war Sherman expressed his opinion of McClernand to Dr. John W. Draper, who was writing a history of the Civil War: "As to McClernand, he was and is the meanest man we ever had in the west — with a mean, gnawing ambition, ready to destroy everybody who could cross his path."[13] Sherman's enmity toward McClernand continued into the postwar era.

Of those in the administration, General-in-Chief Henry W. Halleck despised McClernand the most. His first real contact with the Illinoisan came when he took field command of the Army of the Tennessee after Shiloh. During the ensuing Corinth campaign McClernand commanded the Reserve Corps. Because he led a corps this was a promotion, but McClernand still complained that his command was too small.[14] Following the capture of Corinth Halleck was appointed general-in-chief, and in that position his dislike for the Illinois general escalated. Halleck did not believe McClernand was competent, but he opposed the general even more because he constantly bypassed the chain of command and wrote directly to Lincoln. In August 1862 McClernand requested a leave of absence from Lincoln directly. The general-in-chief rebuked his subordinate for that, reminding him that "in sending this application directly to the President, instead of transmitting it through the prescribed channels, you have violated the Army regulations. This is not the first instance of this kind...."[15]

Halleck's frustrations with McClernand increased as the war progressed. As late as April 1864 he explained to Grant that McClernand was, in essence, a troublemaker.[16] The basis for Halleck's dislike of McClernand was a fundamental distrust of political generals. He was part of a West Point bias against politicians in uniform, especially those of high rank. Halleck's biographer explained that the general was "petty, vindictive, and unforgiving" toward political generals, "as his relations with Hooker, McClernand, Banks, and Butler demonstrated." This historian explained how by 1865 "Halleck, aided by his fellow West Pointers, had eliminated all amateurs from independent commands — the heroes of the war were West Point graduates. Grant, Sherman, Thomas, and Sheridan led the victorious armies; Banks, Butler, McClernand, and Frémont watched from the sidelines."[17] So while McClernand certainly contributed to antagonizing Halleck, it seems the general-in-chief had his own agenda — elimination of all political generals.

McClernand's greatest rival in the army was his immediate superior and fellow Illinoisan, General Ulysses S. Grant. The feud between these two men was legendary. Much has been made about the break between Grant and McClernand, and some historians have attempted to pinpoint a specific incident that led to this estrangement.[18] Most likely there was not a single event that caused the break, but rather an accumulation of incidents. It started with McClernand's congratulatory order after the Battle of Belmont in November 1861 and continued to build up throughout the course of the war until Grant finally had enough of McClernand's actions and removed him in June 1863.

The series of events that antagonized Grant the most was McClernand's politicking for a command in the autumn of 1862. In December 1862 Grant informed Halleck that he believed McClernand was "unmanageable and incompetent," and asked that no new officers be sent "into the department who rank those who are now with me."[19] This seems to be an obvious reference to McClernand, who would soon join the department with an independent command. Since McClernand outranked all officers except the department commander, Grant did not want him.

Grant was especially suspicious of McClernand's campaign against Arkansas Post and disapproved of it until he discovered that Sherman supported the move. He even wrote out an order relieving McClernand but did not send it. The fact that McClernand succeeded in taking the fort seemed to irritate Grant even more.

The feud between Grant and McClernand reached new heights during the Vicksburg campaign. McClernand tried to get Grant removed and Grant portrayed McClernand in the worst possible light. Grant had a new ally in the effort — War Department correspondent/spy Charles A. Dana. Acting in his official capacity Dana served as a conduit for information to the War Department. He became a staunch Grant supporter, so without having to write as much as one report Grant could get information to Washington. And the information Dana sent was that "McClernand has not the qualities necessary for a good commander, even of a regiment."[20] Grant had the same opinion of McClernand and told Halleck that his subordinate was "entirely unfit for the position of corps commander, both on the march and on the battle-field."[21] The solution, Grant decided, was to "especially supervise" McClernand's corps, activity that caused him "more labor and infinitely more uneasiness than all the remainder of my department."[22]

There are several inconsistencies with this declaration. If Grant believed McClernand unfit to command a corps, why did he wait so long before removing him? Why, also, did he allow McClernand's corps to function as the advance through most of the Vicksburg campaign? If Grant really distrusted McClernand he easily could have had McPherson's corps pass McClernand's and assume the advance in the early stages of the campaign. It would have been relatively easy to relegate the 13th Corps to rearguard activity. There are also questions about Grant's actions during the May 22 assault on Vicksburg. If Grant truly distrusted McClernand why did he spend the day on the right wing with Sherman and McPherson? If Grant believed he had to personally supervise McClernand's actions he should have been on the left during the attack. Had Grant been with McClernand he could have evaluated for himself the need to renew the attacks as McClernand requested. Even after McClernand asked for the renewed assaults Grant did not consult with his 13th Corps commander. Instead he stayed with Sherman. So while Grant, Sherman, and McPherson blamed McClernand for the high casualties on May 22, Grant certainly did nothing to personally verify the claims of his "unfit" subordinate.

Even though McClernand aided Grant in maintaining his 21st Illinois Regiment back in June 1861 Grant probably always doubted McClernand's ability to command, simply because his second-in-command was a politician. Grant always disliked politicians because they were "selfish, narrow-minded, calculating, manipulative, and always looking out for themselves."[23] Much of that description is accurate for McClernand. Grant therefore did not think highly of McClernand's ability as a general simply because he was a politician.

Why did Grant keep McClernand so long? The answer is that Grant understood the political nature of the war, such as the necessity of tolerating political generals. Grant's future would be severely hampered if he removed McClernand without good cause. For that reason Grant sent John Rawlins to meet with Lincoln after Vicksburg fell, in part to explain McClernand's removal.[24] Grant could do some politicking of his own.

Although the rivalry between Grant and McClernand turned bitter, fighting under Grant did have some benefits. The most obvious was that Grant won. Starting with Belmont his army had a series of successes — Forts Henry and Donelson, Shiloh, and a string of victories during the Vicksburg campaign. As Grant's second-in-command McClernand played a large role in those victories. And he reaped the benefits of fighting under Grant, the most tangible of which was an early promotion to major general. So while McClernand's bitterness toward Grant was great (and vice versa), so were the advantages of fighting under a winner.

Lincoln was one source of hope and support for McClernand during and before the war. Throughout the secession crisis McClernand remained loyal to the Union, and this loyalty Lincoln gladly rewarded with a general's commission. This was purely politically motivated. McClernand was a Democrat who supported the war, and more important he had a large following in southern Illinois. It was important to hold southern Illinois, which had strong Confederate sympathies during the war. Two historians suggested that Lincoln issued McClernand a commission simply to keep this area loyal to the Union.[25] John McClernand's commission was an example of what one historian called Lincoln's "ability to maneuver and to balance factions."[26] Democrats had to be kept in the fold and Lincoln knew exactly how to do it.

And the manner in which the general dealt with the president caused many of McClernand's problems. From the very beginning of the war the general did not hesitate to correspond directly with the president, even though it was against regulations. He constantly kept Lincoln updated on the army's movements and sent a steady stream of letters to Washington. The motive for this was politics. McClernand believed he had a special association with Lincoln since the two served in the state assembly together, worked many of the same legal cases as opposing or co-counsel, and McClernand owed his commission to Lincoln. Because McClernand and Lincoln were prewar acquaintances the new general apparently believed this gave him unlimited access to the president. McClernand probably considered Lincoln a friend because it was politically expedient, but the relationship probably did not mature to that threshold. The president's secretaries, John G. Nicolay and John Hay, wrote in their biography of Lincoln that McClernand was "an acquaintance and fellow-townsman of Mr. Lincoln, but they were never intimate friends; their relations were those of lifelong political opponents."[27]

McClernand may have believed that he need not respect the military chain of command because Grant was not his social equal. McClernand was a nationally known politician and Grant had known few successes when their lives collided in 1861. McClernand's bypassing the chain of command may have started out as a simple breach of protocol that continued for the duration of the war.

In McClernand's defense, Lincoln never dissuaded the general from direct correspondence with the White House. He never instructed McClernand that his letters were inappropriate and that he should go through regular channels, and the general may have interpreted the president's silence on the matter as tacit approval. This also brings up the intriguing possibility that Lincoln used McClernand to spy on Grant, since the president was aware of Grant's reputation as a drinker.

Lincoln was shrewd in his dealings with McClernand, especially with regard to the Mississippi Expedition. The president awarded command of the expedition to his hometown acquaintance, but included numerous conditions in the order. These conditions allowed either Grant or Halleck to supplant McClernand or confiscate his troops. If this happened Lincoln could claim that he could not overrule the action, thereby shifting responsibility to Grant and/or Halleck and allowing Lincoln to keep his association with McClernand intact.

McClernand did not realize that when he became a soldier he ceased to be a politician in the way he was used to. He believed he could use traditional political maneuvering to get what he wanted as a soldier. When he had a plan he believed was valuable he sent it to Lincoln and after virtually every battle he sent a report to the president. If he felt he was the victim of a West Point bias Lincoln heard about it; McClernand even counseled the president to fire General-in-Chief Halleck. When the general believed Grant was drunk Lincoln was the first informed. He even visited Washington in person to request command of the Mississippi Expedition. He simply did not respect the concept of military channels. This alienated almost every general officer in the army and was at the heart of the opposition to him. Politicking for a command had no place in the Army of the Tennessee.

Another source of the intense hatred toward McClernand was his ambition. He probably wanted to use military heroics to get to the White House, so he took credit for virtually all victories won on the battlefield. His congratulatory orders after every engagement were studies in self-adulation. He heaped recognition upon himself and his own troops to the exclusion of the rest of the army. Most of these orders did not even mention that Grant had been on the field, and it was one of these orders that caused Grant to remove him in June 1863.

By the time Grant removed McClernand he had made enemies of many influential army and navy officers. His ambition and politicking did him in. No matter how well he fought he could not surmount the mountain of hatred stacked against him. The combination of Halleck, Grant, Sherman, and Porter constituted a vitriolic anti–McClernand bloc that not even Lincoln could overcome, even if he had wanted to.

McClernand's superiors were not the only men who appraised the general's conduct. The opinions McClernand's troops held of him varied, as some supported him without hesitation while others made uncomplimentary remarks. One of the flash points of McClernand's contentious relationship with Grant was the assault on the Vicksburg trenches on May 22, 1863. Grant did not believe McClernand's claim that part of his 13th Corps carried and occupied Confederate trenches. No less than three officers of the 22nd Iowa Infantry Regiment backed McClernand's report. Colonel William M. Stone, who commanded the unit, reported that his men captured an enemy fort and held it for over an hour. Stone also wrote that the 11th Wisconsin Infantry Regiment also captured a rebel fort during the same assault.[28] The next two ranking officers of the 22nd Iowa, Lieutenant Colonel Harvey Graham and Major J.B. Atherton, made the same claim — that their troops carried portions of the Confederate works on May 22. Graham reported that his men planted two Union flags upon the fort's parapet by 11:00 A.M. and "remained there all day, in spite of all the efforts of the enemy to capture them."[29] All three claimed that with proper support they could have held onto the captured ground.

Officers and men often made disparaging remarks about generals and Captain R.B. Beck of the 30th Missouri Infantry Regiment joined in this criticism of general officers during the Arkansas Post campaign. The 30th Missouri was part of General Sherman's corps, General Frederick Steele's division, General Frank P. Blair's brigade, and was held in reserve during the assault on the Confederate fort. On January 10, 1863, Beck caustically noted in his journal that "Brigadier Generals have made themselves quite conspicuous to-day; dashing around in all directions with large and imposing Staffs and Body Guards. Some of them have Cavalry enough to form a full Co. in a Cavalry Reg." Beck concluded his tirade by claiming that many of these generals "would not make compitent [sic] Corperals."[30] Although not specifically an indictment of McClernand, Captain Beck did not have a high opinion of general officers.

General John A. McClernand, 1862 or 1863 (Library of Congress).

Some of the most damaging reflections of General McClernand came, surprisingly enough, from one of his staff members, Henry Clay Warmoth. During the Vicksburg campaign Warmoth, whose father was an old friend of McClernand, was attached to the 13th Corps commander's staff. On April 11, 1863, Warmoth recorded the appearance of Adjutant General Lorenzo Thomas. While visiting the adjutant general McClernand did not introduce his staff, which Warmoth called "selfishness that is not to be respected."[31] Eleven days later Warmoth found McClernand in a foul mood because of a misunderstanding over when a transport ship would arrive. The staff officer remembered that his commander had "acted the Damned fool about the matter and I believe I would have given him my mind in full if he had not been so far my superior officer."[32] Though a member of McClernand's staff, and one would think sympathetic to the general, Warmoth paints an unappealing portrait of General McClernand.

Other soldiers under McClernand reported similar incidents that reflect poorly on the general's demeanor and character. One man in the 20th Illinois Infantry Regiment, Allen M. Geer, recorded that McClernand "swore and stormed" when a heavy rain forced several soldiers into the his tent shortly after the Battle of Shiloh.[33] Many soldiers also remembered the speeches McClernand habitually gave to his troops and Private Geer noted several in his diary. The occasion for one speech was a visit by Illinois governor Richard Yates in May 1862.[34] One particular address, on August 22, 1862, caused Geer to reflect that McClernand "inspired them with new confidence."[35] It seems that the troops remembered and recorded a wide range of the general's activities, good and bad.

So where does McClernand belong in the framework of Civil War political generals? As a group, political generals have a bad reputation and the records of some bear out this generalization. Nathaniel P. Banks, under whom McClernand served in the ill-fated Red River campaign, was one example of a horrible commander. Benjamin F. Butler was yet another politician who received a general's commission. His service, while not as completely inept as Banks', was by no means laudatory and his conduct in New Orleans was controversial. General Grant sent Butler home in January 1865. A final example of poor military leadership by a political general was John C. Frémont, under whom McClernand served for a time. He was moved from one command to another until he resigned his commission in June 1864.

In comparing McClernand's service to that of Banks, Butler, and Frémont, the Illinoisan was almost brilliant. Though he suffered the same fate as those three — early removal from command and resignation of his commission — his leadership was more sound and his combat actions more reliable. Whereas McClernand did succeed in capturing Arkansas Post — the zenith of his military career — Banks, Butler, and Frémont all suffered humiliating defeats on the battlefield. One primary difference between these four generals is that Banks, Butler, and Frémont commanded entire departments and armies. This gave them the latitude to make poor decisions. McClernand, on the other hand, was under the watchful eye of Grant for most of his service and did not have the same opportunity to make costly errors. Another distinction is that Banks and Frémont faced "Stonewall" Jackson and Butler fought P.G.T. Beauregard and Robert E. Lee, while McClernand's opponents were not as skilled. In the end McClernand probably compares favorably to Banks, Butler, and Frémont.

An obvious and natural comparison to McClernand was General John A. Logan, who served under McClernand for a time. Logan was also an Illinois politician who joined the army when the war started. He began his Civil War service as a colonel commanding the 31st Illinois Infantry Regiment. Logan fought hard and was promoted through the ranks, ultimately reaching major general in March 1863 to rank from the preceding November. One important difference between these two Illinoisans is that throughout the war McClernand politicked for a larger command while Logan did not. That is not to say that Logan did not get involved in politics during the war, he did. He simply did not use his political connections for self promotion. Logan, like McClernand, suffered because he was a political general. In 1864 he was denied command of the Army of the Tennessee because General Sherman wanted a West Pointer in that position. This caused Logan, like McClernand, to hate West Pointers, and both came around to believe in a West Point bias in the conduct of the war. In the end, any comparison between McClernand and Logan, in terms of military effectiveness, must favor Logan.[36]

In the final analysis, John A. McClernand as a political general should be evaluated as a competent leader. As a brigade, division, and corps commander his actions on the battlefield, with few exceptions, were solid. What kept McClernand from reaching his military potential was his political nature. If he could have confined his wartime efforts to his military duties he may have accomplished everything he expected of himself.

Epilogue

The postwar era was a time of frustration for John McClernand. After he tendered his resignation and it was accepted he sat out the rest of the war in Springfield getting involved in politics and trying to clear his name. He was not entirely successful at either. That failure foreshadowed a postwar period filled with setbacks. Because Grant was the war's hero there was little chance of any rival, especially John McClernand, getting his due. The old animosities never faded away, as Grant's 1885 memoirs made clear.

McClernand stayed active and visible after the war in politics and the law. In 1866 he supported the erection of a monument in memory of Illinois soldiers who died during the war.[1] The next year was a flurry of activity and a multitude of possibilities for McClernand to serve the state or country in some capacity. McClernand's name was mentioned in connection with a vacancy on the Illinois Canal Commission.[2] Though this never materialized, McClernand was considered for several U.S. diplomatic missions in Austria, Prussia, and Mexico. President Andrew Johnson nominated McClernand for the Mexico post.[3] In the confirmation hearings, however, McClernand's old Civil War enemies worked against him, as John A. Logan and Ulysses S. Grant both opposed the appointment. Grant, not a member of the Senate, appeared on the floor to blast McClernand.[4]

Pushing these disappointments aside McClernand focused his energies on his law practice. When this did not satisfy him he ran, unopposed, for judge of the circuit court in 1870. The circuit included Sangamon County and he held this office until June 1873. McClernand's law partner described his performance as a judge:

> He was a just and able judge; he was impartial in the discharge of his
> duties, and no decision came from him in any case without his first having
> given the same full, fair and impartial consideration. No matter how power-

ful and influential the litigants, either plaintiffs or defendants, that fact made no impression upon McClernand as a judge or citizen; he was entirely impartial. No inducements held out to him of place or power could swerve him from the discharge of his legal and moral duty as a judge or man. He was entirely fearless in the discharge of his duty.[5]

After retiring from the bench McClernand remained active in politics, the law, and business. During the 1876 presidential campaign he served as president of the Democratic nominating convention in St. Louis. In business McClernand became president of a Texas venture in 1884 called the Midland Town Company and in May of that year he purchased 5 lots in Midland, Texas, for this business.[6]

When Grover Cleveland was elected president in 1884 McClernand began to correspond with the new chief executive in a series of letters that seemed awfully similar to those written twenty years before to President Abraham Lincoln. Cleveland was the first Democratic president since Andrew Johnson and because McClernand was still a Democrat he felt comfortable writing to President Cleveland. This correspondence seems innocuous enough — McClernand first offered congratulations to Cleveland for winning the 1884 election. The Illinoisan then wrote with advice on cabinet appointments and the removal of an associate justice in New Mexico, and he recommended John Gibbon for major general in the U.S. Army when a vacancy opened.[7] Was McClernand angling for some government appointment with his lengthy correspondence? He never requested an appointment outright, but he received one. In an appointment dated April 19, 1886, the Department of the Interior appointed McClernand a member of the Board of Registration and Election in the Territory of Utah.[8] This board was more commonly called the Utah Commission and was tasked with investigating the institution of polygamy among Mormons in Utah. The Illinoisan immediately thanked President Cleveland for his appointment and periodically updated

John A. McClernand later in life (Abraham Lincoln Presidential Library and Museum).

Cleveland on affairs in Utah.[9] Shortly after the appointment McClernand received a letter that must have surprised him. In a shameless display of generosity and praise John A. Logan assured McClernand that "it was with pleasure I supported your nomination, and heartily congratulate the Administration upon your selection."[10]

In the later years of his life McClernand relied on a $100 monthly pension the U.S. Congress granted him in 1896, and he was appointed president of the Shiloh Battlefield Commission. He grew increasingly feeble in the last years of his life and in 1898 suffered "an attack which nearly ended fatally." The last 24 hours of his life the old general was unconscious and was kept alive only through strychnine injections. On September 20, 1900, at 1:10 A.M. McClernand passed away at his home in Springfield.[11] He was survived by his wife, Minerva McClernand, two sons, Edward J. McClernand and John F. McClernand, and two daughters, Rose Fox and Helen Williams. Though his will does not list the value of his property, he left it all to his wife.[12]

John Alexander McClernand lived for 88 years, many of those in the service of his state and country. Most people will remember him for politicizing his Civil War service or for being the hated rival of Ulysses S. Grant. Many will overlook his role in the Compromise of 1850 and his attempt at conciliation during the winter of 1860–1861. Many will never know the great act of kindness McClernand showed in arranging the burial of Colonel Warren Stuart in January 1863. The general purchased a cemetery plot for Stuart next to his own in Oak Ridge Cemetery in Springfield and sent a blank check to pay for the plot.[13] Even though the general detected a West Point bias during the Civil War, his son Edward attended the academy. His two daughters were college-educated, illustrating McClernand's progressiveness. For over 50 years McClernand's state and country needed him, and he never failed to answer the calls.

Appendix

Organization of Troops Commanded by General John A. McClernand

BATTLE OF BELMONT

First Brigade: Brigadier General John A. McClernand

27th Illinois Infantry
30th Illinois Infantry
31st Illinois Infantry
Dollins' Company Independent Illinois Cavalry
Delano's Company Adams County Illinois Cavalry

FORTS HENRY AND DONELSON

First Division: Brigadier General John A. McClernand

First Brigade

8th Illinois Infantry
18th Illinois Infantry
29th Illinois Infantry
30th Illinois Infantry
31st Illinois Infantry
Batteries A, E, 2nd Illinois Light Artillery

Companies A, B, 2nd Illinois Cavalry
Company C, 2nd U.S. Cavalry
Company I, 4th U.S. Cavalry
Dollins' Illinois Cavalry
O'Harnett's Illinois Cavalry
Stewart's Illinois Cavalry

Second Brigade

11th Illinois Infantry
45th Illinois Infantry
48th Illinois Infantry
Batteries B, D, 1st Illinois Light Artillery
4th Illinois Cavalry

Third Brigade

17th Illinois Infantry
49th Illinois Infantry

BATTLE OF SHILOH

First Division: Major General John A. McClernand

First Brigade

8th Illinois Infantry
18th Illinois Infantry

173

11th Iowa Infantry
13th Iowa Infantry

Second Brigade

11th Illinois Infantry
20th Illinois Infantry
45th Illinois Infantry
48th Illinois Infantry

Third Brigade

17th Illinois Infantry
29th Illinois Infantry
43rd Illinois Infantry
49th Illinois Infantry

Unattached

Dresser's Battery, 2nd Illinois Light Artillery
McAllister's Battery, 1st Illinois Light Artillery
Schwartz's Battery, 2nd Illinois Light Artillery
Burrows' Battery, 14th Ohio Light Artillery
1st Battalion, 4th Illinois Cavalry
Carmichael's Company Illinois Cavalry
Stewart's Company Illinois Cavalry

CORINTH CAMPAIGN

Reserve Corps: Major General John A. McClernand

First Division

First Brigade

8th Illinois Infantry
18th Illinois Infantry
30th Illinois Infantry
31st Illinois Infantry
12th Michigan Infantry

Second Brigade

11th Illinois Infantry
20th Illinois Infantry
45th Illinois Infantry
48th Illinois Infantry

Third Brigade

17th Illinois Infantry
29th Illinois Infantry
43rd Illinois Infantry
49th Illinois Infantry
61st Illinois Infantry

Artillery

1st Illinois, Battery D
2nd Illinois, Battery E
14th Indiana Battery
14th Ohio Battery

Cavalry

4th Illinois, 1st Battalion
Carmichael's Company
Dollins' Company
O'Harnett's Company
Stewart's Company

Third Division

FIRST BRIGADE

11th Indiana Infantry
24th Indiana Infantry
8th Missouri Infantry

Second Brigade

23rd Indiana Infantry
1st Nebraska Infantry
20th Ohio Infantry
58th Ohio Infantry

Third Brigade

56th Ohio Infantry
68th Ohio Infantry
76th Ohio Infantry
78th Ohio Infantry

Artillery

1st Illinois, Batteries A, F, M
9th Indiana Battery
8th Ohio Battery

Cavalry

11th Illinois, 3rd Battalion

ARKANSAS POST CAMPAIGN

Army of the Mississippi: Major General John A. McClernand

First Corps

First Division

FIRST BRIGADE

16th Indiana Infantry
60th Indiana Infantry
67th Indiana Infantry
83rd Ohio Infantry
96th Ohio Infantry
23rd Wisconsin Infantry

SECOND BRIGADE

77th Illinois Infantry
97th Illinois Infantry
108th Illinois Infantry
131st Illinois Infantry
19th Kentucky Infantry
48th Ohio Infantry

ARTILLERY

Illinois Light Artillery, Mercantile Battery
Ohio Light Artillery, 17th Battery

CAVALRY

6th Missouri (squadron)

Second Division

FIRST BRIGADE

118th Illinois Infantry
69th Indiana Infantry
120th Ohio Infantry

SECOND BRIGADE

49th Indiana Infantry
3rd Kentucky Infantry
114th Ohio Infantry

THIRD BRIGADE

54th Indiana Infantry
22nd Kentucky Infantry
16th Ohio Infantry
42nd Ohio Infantry

ARTILLERY

Michigan Light Artillery, 7th Battery

Wisconsin Light Artillery, 1st Battery

Second Corps

First Division

FIRST BRIGADE

13th Illinois Infantry
29th Missouri Infantry
30th Missouri Infantry
31st Missouri Infantry
32nd Missouri Infantry
58th Ohio Infantry
Ohio Light Artillery, 4th Battery

SECOND BRIGADE

25th Iowa Infantry
31st Iowa Infantry
3rd Missouri Infantry
12th Missouri Infantry
17th Missouri Infantry
76th Ohio Infantry
2nd Missouri Light Artillery, Battery F

THIRD BRIGADE

4th Iowa Infantry
9th Iowa Infantry
26th Iowa Infantry
30th Iowa Infantry
34th Iowa Infantry
Iowa Light Artillery, First Battery

CAVALRY

3rd Illinois Cavalry

Second Division

FIRST BRIGADE

113th Illinois Infantry
116th Illinois Infantry
6th Missouri Infantry
8th Missouri Infantry
13th U.S., 1st Battalion

SECOND BRIGADE

55th Illinois Infantry
127th Illinois Infantry
83rd Indiana Infantry
54th Ohio Infantry
57th Ohio Infantry

ARTILLERY

1st Illinois Light Artillery, Batteries A, B, H

Ohio Light Artillery, 8th Battery

VICKSBURG CAMPAIGN

13th Corps: Major General John A. McClernand

Escort: Company L, 3rd Illinois Cavalry

Pioneers: Kentucky Infantry (independent company)

Ninth Division

FIRST BRIGADE

118th Illinois Infantry
49th Indiana Infantry
69th Indiana Infantry
7th Kentucky Infantry
120th Ohio Infantry

SECOND BRIGADE

54th Indiana Infantry
22nd Kentucky Infantry
16th Ohio Infantry
42nd Ohio Infantry
114th Ohio Infantry

CAVALRY

2nd Illinois Cavalry (5 companies)
3rd Illinois Cavalry (3 companies)
6th Missouri Cavalry (7 companies)

ARTILLERY

Michigan Light Artillery, 7th Battery
Wisconsin Light Artillery, 1st Battery

Tenth Division

Escort: Company C, 4th Indiana Cavalry

FIRST BRIGADE

16th Indiana Infantry
60th Indiana Infantry
67th Indiana Infantry
83rd Ohio Infantry
96th Ohio Infantry
23rd Wisconsin Infantry

SECOND BRIGADE

77th Illinois Infantry
97th Illinois Infantry

130th Illinois Infantry
19th Kentucky Infantry
48th Ohio Infantry

ARTILLERY

Illinois Light Artillery, Chicago Mercantile Battery
Ohio Light Artillery, 17th Battery

Twelfth Division

Escort: Company C, 1st Indiana Cavalry

FIRST BRIGADE

11th Indiana Infantry
24th Indiana Infantry
34th Indiana Infantry
46th Indiana Infantry
29th Wisconsin Infantry

SECOND BRIGADE

87th Illinois Infantry
47th Indiana Infantry
24th Iowa Infantry
28th Iowa Infantry
56th Ohio Infantry

ARTILLERY

1st Missouri Light Artillery, Battery A
Ohio Light Artillery, 2nd and 16th Battery

Fourteenth Division

Escort: Company G, 3rd Illinois Cavalry

FIRST BRIGADE

33rd Illinois Infantry
99th Illinois Infantry
8th Indiana Infantry
18th Indiana Infantry
1st U.S. (siege guns)

SECOND BRIGADE

21st Iowa Infantry
22nd Iowa Infantry
23rd Iowa Infantry
11th Wisconsin Infantry

ARTILLERY

2nd Illinois Light Artillery, Battery A
Indiana Light Artillery, 1st Battery

Chapter Notes

Introduction

1. Nathaniel C. Hughes, *The Battle of Belmont: Grant Strikes South* (Chapel Hill: University of North Carolina Press, 1991), 13; Benjamin F. Cooling, *Forts Henry and Donelson: The Key to the Confederate Heartland* (Knoxville: University of Tennessee Press, 1987), 250; Edward G. Longacre, "Congressman Becomes General: John A. McClernand," *Civil War Times Illustrated* (November 1982), 30.

2. Victor Hicken, "John A. McClernand and the House Speakership Struggle of 1859," *Journal of the Illinois State Historical Society* (Summer 1960): 164; Allan Nevins, *The Emergence of Lincoln*, vol. 2 (New York: Charles Scribner's Sons, 1950), 114.

3. Herman Hattaway and Archer Jones, *How the North Won: A Military History of the Civil War* (Urbana: University of Illinois Press, 1983), 293.

4. Steven E. Woodworth, *Nothing but Victory: The Army of the Tennessee, 1861–1865* (New York: Knopf, 2005), 87.

5. Allan Nevins, *The War for the Union*, vol. 1 (New York: Charles Scribner's Sons, 1959), 323; Edward Longacre, "Congressman Becomes General: John A. McClernand," 30.

6. Richard L. Kiper, "Prelude to Vicksburg: The Louisiana Campaign of Major General John Alexander McClernand," *Louisiana History* (Summer 1996), 307–308.

7. William L. Shea and Terrence J. Winschel, *Vicksburg Is the Key: The Struggle for the Mississippi River* (Lincoln: University of Nebraska Press, 2003), 152.

Chapter 1

1. There are many references to this dispatch, but no specific details. See undated letter, "Statement of his participation in military affairs," John A. McClernand Collection, Archives/Manuscript Department, Chicago Historical Society; Joseph Wallace, "Sketch of John A. McClernand," unpublished manuscript, Abraham Lincoln Presidential Library, 4; Schwartz, "Biography of John A. McClernand," unpublished manuscript, Abraham Lincoln Presidential Library, 13.

2. Schwartz, "Biography of John A. McClernand," 12; Wallace, "Sketch of John A. McClernand," 1; Alfred Orendorff, "General John A. McClernand," *Transactions of the Illinois State Historical Society* (Springfield: Phillips Bros., State Printers, 1901), 80.

3. Her maiden name was Fatina Cummins.

4. Wallace, "Sketch of John A. McClernand," 3–4n.

5. Although a "free" state, the 1818 state constitution allowed slaves and indentured servants who were brought in during the territorial period to remain enslaved. The introduction of slaves was prohibited except for slaves who could be used at the salt springs in Shawneetown until 1825. This may explain

slaves in the McClernand household. See Robert P. Howard, *Illinois: A History of the Prairie State* (Grand Rapids: William B. Eerdmans, 1972), 103.

6. See Judge Charles A. Keys, "McClernand as a Lawyer," in *Arbor Day Exercises at Springfield, Illinois, April 25th, 1902 in Honor of Gen. John M. Palmer and Gen. John A. McClernand* (Springfield, 1902), 42. Charles Keys was McClernand's law partner in the 1870s and 1880s.

7. This battle is frequently called a massacre because helpless women and children were among those slaughtered as they attempted to escape.

8. Black Hawk War service record of John A. McClernand, National Archives; Ellen M. Whitney, ed., *The Black Hawk War, 1831–1832*, vol. 1 (Springfield: Illinois State Historical Library, 1970), 258–259; Schwartz, "Biography of John A. McClernand," 13.

9. *Gallatin Democrat*, December 5, 1835. The only two issues in the newspaper collection at the Abraham Lincoln Presidential Library are December 5 and 19, 1835.

10. Land deeds, November 15, 1834, and November 9, 1837; John A. McClernand to Mr. David, June 20, 1836, John A. McClernand Papers, Abraham Lincoln Presidential Library.

11. Election Returns, vol. 27, p. 58, Illinois State Archives. McClernand finished first in the following precincts: Shawneetown, Monroe, Rock Cave, Bear Creek, North Fork, and Cane Creek. He finished second in the Equality and Saline precincts.

12. Wallace, "Sketch of John A. McClernand," 5.

13. Quoted in *Illinois State Journal*, September 20, 1900; quoted in Schwartz, "Biography of John A. McClernand," 16–17.

14. Quoted in Robert W. Johannsen, *Stephen A. Douglas* (Urbana: University of Illinois Press, 1973), 47.

15. *Journal of the House of Representatives*, Tenth General Assembly, First Session (Vandalia, 1836), 28, 29.

16. Ibid., 114.

17. The committee's report can be found in *Journal of the House of Representatives*, Tenth General Assembly, First Session, 202–215.

18. The vote can be found in ibid., 754–758.

19. McClernand's election can be found in ibid., 833; his commission as treasurer can be found in Executive Record, 1832–1837, vol. 2, p. 319, Illinois State Archives.

20. *Illinois State Register*, June 8, 1838.

21. Statement of political principles, 1846, John A. McClernand Papers, Abraham Lincoln Presidential Library (underline in the original).

22. For Douglas' role see Johannsen, *Stephen A. Douglas* (New York: Oxford University Press, 1973), 84–87.

23. Bond document filed with the Sangamon County sheriff, July 5, 1839, John A. McClernand Papers, Abraham Lincoln Presidential Library. This document was also signed by Stephen A. Douglas.

24. When Field resigned in 1841 Governor Carlin appointed Stephen A. Douglas, not McClernand, as his replacement; see Thomas Ford, *A History of Illinois* (Chicago: S.C. Griggs, 1854), 213–214.

25. McClernand's commission as presidential elector can be found in Executive Record, 1837–1843, vol. 3, p. 225, Illinois State Archives.

26. The *Illinois State Journal*, a Whig newspaper, claimed victory for Lincoln, while the *Illinois State Register*, a Democratic newspaper, proclaimed McClernand the victor. Both were Springfield newspapers.

27. For a vote tabulation see Election Returns, vol. 42, p. 1, Illinois State Archives.

28. *Journal of the House of Representatives*, Twelfth General Assembly (Springfield, 1840), 34.

29. See Stephen A. Douglas to John A. McClernand, January 29, 1841, in Robert W. Johannsen, ed., *The Letters of Stephen A. Douglas* (Urbana: University of Illinois Press, 1961), 95–96; see also Alexander Davidson and Bernard Stuve, *A Complete History of Illinois from 1673 to 1873* (Springfield: Illinois Journal, 1874), 455–461. The number of aliens, 10,000, seems high, and this figure comes from Davidson and Stuve, 455.

30. *Illinois State Register*, March 26, 1841.

31. (Shawneetown) *Illinois Republican*, March 13, 1841; Davidson and Stuve, *A Complete History of Illinois from 1673 to 1873*, 622–623.

32. Douglas resigned the secretary of state's office to accept the judgeship. Governor Car-

lin appointed Lyman Trumbull to succeed Douglas, again overlooking McClernand.

33. For election returns see (Shawnee-town) *Illinois Republican*, August 6, 1842; for committee assignments see *Journal of the House of Representatives*, Thirteenth General Assembly (Springfield, 1842), 60.

34. Governor Ford described a "milk and water man" as "clever, timid, moderate, and accommodating ... agree for the time being, to anything, and with anybody.... They make it a matter of calculation never to contradict, to advocate no opinion, to give no offence, to make no enemies, and to be amiable and agreeable to all." See Thomas Ford, *A History of Illinois*, 289.

35. Ibid., 306.

36. See ibid., 303–309; see also Davidson and Stuve, *A Complete History of Illinois from 1673 to 1873*, 468–470.

37. For the vote distribution see *Illinois State Register*, December 23, 1842; see also Johannsen, *Stephen A. Douglas*, 112–114, and George F. Milton, *The Eve of Conflict: Stephen A. Douglas and the Needless Conflict* (Boston: Houghton Mifflin, 1934), 26.

38. For an overall discussion of the Whig party see Michael F. Holt, *The Rise and Fall of the American Whig Party: Jacksonian Politics and the Onset of the Civil War* (New York: Oxford University Press, 1999) and *Political Parties and American Political Development from the Age of Jackson to the Age of Lincoln* (Baton Rouge: Louisiana State University Press, 1992), 192–236.

39. Quoted in Holt, *The Rise and Fall of the American Whig Party*, 214, 215.

40. See Theodore C. Pease, *The Story of Illinois* (Chicago: University of Chicago Press, 1925), 113–114, 263–265.

41. These fourteen counties were Edwards, Franklin, Gallatin, Hamilton, Hardin, Jefferson, Johnson, Marion, Massac, Pope, Wabash, Wayne, White, and Williamson.

42. *Illinois State Register*, May 12, 1843.

43. Quoted in Victor Hicken, "From Vandalia to Vicksburg: The Political and Military Career of John A. McClernand" (PhD diss., University of Illinois, 1955), 37.

44. *Illinois State Register*, July 14, 1843.

45. Theodore C. Pease, ed., *Illinois Election Returns, 1818–1848* (Springfield: Trustees of the Illinois Historical Library, 1923), 136.

46. Pease, *The Story of Illinois*, 114.

Chapter 2

1. Allan Nevins, *Ordeal of the Union: Fruits of Manifest Destiny*, vol. 1 (New York: Charles Scribner's Sons, 1947), 39; Robert Johannsen, *Stephen A. Douglas*, 124.

2. Frances Trollope, *Domestic Manners of the Americans* (New York: Knopf, 1949), 216; Charles Dickens, *American Notes* (Gloucester: Peter Smith, 1968), 139, 137; Alexis de Tocqueville, *Democracy in America*, vol. 2 (New York: Knopf, 1945), 56.

3. Dickens, *American Notes*, 140.

4. See Johannsen, *Stephen A. Douglas*, 125–126.

5. Milton, *The Eve of Conflict*, 23; Johannsen, *Stephen A. Douglas*, 73.

6. It is interesting to note that Sarah Dunlap and Mary Todd were friends. One wonders how much influence Sarah McClernand and Mary Lincoln exerted on John McClernand and Abraham Lincoln to remain friendly despite being political opponents. James Dunlap, Sarah's father, later served as McClernand's quartermaster during the Civil War.

7. *Illinois State Register*, May 3, 1844.

8. Ibid.

9. *Congressional Globe*, 28th Congress, First Session, 2, 1.

10. Ibid., 3.

11. John A. McClernand to L.J. Cist, June 13, 1865, John A. McClernand Collection, Archives/Manuscript Department, Chicago Historical Society.

12. For a brilliant discussion of the breakdown of the Second Party System and the resulting political crisis see Michael F. Holt, *The Political Crisis of the 1850s* (New York: John Wiley & Sons, 1978).

13. *Congressional Globe*, 28th Congress, First Session, 117–118, Appendix, 27–28.

14. Ibid., Appendix, 28.

15. Ibid.; vote in Ibid., 123.

16. *Illinois State Register*, January 26, 1844.

17. Ibid., March 22, 1844.

18. Quoted in *Illinois State Register*, February 2, 1844.

19. *Illinois State Gazette*, April 4, 1844.

20. McClernand's remarks in *Congressional Globe*, 28th Congress, First Session, 567–568; vote on 568.

21. Ibid., Appendix, 624.

22. See *Illinois State Register*, May 24, 1844.

23. For McClernand's June 4, 1844, speech see *Illinois State Gazette*, July 25, 1844.

24. Pease, ed., *Illinois Election Returns, 1818–1848*, 143.

25. On the election see Charles G. Sellers, *James K. Polk, Continentalist, 1843–1846* (Princeton: Princeton University Press, 1966), 108–161, and Paul F. Boller, Jr., *Presidential Campaigns*, revised edition (New York: Oxford University Press, 1996), 78–81.

26. *Illinois State Register*, June 21, 1844.

27. See *Illinois State Register*, September 6, 1844, and October 18, 1844; quotation from November 1, 1844.

28. For a succinct analysis see David M. Potter, *The Impending Crisis, 1848–1861* (New York: Harper & Row, 1976), 24–26.

29. For an analysis of the importance of party in the Texas question see Holt, *The Political Crisis of the 1850s*, 43–44.

30. (Washington, D.C.) *Daily Globe,* February 28, 29, 1845.

31. *Congressional Globe*, 28th Congress, First Session, Appendix, 621.

32. Ibid., 622.

33. Ibid., 28th Congress, Second Session, 190–194, 362–363, 372.

34. See Michael F. Holt, *The Political Crisis of the 1850s*, especially the chapter "Slavery Extension and the Second Party System, 1843–1848."

35. (Washington, D.C.) *Daily Union,* January 9, 1846; McClernand expounds on this theme in *Congressional Globe*, 29th Congress, First Session, Appendix, 274.

36. *Congressional Globe*, 29th Congress, First Session, 168; Appendix, 275.

37. Ibid., 28th Congress, Second Session, 222.

38. Ibid., 29th Congress, First Session, 720.

39. Ibid., Appendix, 670; Wentworth quoted in Potter, *The Impending Crisis, 1848–1861*, 25.

Chapter 3

1. See *Illinois State Gazette*, March 20, 1845. This speech on the Oregon issue can be found in *Congressional Globe*, 29th Congress, First Session, Appendix, 202–206.

2. The letter was dated July 11, 1845. See *Illinois State Register*, August 1, 1845, and *Illinois State Gazette*, July 31, 1845.

3. See *Illinois State Register*, July 24, 1846.

4. *Illinois State Gazette*, August 20, 1846; *Illinois State Register*, August 28, 1846.

5. The House vote on the war declaration is in *Congressional Globe*, 29th Congress, First Session, 795; on the Supplemental War Bill see ibid., 924–925, 984–985.

6. Ibid., Appendix, 671.

7. Ibid., 30th Congress, First Session, 914. For the Whig position on the war see Holt, *The Rise and Fall of the American Whig Party*, especially 248–250.

8. Ibid., 29th Congress, Second Session, 202–204; see also *Illinois State Register*, March 12, 1847.

9. *Wabash Democrat and Shawneetown Gazette*, July 21, 1847. The speech was given in Fairfield on June 26, 1847.

10. For a discussion of the northern and southern positions on the Wilmot Proviso see Potter, *The Impending Crisis, 1848–1861*, 59–62, and James M. McPherson, *Battle Cry of Freedom* (New York: Oxford University Press, 1988), 52–60.

11. See *Congressional Globe*, 29th Congress, First Session, 1217–1218 (3 votes); Ibid., 29th Congress, Second Session, 303 (1 vote), 424–425 (3 votes), 573 (2 votes); Ibid., 30th Congress, First Session, 391 (1 vote); Ibid., 31st Congress, First Session, 276 (1 vote).

12. John A. McClernand to Charles H. Lanphier, May 30, 1848, Charles H. Lanphier Papers, Abraham Lincoln Presidential Library (underline in the original).

13. Ibid.; *Congressional Globe*, 29th Congress, Second Session, 188, Appendix, 103.

14. *Congressional Globe*, 30th Congress, First Session, 1015.

15. Lewis Cass first espoused this doctrine in December 1847 in the famous "Nicholson letter," which was printed in the December 24, 1847, issue of the *Washington Union*. For an analysis of these questions see David M. Potter, *The Impending Crisis, 1848–1861*, 56–62.

16. *Illinois State Register*, October 13, 1848.

17. See *Illinois State Register*, January 20, 1849, for the tabulations.

18. For this tabulation see *Illinois State Register*, November 1, 1849.

19. *Congressional Globe*, 31st Congress, First Session, 1.

20. John A. McClernand to Charles H. Lanphier, December 9, 1849, Charles H. Lanphier Papers, Abraham Lincoln Presidential Library.

21. The speakership votes are in *Congressional Globe*, 31st Congress, First Session, 2–66, while the committee assignments are listed on 87–88.

22. Ibid., 30th Congress, Second Session, 606.

23. See ibid., 31st Congress, First Session, 244–247 for the content of the resolutions.

24. For details and analysis of the negotiations and speeches see John C. Waugh, *On the Brink of Civil War: The Compromise of 1850 and How It Changed the Course of American History* (Wilmington, DE: Scholarly Resources, 2003); Holman Hamilton, *Prologue to Conflict: The Crisis and Compromise of 1850* (Lexington: University of Kentucky Press, 1964); Potter, *The Impending Crisis, 1848–1861*, 90–120; and Johannsen, *Stephen A. Douglas*, 262–303.

25. Alexander H. Stephens, *A Constitutional View of the Late War Between the States*, vol. 2 (Philadelphia: National, 1870), 202–204.

26. Ibid.

27. The remarks and plan are in *Congressional Globe*, 31st Congress, First Session, 628–629.

28. For this claim see John A. McClernand to L.J. Cist, June 13, 1865, John A. McClernand Collection, Archives/Manuscript Department, Chicago Historical Society. In this letter McClernand wrote, "In 1850, I drew up and presented the original plan of the 'Compromise Measures' adopted by Congress in that year." Douglas made certain that it was known that McClernand's proposal was not the first, nor was it different from any other plan, as he told Charles Lanphier: "It is true Col. McClernand at one time thought that he could get up a better one, but soon gave it up. His Bill was substantially the same as Mr. Clay's, differing a little in the details." See Stephen A. Douglas to Charles H. Lanphier, August 3, 1850, Charles H. Lanphier Papers, Abraham Lincoln Presidential Library.

29. *Congressional Globe*, 31st Congress, First Session, 1700.

30. For the House votes on these bills see ibid., 1764 (Texas/New Mexico), 1772 (California), 1776 (Utah), 1807 (fugitive slave bill), and 1837 (slavery in Washington, D.C.).

31. Holt, *The Political Crisis of the 1850s*, 87–88. See also Hamilton, *Prologue to Conflict:*

The Crisis and Compromise of 1850, 191–200, and Waugh, *On the Brink of Civil War*, 179–184.

32. For this report see George F. Milton, *The Eve of Conflict: Stephen A. Douglas and the Needless War* (Boston: Houghton Mifflin, 1934), 57.

33. A.G. Sloo to John A. McClernand, May 14, 1850, John A. McClernand Papers, Abraham Lincoln Presidential Library.

34. John A. McClernand to Charles H. Lanphier, June 25, 1850, Charles H. Lanphier Papers, Abraham Lincoln Presidential Library.

35. See James Buchanan to John A. McClernand, June 29, 1850, John A. McClernand Papers, Abraham Lincoln Presidential Library.

36. *Congressional Globe*, 31st Congress, Second Session, 668, Appendix, 96–98.

37. See Deed Books, Book WW, pg. 238 (2 lots); Book YY, pgs. 145–146 (80 acres), 335–336 (40 acres); Book ZZ, pgs. 156–157 (3 lots), 624–625 (93 acres); Book 1, pgs. 150–151 (1 lot), 433–435 (1 lot); Book 3, pgs. 447–448 (8 lots); Book 6, pgs. 424–425 (40 acres), 471–472 (3 lots), University of Illinois at Springfield Archives. By the end of the 1860s McClernand had more than doubled his landholdings in Springfield and Sangamon County. He had also purchased 1 cemetery plot.

38. See tax statement for Monroe County dated January 13, 1858, Pulaski and Massac counties for 1862, in John A. McClernand Papers, Abraham Lincoln Presidential Library.

39. Executive Record, 1852–1856, volume 6, page 86, Illinois State Archives.

40. *Illinois State Register*, April 20, 24, 1852; Alexander Davidson and Bernard Stuve, *A Complete History of Illinois from 1673–1873*, 599–600.

41. *Illinois State Register*, June 21, 1852.

42. *Southern Illinoisan*, August 20, 1852.

43. *Illinois State Register*, December 3, 1852.

44. See ibid., December 21, 1852.

45. For a detailed analysis of the destruction of the Second Party System and party realignment, see Holt, *The Political Crisis of the 1850s*, 101–181. On the destruction of the Whig party see Holt, *The Rise and Fall of the American Whig Party*, 951–985.

46. Stephen A. Douglas to Charles H. Lanphier, November 11, 1853, Charles H. Lanphier Papers, Abraham Lincoln Presidential Library.

47. Stephen A. Douglas to Charles H. Lanphier, February 13, 1854, Charles H. Lanphier Papers, Abraham Lincoln Presidential Library.

48. *Illinois State Register*, October 17, 1854.

49. See *Daily Jacksonville Constitutionist*, November 6, 1854.

50. Ibid.; for the claim that McClernand followed Douglas around the state see *Illinois State Journal*, December 18, 1855.

51. For more on Douglas' speaking tour see Eric H. Walther, *The Shattering of the Union: America in the 1850s* (Wilmington, DE: Scholarly Resources, 2004), 50–51.

52. Robert W. Johannsen, ed., *The Letters of Stephen A. Douglas* (Urbana: University of Illinois Press, 1961), 371.

53. *Illinois Sentinel*, October 17, 1856.

54. *Ottawa* (Illinois) *Free Trader*, March 24, 1857.

55. Johannsen, ed., *The Letters of Stephen A. Douglas*, 375.

56. See ibid., 381; Thomas L. Harris to John A. McClernand, March 10, 1857, John A. McClernand Papers, Abraham Lincoln Presidential Library; Stephen A. Douglas to John A. McClernand, April 26, 1857, John A. McClernand Papers, Abraham Lincoln Presidential Library.

57. Johannsen, ed., *The Letters of Stephen A. Douglas*, 371.

58. See advertisements for the law firm in *Illinois State Journal*, July 3, 1856, and *Illinois Sentinel*, July 11, 1856.

59. See advertisement in *Illinois Sentinel*, July 11, 1856.

60. *Illinois State Journal*, December 16, 1857.

61. "Case File Information," *Holt v. Dale*, Lincoln Legal Papers, Springfield, Illinois.

62. John A. Lupton, "Abraham Lincoln's Law Practice in Macoupin County" (MA thesis, Sangamon State University, 1992), 40–47.

63. "Case File Information," *Van Brunt & Watrons v. Madux*, Lincoln Legal Papers, Springfield, Illinois.

64. Johannsen, ed., *The Letters of Stephen A. Douglas*, 403.

65. Ibid., 417n–418n.

66. *Illinois State Register*, February 12, 1858 (italics in the original).

67. See Potter, *The Impending Crisis, 1848–1861*, 299.

68. Stephen A. Douglas to John A. McClernand, February 21, 1858, John A. McClernand Papers, Abraham Lincoln Presidential Library.

69. *Illinois State Register*, September 29, 1859.

70. For this schedule see ibid., October 3, 1859.

71. Stephen A. Douglas to John A. McClernand, October 1, 1859, John A. McClernand Papers, Abraham Lincoln Presidential Library.

72. For this claim see John M. Palmer, *Personal Recollections of John M. Palmer* (Cincinnati: Robert Clarke, 1901), 80.

73. *Illinois State Register*, November 1, 1859.

74. Ibid., November 12, 1859.

75. See Johannsen, *Stephen A. Douglas*, 158–159.

Chapter 4

1. For the party breakdown in the House see *Congressional Globe*, 36th Congress, First Session, 1–2.

2. John A. McClernand to Capt. John Henry, January 14, 1860, John A. McClernand Papers, Abraham Lincoln Presidential Library.

3. Victor Hicken, "John A. McClernand and the House Speakership Struggle of 1859," *Journal of the Illinois State Historical Society* (Summer 1960): 168.

4. Missouri's John B. Clark offered the resolution, which can be found in *Congressional Globe*, 36th Congress, First Session, 3; for the significance of the Helper resolution see David M. Potter, *The Impending Crisis, 1848–1861*, 386–387.

5. Allan Nevins, *The Emergence of Lincoln: Prologue to Civil War, 1859–1861*, vol. 2 (New York: Charles Scribner's Sons, 1950), 121.

6. James M. McPherson, *Battle Cry of Freedom* (New York: Oxford University Press, 1988), 200.

7. John A. McClernand to Charles H. Lanphier, December 15, 1859, Charles H. Lanphier Papers, Abraham Lincoln Presidential Library.

8. *Congressional Globe*, 36th Congress, First Session, 209.

9. John A. McClernand to Charles H. Lanphier, December 22, 1859, Charles H. Lanphier Papers, Abraham Lincoln Presidential Library.

10. Hicken, "John A. McClernand and the House Speakership Struggle of 1859," 173–174.

11. John A. McClernand to Charles H. Lanphier, January 3, 1860, Charles H. Lanphier Papers, Abraham Lincoln Presidential Library.

12. See Hicken, "John A. McClernand and the House Speakership Struggle of 1859," 174.

13. *Congressional Globe*, 36th Congress, First Session, 513.

14. John A. McClernand to Capt. John Henry, January 14, 1860, John A. McClernand Papers, Abraham Lincoln Presidential Library.

15. Ibid.

16. John A. Logan to Mary Logan, December 10, 1859, John A. Logan Family Papers, Library of Congress. On Logan's remarks see James P. Jones, *"Black Jack": John A. Logan and Southern Illinois in the Civil War Era* (Tallahassee: University Presses of Florida, 1967), 42–46. For a discussion of Greeley's role in the 1858 election see Johannsen, *Stephen A. Douglas*, 632–635 and Don E. Fehrenbacher, *Prelude to Greatness: Lincoln in the 1850s* (Stanford: Stanford University Press, 1962), 49–50, 60–64.

17. *Congressional Globe*, 36th Congress, First Session, Appendix, 164–165.

18. *Illinois State Register*, January 5, 7, 1860; for analysis see Johannsen, *Stephen A. Douglas*, 735–737, and Milton, *The Eve of Conflict*, 404–405.

19. John Moore to John A. McClernand, January 17, 1860, John A. McClernand Papers, Abraham Lincoln Presidential Library.

20. William B. Hesseltine, ed., *Three Against Lincoln: Murat Halstead Reports the Caucuses of 1860* (Baton Rouge: Louisiana State University Press, 1960), 9.

21. Ibid., 7–8.

22. Ibid., 12, 13.

23. Ibid., 70.

24. Ibid., 74.

25. Johannsen, *Stephen A. Douglas*, 769.

26. *Illinois State Register*, December 11, 1860.

27. John A. McClernand to Charles H. Lanphier, December 3, 1860, Charles H. Lanphier Papers, Abraham Lincoln Presidential Library (underline in the original).

28. *Congressional Globe*, 36th Congress, Second Session, 6.

29. Ibid., 40.

30. Ibid., 6.

31. Ibid., 39; also John A. McClernand to Charles H. Lanphier, December 10, 1860, Charles H. Lanphier Papers, Abraham Lincoln Presidential Library.

32. Nevins, *The Emergence of Lincoln*, vol. 2, 405.

33. John A. McClernand to Charles H. Lanphier, December 25, 1860, Charles H. Lanphier Papers, Abraham Lincoln Presidential Library.

34. *Congressional Globe*, 36th Congress, Second Session, 367, 369.

35. He expounds on this belief in ibid., 367–370.

36. Ibid., 372, 370.

37. John A. McClernand to Mason Brayman, January 27, 1861, Mason Brayman Collection, Archives/Manuscript Department, Chicago Historical Society.

38. Ibid.

39. Ibid.

40. *Congressional Globe*, 36th Congress, Second Session, 690–691; Carl Sandburg, *Abraham Lincoln: The Prairie Years*, vol. 2 (New York: Harcourt, Brace, 1926), 407, states, "Next to Trumbull, Congressman William Kellogg of Canton, Illinois was closer to Lincoln than any other Republican...." If that was the case, perhaps McClernand was correct in his assumption.

41. John A. McClernand to Charles H. Lanphier, February 8, 1861, Charles H. Lanphier Papers, Abraham Lincoln Presidential Library.

42. Carl Sandburg, *Abraham Lincoln: The Prairie Years*, vol. 2, 408.

43. John A. McClernand to Abraham Lincoln, April 10, 1861, John A. McClernand Papers, Abraham Lincoln Presidential Library.

44. Ibid.

45. Governor Richard Yates to John A. McClernand, April 22, 1861, John A. McClernand Papers, Abraham Lincoln Presidential Library, and Richard Yates to Abraham Lincoln, May 15, 1861, ibid.

46. Roy P. Basler, ed., *The Collected Works of Abraham Lincoln*, vol. 4 (New Brunswick: Rutgers University Press, 1953), 381.

47. Ulysses S. Grant, *Personal Memoirs of U.S. Grant* (New York: Da Capo, 1982), 125; Lloyd Lewis, *Captain Sam Grant* (Boston: Little, Brown, 1950), 429; James P. Jones, *"Black Jack": John A. Logan and Southern Illinois in the Civil War Era*, 88.

48. *Congressional Globe*, 37th Congress, First Session, 131.

49. John A. McClernand to Abraham Lincoln, August 2, 1861, Abraham Lincoln Papers, Library of Congress.

50. Theodore C. Pease and James G. Randall, eds., *The Diary of Orville Hickman Browning*, vol. 1 (Springfield: Abraham Lincoln Presidential Library, 1925), 487–491; Basler, ed., *The Collected Works of Abraham Lincoln*, vol. 4, 593–594; Abraham Lincoln to John A. McClernand, August 7, 1861, John A. McClernand Papers, Abraham Lincoln Presidential Library.

Chapter 5

1. Henry Clay Whitney, *Life on the Circuit with Lincoln* (Caldwell: Claxton, 1940), 372.

2. Quoted in Carl Sandburg, *Abraham Lincoln: The War Years*, vol. 2 (New York: Harcourt, Brace, 1939), 52.

3. Abraham Lincoln to John A. McClernand, August 7, 1861, John A. McClernand Papers, Abraham Lincoln Presidential Library.

4. Basler, *The Collected Works of Lincoln*, vol. 4, 480, 492, 517, 527; John A. McClernand to Richard Yates, September 7, 1861, John A. McClernand Papers, Abraham Lincoln Presidential Library, and John A. McClernand to Abraham Lincoln, September 10, 1861. It is important to note that in the Black Hawk War McClernand served in Captain Harrison Wilson's company. Harrison Wilson was James Wilson's father. See chapter 1.

5. John Wood to Capt. James Dunlap, August 20, 1861, John A. McClernand Papers, Abraham Lincoln Presidential Library, and John A. McClernand to M.C. Meigs, August 23, 1861.

6. John A. McClernand to Richard Yates, September 22, 1861, Richard Yates Papers, Abraham Lincoln Presidential Library.

7. Philip Fouke to John A. McClernand, August 12, 1861, John A. McClernand Papers, Abraham Lincoln Presidential Library.

8. General Order No. 3 (by Grant), September 4, 1861, John A. McClernand Papers, Abraham Lincoln Presidential Library; John A. McClernand to Ulysses S. Grant, September 4, 1861, National Archives, RG 94, Generals Papers and Books, John A. McClernand, and General Order No. 1 (by McClernand), September 5, 1861.

9. *War of the Rebellion: A Compilation of the Official Records of the Union and Confederate Armies*, series 1, vol. 3 (Washington, D.C.: Government Printing Office, 1880–1901), 558 (hereinafter cited as *Official Records*; unless otherwise noted all references are to series 1).

10. Whitney, *Life on the Circuit with Lincoln*, 383, 384.

11. *Official Records*, vol. 4, 196–197.

12. Ibid., 197.

13. Harry B. Smith to General John C. Fremont, September 3, 1861, John A. McClernand Papers, Abraham Lincoln Presidential Library.

14. John Y. Simon, ed., *The Papers of Ulysses S. Grant*, vol. 2 (Carbondale: Southern Illinois University Press, 1969), 210–212.

15. Ibid., 327–328.

16. John A. McClernand to John C. Fremont, September 2, 1861, John A. McClernand Papers, Abraham Lincoln Presidential Library.

17. Simon, ed., *The Papers of Ulysses S. Grant*, vol. 2, 276–277.

18. *Official Records*, vol. 3, 507.

19. John A. McClernand to Mason Brayman, October 14, 1861, Mason Brayman Papers, Chicago Historical Society.

20. *Official Records*, vol. 3, 267.

21. The existence of this message has been called into question. The document itself has never been found, Grant's staff apparently did not make a verbatim copy, and it does not appear in Fremont's letter-books. See William B. Feis, "Grant and the Belmont Campaign: A Study in Intelligence and Command," in *The Art of Command in the Civil War*, ed. Steven E. Woodworth (Lincoln: University of Nebraska Press, 1998), 36.

22. *Official Records*, vol. 3, 267 (Oglesby), 268 (Plummer), 269 (Smith and Wallace).

23. Ibid., 277.

24. Nathaniel C. Hughes (*The Battle of Belmont: Grant Strikes South* [Chapel Hill: University of North Carolina Press, 1991], 49) characterizes the *Belle Memphis* as large and luxurious.

25. Robert U. Johnson and Clarence C. Buel, eds., *Battles and Leaders of the Civil War*, vol. 1 (Secaucus: Castle, 1887), 348.

26. This message, like the November 5 telegram from Fremont, has been called into question. The document has not been found and, like the November 5 telegram, it first appears in Grant's official report that he wrote in May 1864. See William B. Feis, "Grant and the Belmont Campaign," 37–38.

27. Grant, *Personal Memoirs*, 139.

28. Grant's justifications for fighting seem to have changed after the battle. His report and a letter he wrote to his father on November 8 emphasized his preventing Confederate troops from reinforcing Confederate General Sterling Price. This was not mentioned as a reason for his movements prior to the November 7 battle. See William B. Feis, *Grant's Secret Service: The Intelligence War from Belmont to Appomattox* (Lincoln: University of Nebraska Press, 2002), 46–47.

29. Unnumbered Special Order, November 7, 1861, John A. McClernand Papers, Abraham Lincoln Presidential Library.

30. *Official Records*, vol. 3, 278, 275–276.

31. Johnson and Buel, eds., *Battles and Leaders of the Civil War*, vol. 1, 348–350; Nathaniel C. Hughes and Roy P. Stonesifer, Jr., *The Life and Wars of Gideon J. Pillow* (Chapel Hill: University of North Carolina Press, 1993), 197.

32. "Report of Capt. Schwartz," Mason Brayman Papers, Chicago Historical Society. Captain Adolph Schwartz was an aide to General McClernand at Belmont.

33. Ibid.

34. *Official Records*, vol. 3, 278.

35. Ibid.

36. Ibid., 279.

37. "Report of Capt. Schwartz," Mason Brayman Papers, Chicago Historical Society; *Official Records*, vol. 3, 279–280, 288.

38. *Official Records*, vol. 3, 280; Victor Hicken (*Illinois in the Civil War* [Urbana: University of Illinois Press, 1966], 22) states that McClernand "theatrically mounted a captured cannon" to give the three cheers. No other source corroborates this claim, but it would hardly come as a surprise if a politician of McClernand's stature seized such an opportunity. Captain Schwartz, who wrote extensively in his report about captured rebel artillery pieces, did not mention this acrobatic act.

39. *Official Records*, vol. 3, 281; Nathaniel C. Hughes, *The Battle of Belmont: Grant Strikes South* (Chapel Hill: University of North Carolina Press, 1991), 154. Many officers had body servants, including Grant. Hughes reports there were some forty servants involved at Belmont.

40. McClernand's claim to be the last man on board is in his official report, *Official Records*, vol. 3, 281. Grant also claims to have been the last man to board the transports. Grant's claims can be found in Grant, *Personal Memoirs*, 142; William S. McFeely, *Grant: A Biography* (New York: W.W. Norton, 1981), 93; and Brooks D. Simpson, *Ulysses S. Grant: Triumph Over Adversity, 1822–1865* (New York: Houghton Mifflin, 2000), 101. Since both men sailed on different transports it seems safe to presume each man was the last on board his transport.

41. *Official Records*, vol. 3, 281, 285; "Report of Capt. Schwartz," Mason Brayman Papers, Chicago Historical Society.

42. *Official Records*, vol. 3, 274; General Order No. 15, November 8, 1861, John A. McClernand Papers, Abraham Lincoln Presidential Library.

43. John A. McClernand to Leonidas Polk, November 14, 16, 1861; John A. McClernand to Mrs. Bielaski, November 19, 1861; Leonidas Polk to John A. McClernand, November 29, 1861, Mason Brayman Papers, Chicago Historical Society.

44. John A. Logan, *The Volunteer Soldier of America, with Memoir of the Author and Military Reminiscences from General Logan's Private Journal* (Chicago: R.S. Peale, 1887), 625.

45. Johnson and Buel, eds., *Battles and Leaders of the Civil War*, vol. 1, 355.

46. *Official Records*, vol. 3, 271.

47. Simon, ed., *The Papers of Ulysses S. Grant*, vol. 3, 138.

48. John A. McClernand to George B. McClellan, November 8, 1861, John A. McClernand Papers, Abraham Lincoln Presidential Library.

49. Abraham Lincoln to John A. McClernand, November 10, 1861; John A. McClernand to Abraham Lincoln, November 22, 1861, Abraham Lincoln Papers, Library of Congress.

50. John A. McClernand to Abraham Lincoln, November 20, 1861, John A. McCler-

nand Papers, Abraham Lincoln Presidential Library.

51. John A. McClernand to Abraham Lincoln, November 22, 1861, Abraham Lincoln Papers, Library of Congress.

52. Ibid., John A. McClernand to Abraham Lincoln, December 3, 1861 (underline in the original).

53. Simon, ed., *The Papers of Ulysses S. Grant*, vol. 3, 214–217.

54. See John A. Logan to John A. McClernand, December 27, 1861, John A. McClernand Papers, Abraham Lincoln Presidential Library.

55. Report dated December 1, 1861, Mason Brayman Papers, Chicago Historical Society; *Official Records*, vol. 8, 416, 433, 457.

Chapter 6

1. See Thomas L. Connelly, *Army of the Heartland: The Army of Tennessee, 1861–1862* (Baton Rouge: Louisiana State University Press, 1967), 50.

2. Thomas L. Connelly and Archer Jones, *The Politics of Command: Factions and Ideas in Confederate Strategy* (Baton Rouge: Louisiana State University Press, 1973), 96; Archer Jones, *Confederate Strategy from Shiloh to Vicksburg* (Baton Rouge: Louisiana State University Press, 1961), 52.

3. John A. McClernand to Abraham Lincoln, January 3, 1862, Abraham Lincoln Papers, Library of Congress.

4. John A. McClernand to John A. Logan, January 3, 1861, John A. Logan Family Papers, Library of Congress.

5. John A. McClernand to John A. Logan, January 8, 1861, John A. Logan Family Papers, Library of Congress.

6. Ibid. (underline in the original).

7. John A. Logan to John A. McClernand, January 14, 1862, John A. McClernand Papers, Abraham Lincoln Presidential Library.

8. John A. McClernand to John A. Logan, January 8, 1862, John A. Logan Family Papers, Library of Congress.

9. *Official Records*, vol. 7, 68.

10. Grant, *Personal Memoirs*, 146; *Official Records*, vol. 7, 69–70.

11. John A. McClernand to W.D. Porter, January 14, 1862, John A. McClernand Papers, Abraham Lincoln Presidential Library.

12. *Official Records*, vol. 7, 69.

13. Ibid.

14. Ibid., 71.

15. John A. McClernand to Abraham Lincoln, January 28, 1862, Abraham Lincoln Papers, Library of Congress.

16. Ibid.

17. Grant, *Personal Memoirs*, 147.

18. *Official Records*, vol. 7, 120–122.

19. Connelly, *Army of the Heartland: The Army of Tennessee, 1861–1862*, 78–85.

20. Johnson and Buel, eds., *Battles and Leaders of the Civil War*, vol. 1, 369.

21. *Official Records*, vol. 7, 126.

22. Ibid., 126–127, 128.

23. Feis, *Grant's Secret Service*, 67. Two of the Jessie Scouts, Carpenter and L.F. Scott remained with the army until March 25, when Grant arrested them and shipped them to St. Louis. See also 89–90.

24. *Official Records*, vol. 7, 127–128.

25. Richard J. Oglesby to Major Mason Brayman, February 5, 1862, John A. McClernand Papers, Abraham Lincoln Presidential Library.

26. John A. McClernand to Ulysses S. Grant, February 5, 1862, John A. McClernand Papers, Abraham Lincoln Presidential Library.

27. *Official Records*, vol. 7, 125; Field Order No. 20, February 5, 1862, John A. McClernand Papers, Abraham Lincoln Presidential Library.

28. John A. Logan, *The Volunteer Soldier of America*, 631.

29. John A. McClernand to Ulysses S. Grant, February 6, 1862, John A. McClernand Papers, Abraham Lincoln Presidential Library; *Official Records*, vol. 7, 129.

30. *Official Records*, vol. 7, 129–130.

31. Ibid., 123 (Foote's report), 130 (McClernand's report).

32. John A. McClernand to Andrew H. Foote, February 7, 1862, John A. McClernand Papers, Abraham Lincoln Presidential Library.

33. John A. McClernand to Ulysses S. Grant, February 7, 1862, John A. McClernand Papers, Abraham Lincoln Presidential Library.

34. John A. McClernand to Abraham Lincoln, February 8, 1862, Abraham Lincoln Papers, Library of Congress.

35. John A. McClernand to Ulysses S. Grant, February 9, 1862, John A. McClernand Papers, Abraham Lincoln Presidential Library.

36. Johnson and Buel, eds., *Battles and Leaders of the Civil War*, vol. 1, 404–405; McFeely, *Grant*, 98–99.

37. General Field Orders No. 12, February 11, 1862, John A. McClernand Papers, Abraham Lincoln Presidential Library.

38. *Official Records*, vol. 7, 161 (McPherson's report).

39. Field Order No. 125, February 11, 1862, John A. McClernand Papers, Abraham Lincoln Presidential Library.

40. *Official Records*, vol. 7, 170–171.

41. Ibid., 172.

42. Grant, *Personal Memoirs*, 153.

43. *Official Records*, vol. 7, 172–173, 193–194, 212–213.

44. Ibid., 173.

45. Ibid.

46. Ibid., 185.

47. Report of Andrew H. Foote, February 16, 1862, Andrew H. Foote Papers, Library of Congress.

48. M.F. Force to "My dear James," February 16, 1862, Peter Force Papers, Library of Congress.

49. McFeely, *Grant*, 99.

50. *Official Records*, vol. 7, 175, 237.

51. Ibid., 177–178, 195–196.

52. Ibid., 178–179, 187, 195–196, 237–238; also Johnson and Buel, eds., *Battles and Leaders of the Civil War*, vol. 1, 419–421. Grant did not record the time he arrived on the battlefield in his official report or his memoirs, and neither did William S. McFeely in *Grant* or Bruce Catton in *Grant Moves South*.

53. Quoted in Brooks Simpson, *Ulysses S. Grant: Triumph Over Adversity, 1822–1865* (New York: Houghton Mifflin, 2000), 115.

54. Johnson and Buel, eds., *Battles and Leaders of the Civil War*, vol. 1, 422–425; Grant, *Personal Memoirs*, 156–157.

55. *Official Records*, vol. 7, 182.

56. Field Order No. 145, February 17, 1862, John A. McClernand Papers, Abraham Lincoln Presidential Library.

57. John A. McClernand to Ulysses S. Grant, February 19, 1862, John A. McClernand Papers, Abraham Lincoln Presidential Library.

58. John A. McClernand to Abraham Lincoln, February 18, 1862, Abraham Lincoln Papers, Library of Congress.

59. Robert R. McCormick, *Ulysses S.*

Grant: The Great Soldier of America (New York: D. Appleton-Century, 1934), 34; see also Grant, *Personal Memoirs*, 148.

60. Benjamin F. Cooling, *Forts Henry and Donelson: The Key to the Confederate Heartland* (Knoxville: University of Tennessee Press, 1987), 116–117.

Chapter 7

1. Grant, *Personal Memoirs*, 163.

2. General Orders No. 7, February 21, 1862, John A. McClernand Papers, Abraham Lincoln Presidential Library (it is labeled General Orders No. 6 in *The Papers of Ulysses S. Grant*, ed. John Y. Simon, vol. 4, 253–254); *Official Records*, vol. 10, part 1, 112.

3. Isabel Wallace, *The Life and Letters of General W.H.L. Wallace* (Chicago: R.R. Donnelley & Sons, 1909), 166.

4. Simon, ed., *The Papers of Ulysses S. Grant*, vol. 4, 225.

5. I. Wallace, *The Life and Letters of General W.H.L. Wallace*, 171.

6. John A. McClernand to Abraham Lincoln, February 27, 1862, Abraham Lincoln Papers, Library of Congress.

7. John A. McClernand to Ulysses S. Grant, March 6, 1862, John A. McClernand Papers, Abraham Lincoln Presidential Library.

8. John A. McClernand to C.F. Smith, March 26, 1862, John A. McClernand Papers, Abraham Lincoln Presidential Library.

9. On Smith's commission see Ezra J. Warner, *General in Blue: Lives of the Union Commanders* (Baton Rouge: Louisiana State University Press, 1964), 455; on McClernand's commission see chapter 4 above.

10. Wiley Sword, *Shiloh: Bloody April* (New York: William Morrow, 1974), 118; Larry J. Daniel, *Shiloh: The Battle That Changed the Civil War* (New York: Simon & Schuster, 1997), 139.

11. Simon, ed., *The Papers of Ulysses S. Grant*, vol. 4, 275; Basler, ed., *The Collected Works of Abraham Lincoln*, vol. 5, 142.

12. Copy of McClernand's major general's commission in John A. McClernand Papers, Abraham Lincoln Presidential Library; original in Abraham Lincoln Papers, Abraham Lincoln Presidential Library.

13. Simon, ed., *The Papers of Ulysses S. Grant*, vol. 4, 338.

14. John A. McClernand to Ulysses S. Grant, March 14, 1862, John A. McClernand Papers, Abraham Lincoln Presidential Library.

15. Simon, ed., *The Papers of Ulysses S. Grant*, vol. 4, 369.

16. Ibid., 399. Grant was reinstated on March 13 and resumed command on March 17.

17. John A. McClernand to C.F. Smith, March 26, 1862, John A. McClernand Papers, Abraham Lincoln Presidential Library; John Y. Simon, ed., *The Papers of Ulysses S. Grant*, vol. 4, 429.

18. *Official Records*, vol. 10, part 2, 67.

19. John A. McClernand to Ulysses S. Grant, March 27, 1862, National Archives, RG 94, Generals Papers and Books, John A. McClernand.

20. Simon, ed., *The Papers of Ulysses S. Grant*, vol. 4, 430–431; *Official Records*, vol. 10, part 2, 94.

21. John A. McClernand to Abraham Lincoln, March 31, 1862, Abraham Lincoln Papers, Library of Congress.

22. For analysis and details of General Buell's movements see Stephen D. Engle, *Don Carlos Buell: Most Promising of All* (Chapel Hill: University of North Carolina Press, 1999).

23. Larry J. Daniel, *Shiloh*, 322, puts Grant's strength at 48,894, including Lew Wallace and Buell's at 17,918.

24. John A. McClernand to William T. Sherman, March 31, 1862, John A. McClernand Papers, Abraham Lincoln Presidential Library; Daniel, *Shiloh*, 176.

25. *Official Records*, vol. 10, part 1, 249 (Sherman's report). William S. McFeely, *Grant: A Biography* (New York: W.W. Norton, 1981), 112, Sword, *Shiloh: Bloody April*, 217, and Daniel, *Shiloh*, 175, all put Grant's arrival at Pittsburg Landing at about 9:00 A.M., while James L. McDonough (*Shiloh: In Hell Before Night* [Knoxville: University of Tennessee Press, 1977], 122) puts Grant at Pittsburg Landing at mid-morning.

26. Larry J. Daniel, *Shiloh*, 185.

27. For McClernand's claim of deceptive Confederates see *Official Records*, vol. 10, part 1, 115; McDonough, *Shiloh: In Hell Before Night*, 122.

28. *Official Records*, vol. 10, part 1, 250 (Sherman's report).

29. Daniel, *Shiloh*, 188.

30. *Official Records*, vol. 10, part 1, 117–118, 250.

31. Ibid., 118, 250.

32. Grant, *Personal Memoirs*, 178. Considering the fighting of Prentiss' division, this remark may have just been a postwar compliment to his friend Sherman.

33. *Official Records*, vol. 10, part 1, 119.

34. Ibid., 120.

35. Larry J. Daniel, *Shiloh*, 298.

36. *Official Records*, vol. 10, part 1, 123, for casualties. McClernand wrongly calculated the casualty rate at 371/2 percent; see p. 121.

37. "Report of Ordnance stores captured by the 1st Division," John A. McClernand Papers, Abraham Lincoln Presidential Library.

38. *Official Records*, vol. 10, part 1, 113–114.

39. John A. McClernand to Ulysses S. Grant, April 11, 1862, John A. McClernand Papers, Abraham Lincoln Presidential Library.

40. John A. McClernand to Ulysses S. Grant, April 20, 1862, John A. McClernand Papers, Abraham Lincoln Presidential Library.

41. Special Field Orders No. 35, April 30, 1862, *Official Records*, vol. 10, part 2, 144; see also part 1, 754.

42. Stephen E. Ambrose, *Halleck: Lincoln's Chief of Staff* (Baton Rouge: Louisiana State University Press, 1962), 46, 48.

43. *Official Records*, vol. 10, part 2, 157–159.

44. L. Wallace, *An Autobiography*, vol. 2 (New York: Harper & Brothers, 1906), 576.

45. *Official Records*, vol. 10, part 2, 192–193.

46. Grant, *Personal Memoirs*, 195; L. Wallace, *An Autobiography*, vol. 2, 577.

47. *Official Records*, vol. 10, part 2, 214. The number of Confederate troops at Corinth was taken from James M. McPherson, *Ordeal by Fire: The Civil War and Reconstruction* (New York: Knopf, 1982), 231.

48. *Official Records*, vol. 10, part 1, 756.

49. John A. Logan, *The Volunteer Soldier of America*, 665–666.

50. *Official Records*, vol. 10, part 1, 757; Grant, *Personal Memoirs*, 197.

51. John A. McClernand to Henry W. Halleck, June 1, 1862, National Archives, RG 94, Generals Papers and Books, John A. McClernand (underline in the original).

52. *Official Records*, vol. 10, part 1, 256–257.

53. Ibid., 247, 248.

54. Ibid., 265, 267.

55. Ibid., vol. 17, part 2, 11.

56. John A. McClernand to Abraham Lincoln, June 20, 1862, Abraham Lincoln Papers, Library of Congress.

57. *Official Records*, vol. 17, part 2, 31.

58. Ibid., 56, 60–61.

59. Simon, ed., *The Papers of Ulysses S. Grant*, vol. 5, 154.

60. Ibid., 154–155.

61. Ibid., 331.

62. Pease and Randall, *The Diary of Orville Hickman Browning*, vol. 1, 560.

63. *Official Records*, vol. 17, part 2, 128–136; see also James P. Jones, *"Black Jack": John A. Logan and Southern Illinois in the Civil War Era*, 141–142.

64. John A. McClernand to Richard Yates, August 12, 1862, Richard Yates Papers, Abraham Lincoln Presidential Library.

65. See Richard Yates to Edwin M. Stanton, August 19, 1862, Yates Letterpress Book, Abraham Lincoln Presidential Library; Richard Yates to John A. McClernand, August 19, 1862, John A. McClernand Papers, Abraham Lincoln Presidential Library.

66. Ulysses S. Grant to John A. McClernand, August 25, 1862, John A. McClernand Papers, Abraham Lincoln Presidential Library.

Chapter 8

1. *Official Records*, vol. 17, part 2, 187; John A. McClernand to Henry W. Halleck, September 1, 1862, John A. McClernand Papers, Abraham Lincoln Presidential Library.

2. John A. McClernand to Henry W. Halleck, September 1, 1862, John A. McClernand Papers, Abraham Lincoln Presidential Library.

3. Richard Yates to John A. McClernand, September 5, 1862, John A. McClernand Papers, Abraham Lincoln Presidential Library. See also John A. McClernand to Richard Yates, September 11, 1862, Richard Yates Papers, Abraham Lincoln Presidential Library.

4. *Jacksonville Journal*, September 4, 1862.

5. *Chicago Tribune*, September 8, 1862 (caps and italics in the original).

6. Richard Yates to John A. McClernand, September 22, 1862, John A. McClernand Papers, Abraham Lincoln Presidential Library.

7. John F. Cowan to John A. McClernand, September 25, 1862, John A. McClernand Papers, Abraham Lincoln Presidential Library.

8. David Donald, ed., *Inside Lincoln's Cabinet: The Civil War Diaries of Salmon P. Chase* (New York: Longman's, Green, 1954), 160–161; John Niven, ed., *The Salmon P. Chase Papers*, vol. 1 (Kent: Kent State University Press, 1993), 402–404.

9. Donald, ed., *Inside Lincoln's Cabinet: The Civil War Diaries of Salmon P. Chase*, 161; Niven, ed., *The Salmon P. Chase Papers*, vol. 1, 404.

10. John A. McClernand to L.J. Cist, June 13, 1865, John A. McClernand Collection, Archives/Manuscript Department, Chicago Historical Society.

11. John A. McClernand to Abraham Lincoln, September 28, 1862, Abraham Lincoln Papers, Library of Congress. McClernand began his plan by stating, "My apology for addressing you this communication is in the fact that you were pleased to invite it." This would seem to indicate that Lincoln requested that the plan be reduced to writing and submitted for consideration.

12. Ibid.

13. Ibid. For a discussion of Civil War strategy, Clausewitz, and Jomini see Herman Hattaway and Archer Jones, *How the North Won*, especially Appendix A.

14. John A. McClernand to Abraham Lincoln, September 28, 1862, Abraham Lincoln Papers, Library of Congress.

15. Niven, ed., *The Salmon P. Chase Papers*, vol. 1, 417.

16. Gideon Welles, *Diary of Gideon Welles*, vol. 1 (New York: Houghton Mifflin, 1911), 167; David Dixon Porter Journal, David D. Porter Papers, Library of Congress. See also David D. Porter to John A. McClernand, October 9, 1862, John A. McClernand Papers, Abraham Lincoln Presidential Library. It seems logical that if Porter did not approve of McClernand he would not have written to him later the same day. The admiral also became a strong supporter of Grant, so his criticisms of McClernand in his postwar journal must be considered in that context. Postwar journals

are often unreliable and Porter's appears to be simply a postwar bashing of a Grant opponent.

17. Edwin M. Stanton to Henry W. Halleck, October 11, 1862, John A. McClernand Papers, Abraham Lincoln Presidential Library.

18. *Official Records*, vol. 17, part 2, 274–275.

19. John A. McClernand to Edwin M. Stanton, October 15, 1862, John A. McClernand to Henry W. Halleck, October 16, 1862, John A. McClernand Papers, Abraham Lincoln Presidential Library. McClernand started the letter to Stanton with these words: "In compliance with your order, I have the honor to submit." This suggests that Stanton requested the organizational plan from the general. It also seems to indicate that by that day approval for the expedition had been given.

20. James H. Wilson Diary, Delaware State Historical Society; James H. Wilson, *Under the Old Flag*, vol. 1 (New York: D. Appleton, 1912), 119–123.

21. Quoted in Stephen W. Sears, *George B. McClellan: The Young Napoleon* (New York: Ticknor & Fields, 1988), 335–336. Warren W. Hassler, Jr., in his biography *General George B. McClellan: Shield of the Union* (Baton Rouge: Louisiana State University Press, 1957) does not mention the possibility of McClellan moving to the west.

22. Edwin M. Stanton to John A. McClernand, October 21, 1862, John A. McClernand Papers, Abraham Lincoln Presidential Library.

23. Confidential Order, October 21, 1862, John A. McClernand Papers, Abraham Lincoln Presidential Library.

24. Ibid. Lincoln's endorsement is dated October 20, 1862.

25. Ibid.

26. *Chicago Tribune*, September 29, 1862; *Jacksonville Journal*, November 6, 1862; *New York Times*, January 16, 1863.

27. Kenneth M. Stampp, *Indiana Politics During the Civil War* (Bloomington: Indiana University Press, 1949), 160–161.

28. John A. McClernand to Samuel D. Kirkwood, October 27, 1862, John A. McClernand Papers, Abraham Lincoln Presidential Library.

29. *Official Records*, vol. 17, part 2, 300.

30. Edwin M. Stanton to John A. McClernand, October 29, 1862, John A. McCler-

nand Papers, Abraham Lincoln Presidential Library.

31. See, for example, John A. McClernand to Robert Halsey, October 28, 1862, John A. McClernand Papers, Abraham Lincoln Presidential Library. McClernand asked Halsey, in New York, to meet with and reassure Secretary Chase.

32. *Official Records*, vol. 17, part 2, 309.

33. Basler, ed., *The Collected Works of Abraham Lincoln*, vol. 5, 484 (italics in the original).

34. Walter B. Scates to John A. McClernand, November 8, 1862, John A. McClernand to Edwin M. Stanton, November 10, 1862, John A. McClernand Papers, Abraham Lincoln Presidential Library.

35. John A. McClernand to Edwin M. Stanton, December 24, 1862, John A. McClernand Papers, Abraham Lincoln Presidential Library.

36. John A. McClernand to Edwin M. Stanton, November 10, 1862, John A. McClernand Papers, Abraham Lincoln Presidential Library.

37. *Official Records*, vol. 17, part 2, 345.

38. Ibid., part 1, 467.

39. Ibid., 469.

40. Ulysses S. Grant to William T. Sherman, November 14, 1862, National Archives, RG 393, Department of the Tennessee, Letters Sent, October 1862–October 1863.

41. John A. McClernand to Richard Yates, November 20, 1862, John A. McClernand Papers, Abraham Lincoln Presidential Library.

42. *Official Records*, vol. 17, part 2, 366.

43. Lyman Trumbull to John A. McClernand, December 1, 1862, and Orville H. Browning to John A. McClernand, December 2, 1862, John A. McClernand Papers, Abraham Lincoln Presidential Library.

44. John A. McClernand to Edwin M. Stanton, December 1, 5, 1862, John A. McClernand Papers, Abraham Lincoln Presidential Library.

45. John A. McClernand to Abraham Lincoln, December 12, 1862, and John A. McClernand to Edwin M. Stanton, December 12, 1862, John A. McClernand Papers, Abraham Lincoln Presidential Library.

46. *Official Records*, vol. 17, part 1, 474.

47. Grant, *Personal Memoirs*, 224.

48. Simpson, *Ulysses S. Grant*, 166.

49. Edwin M. Stanton to John A. McClernand, December 15, 1862, John A. McClernand Papers, Abraham Lincoln Presidential Library.

50. John A. McClernand to Henry W. Halleck, December 16, 1862, John A. McClernand Papers, Abraham Lincoln Presidential Library.

51. John A. McClernand to Orville H. Browning, December 16, 1862, John A. McClernand Papers, Abraham Lincoln Presidential Library.

52. John A. McClernand to Jonathan Baldwin Turner, December 17, 1862, Jonathan Baldwin Turner Papers, Abraham Lincoln Presidential Library.

53. *Official Records*, vol. 17, part 2, 420.

54. Ibid., 462.

55. McClernand commanded a corps during the Red River campaign, but because his participation was short it is not included here. For an analysis of the Vicksburg campaign, see chapters 9 and 10.

56. See John A. McClernand to Abraham Lincoln, April 10, 1861, John A. McClernand Papers, Abraham Lincoln Presidential Library; see also chapter 4 for a discussion of the plan.

57. See John A. McClernand to Abraham Lincoln, February 2, 1863, Abraham Lincoln Papers, Library of Congress; see also chapter 10 for a discussion of this proposal.

58. See John A. McClernand to Abraham Lincoln, November 22, 1861, Abraham Lincoln Papers, Library of Congress.

59. See John A. McClernand to John A. Logan, January 8, 1862, John A. Logan Family Papers, Library of Congress.

60. See John A. McClernand to Abraham Lincoln, June 20, 1862, Abraham Lincoln Papers, Library of Congress.

61. See John A. McClernand to Abraham Lincoln, September 28, 1862, Abraham Lincoln Papers, Library of Congress.

Chapter 9

1. John A. McClernand to Ulysses S. Grant, December 28, 1862, John A. McClernand Papers, Abraham Lincoln Presidential Library.

2. See Simpson, *Ulysses S. Grant*, 167.

3. John A. McClernand to Edwin M. Stanton, January 3, 1863, John A. McClernand Papers, Abraham Lincoln Presidential Library.

4. John A. McClernand to Abraham Lincoln, December 29, 1862, Abraham Lincoln Papers, Library of Congress.

5. *Official Records*, vol. 17, part 1, 701, vol. 22, part 1, 887. Confederates called it Arkansas Post while Federals called it Fort Hindman.

6. William T. Sherman, *Memoirs of W. T. Sherman* (repr., New York: Library of America, 1990; first printing, New York: C.L. Webster, 1875), 316–317.

7. John A. McClernand to Edwin M. Stanton, January 3, 1863, John A. McClernand Papers, Abraham Lincoln Presidential Library.

8. *Official Records*, vol. 17, part 2, 534–535.

9. Ibid., 536.

10. Edwin C. Bearss, *The Vicksburg Campaign: Vicksburg Is the Key*, vol. 1 (Dayton, OH: Morningside House, 1985), 361, Richard L. Kiper, *Major General John Alexander McClernand: Politician in Uniform* (Kent, OH: Kent State University Press, 1999), 158–159. John F. Marszalek (*Sherman: A Soldier's Passion for Order* [New York: Free Press, 1993], 208) credits Sherman and Porter with the idea to attack Arkansas Post. Most historians, with the exception of Bearss and Kiper, give Sherman the credit for the idea to attack Arkansas Post. The fort was such an obvious target that both men probably saw the need to reduce it.

11. Sherman, *Memoirs of W. T. Sherman*, 319 (italics in the original).

12. John F. Marszalek, "Sherman Called It the Way He Saw It," *Civil War History* 40, no. 1 (March 1994), 76. See also John F. Marszalek, *Sherman*, 460–478; Albert Castel, *Winning and Losing in the Civil War: Essays and Stories* (Columbia: University of South Carolina Press, 1996), 89–116. The chapter in Castel's book is "Prevaricating Through Georgia: Sherman's Memoirs as a Source on the Atlanta campaign." In this essay Castel points out numerous examples of "deliberate falsehoods" in Sherman's memoirs during the Atlanta campaign. So the logical question for historians is this: if Sherman included falsehoods in his memoirs of the Atlanta campaign, where else are there inaccuracies?

13. David Dixon Porter Journal, David

Dixon Porter Papers, Library of Congress; Sherman, *Memoirs of W. T. Sherman*, 319–320. Did McClernand agree to give up his command in order to get the navy's cooperation? That is a good question, and it is highly unlikely that McClernand would make such an agreement. The best proof is that there are no letters to President Lincoln complaining that he was forced out as commander of the expedition. Certainly if he had been forced to accept Sherman as commander McClernand would have written to Lincoln immediately.

14. *Official Records*, vol. 17, part 2, 537–538, 541.

15. Ibid., vol. 17, part 1, 705, 721; Roger Coleman, *The Arkansas Post Story* (Santa Fe: Southwest Cultural Resources Center, 1987), 103–104.

16. John A. McClernand to Abraham Lincoln, January 7, 1863, Abraham Lincoln Papers, Library of Congress.

17. John A. McClernand to Jonathan Baldwin Turner, December 26, 1862, January 7, 1863, Jonathan Baldwin Turner Papers, Abraham Lincoln Presidential Library.

18. *Official Records*, vol. 17, part 2, 546–547.

19. General Orders No. 30 (issued by Porter), January 7, 1863, John A. McClernand Papers, Abraham Lincoln Presidential Library; Johnson and Buel, eds., *Battles and Leaders of the Civil War*, vol. 3, 560.

20. *Official Records*, vol. 17, part 1, 702.

21. Ibid., 703, 754–755.

22. Ibid., 703–704, 722.

23. Ibid., 706.

24. Ibid., 706–708, 723–724, 756–757.

25. Ibid., 708.

26. John A. McClernand to David D. Porter, January 11, 1863, and David D. Porter to John A. McClernand, January 11, 1863, John A. McClernand Papers, Abraham Lincoln Presidential Library.

27. *Official Records*, vol. 17, part 1, 708.

28. John A. McClernand to Richard Yates, March 16, 1863, Richard Yates Papers, Abraham Lincoln Presidential Library.

29. *Official Records*, vol. 17, part 1, 719.

30. John A. McClernand to Ulysses S. Grant, January 11, 1863, John A. McClernand Papers, Abraham Lincoln Presidential Library.

31. *Official Records*, vol. 17, part 1, 710.

32. Sherman, *Memoirs of W. T. Sherman*, 324.

33. *Official Records*, vol. 22, part 2, 41.

34. Ibid., 66.

35. Ibid., vol. 17, part 2, 553. This communication was written at 3:30 P.M., right in the middle of the battle.

36. Ibid., 553–554. The *Official Records* has this order dated January 11, the day of the battle. However, two other sources date this communication January 12. The other two sources are the Ulysses S. Grant Papers, Library of Congress and National Archives, RG 393, and Department of the Tennessee, Letters Sent, October 1862–October 1863.

37. *Official Records*, vol. 17, part 2, 555.

38. Ulysses S. Grant to John A. McClernand, January 12, 1863, Ulysses S. Grant Papers, Library of Congress. The order read as follows: "In accordance with authority from Headquarters of the Army of Washington D.C. you are hereby relieved from the command of the expedition against Vicksburgh and will turn over the same to your next in rank." Written over the order was the message "Not Sent," and signed by John A. Rawlins, Grant's assistant adjutant general.

39. Ulysses S. Grant to John A. McClernand, January 13, 1863, John A. McClernand Papers, Abraham Lincoln Presidential Library.

40. John A. McClernand to Ulysses S. Grant, January 16, 1863, John A. McClernand Papers, Abraham Lincoln Presidential Library.

41. John A. McClernand to Abraham Lincoln, January 16, 1863, Abraham Lincoln Papers, Library of Congress.

42. *Official Records*, vol. 17, part 2, 570–571. It should be noted that Grant accepted the Arkansas Post campaign only after Sherman defended it.

43. Ibid., vol. 24, part 1, 8–9.

44. Abraham Lincoln to John A. McClernand, January 22, 1863, Abraham Lincoln Papers, Library of Congress.

45. *Official Records*, vol. 24, part 1, 7.

46. John A. McClernand to Ulysses S. Grant, January 30, 1863, John A. McClernand Papers, Abraham Lincoln Presidential Library.

47. General Orders No. 13, January 30, 1863, *Official Records*, vol. 24, part 1, 11.

48. Ibid., 13.

Chapter 10

1. *Official Records*, vol. 24, part 1, 11–14.

2. John A. McClernand to Ulysses S.

Grant, February 1, 1863, Abraham Lincoln Papers, Library of Congress.

3. See John A. McClernand to Abraham Lincoln, February 2, 1863, Abraham Lincoln Papers, Library of Congress.

4. For McClernand's revamped staff see Walter B. Scates to John A. Rawlins, February 12, 1863, National Archives, RG 393, Thirteenth Army Corps, Letters Sent, December 1862–June 1864; on McClernand's plan to invade Arkansas see *Official Records*, vol. 24, part 3, 56–57; on Grant's rejection of the plan see Ulysses S. Grant to John A. McClernand, February 18, 1863, Ulysses S. Grant Papers, Library of Congress.

5. *Official Records*, vol. 24, part 3, 73.

6. John A. McClernand to Abraham Lincoln, February 14, 1863, Abraham Lincoln Papers, Library of Congress.

7. John A. McClernand to Richard Yates, February 16, 1863, Abraham Lincoln Papers, Library of Congress.

8. John A. McClernand to Richard Yates, March 15, 1863, Logan U. Reavis Collection, Archives/Manuscript Department, Chicago Historical Society (underline in the original).

9. John A. McClernand to Abraham Lincoln, March 15, 1863, Abraham Lincoln Papers, Library of Congress. Kountz was a longtime Grant enemy, dating back to late 1861 after the Belmont Campaign. See Simpson, *Ulysses S. Grant*, 107–108, 110, 176.

10. Simon, ed., *The Papers of Ulysses S. Grant*, vol. 8, 322n.

11. See Simon, ed., *The Papers of Ulysses S. Grant*, vol. 8, 324n for Dana's discussion of the timing of the drinking sprees. Grant's biographer, William S. McFeely, does not mention the timing of the binges in his treatment of the general's drinking.

12. Warren Grabau, *Ninety-Eight Days: A Geographer's View of the Vicksburg Campaign* (Knoxville: University of Tennessee Press, 2000), 61; Edwin C. Bearss, *The Vicksburg Campaign: Grant Strikes a Fatal Blow*, vol. 2 (Dayton, OH: Morningside House, 1986), 54.

13. *Official Records*, vol. 24, part 1, 46, 138.

14. For a detailed description of the movements of McClernand's 13th Corps see Richard L. Kiper, "Prelude to Vicksburg: The Louisiana Campaign of General John Alexander McClernand," *Louisiana History* (Summer 1996), 283–308.

15. See Simpson, *Ulysses S. Grant*, 183,

and Bearss, *The Vicksburg Campaign*, vol. 2, 29–30. Warren Grabau (*Ninety-Eight Days*, 61) states that McClernand's corps led the advance "largely by accident."

16. *Official Records*, vol. 24, part 1, 139–140; Paul H. Hass, ed., "The Vicksburg Diary of Henry Clay Warmoth," *The Journal of Mississippi History* (November 1969): 335–336. Henry Warmoth was on McClernand's staff.

17. *Official Records*, vol. 24, part 1, 77, 140–141, 489–490.

18. Grant, *Personal Memoirs*, 245.

19. *Official Records*, vol. 24, part 1, 141. McClernand most likely did not suggest this plan until Grant had already decided to implement it. See Simpson, *Ulysses S. Grant*, 183.

20. *Official Records*, vol. 24, part 1, 75.

21. Grabau, *Ninety-Eight Days*, 82; Bearss, *The Vicksburg Campaign*, vol. 2, 270–271.

22. *Official Records*, vol. 24, part 1, 141; Hass, ed., "The Vicksburg Diary of Henry Clay Warmoth," 346–347.

23. *Official Records*, vol. 24, part 1, 141–142; Grabau, *Ninety-Eight Days*, 85–90.

24. Grant, *Personal Memoirs*, 248.

25. Hass, ed., "The Vicksburg Diary of Henry Clay Warmoth," *Journal of Mississippi History* (February 1970): 62.

26. Grabau, *Ninety-Eight Days*, 146–147.

27. Grant, *Personal Memoirs*, 252.

28. *Official Records*, vol. 24, part 1, 143.

29. Ibid., 143–144.

30. Grabau, *Ninety-Eight Days*, 157.

31. Bearss, *The Vicksburg Campaign*, vol. 2, 385.

32. *Official* Records, vol. 24, part 1, 144–145, 602–603.

33. Ibid., 584.

34. Ibid., 145–146.

35. See Grabau, *Ninety-Eight Days*, 155–160.

36. John A. McClernand to Abraham Lincoln, May 6, 1863, Abraham Lincoln Papers, Library of Congress. In the letter McClernand noted the assistance of part of McPherson's corps. He also exaggerated the amount of stores captured, claiming to have seized 1,200 prisoners, 1,000 small arms, and 4 artillery pieces.

37. Ibid.

38. Wilson, *Under the Old Flag*, vol. 1, 174, 176 (italics in the original).

39. Bearss, *The Vicksburg Campaign*, vol. 2, 428–429.

40. *Official Records*, vol. 24, part 1, 146.

41. Ibid., 147, 50.

42. Ibid., 147, 50–51.

43. Ibid., 148.

44. Ibid., vol. 24, part 2, 13–14, 42–43.

45. Ibid., vol. 24, part 1, 148.

46. Ibid., vol. 24, part 2, 14–15 (Osterhaus' report).

47. Ibid., 42 (Hovey's report).

48. Ibid., 44.

49. Ibid., 7–9. For Logan's part see James P. Jones, *"Black Jack": John A. Logan and Southern Illinois in the Civil War Era*, 164–166.

50. Simpson, *Ulysses S. Grant*, 199–200; Grabau, *Ninety-Eight Days*, 300–301; Edwin C. Bearss, *The Vicksburg Campaign*, vol. 2, 640.

51. Grant, *Personal Memoirs*, 271–272; Grabau, *Ninety-Eight Days*, 306–308. See also Jones, *"Black Jack,"* 167, Kenneth P. Williams, *Lincoln Finds a General*, vol. 4 (New York: Macmillan, 1956), 379, and James M. McPherson, *Battle Cry of Freedom* (New York: Oxford University Press, 1988), 630.

52. Hess, ed., "The Vicksburg Diary of Henry Clay Warmoth," 70–71.

53. *Official Records*, vol. 24, part 1, 152 (McClernand's report), 616–617 (Carr's report).

54. Ibid., 152, 617.

55. John A. McClernand to Abraham Lincoln, May 29, 1863, Abraham Lincoln Papers, Library of Congress.

56. *Official Records*, vol. 24, part 1, 154 (McClernand's report), part 2, 18 (Osterhaus' report).

57. Grant, *Personal Memoirs*, 276.

58. *Official Records*, vol. 24, part 1, 154; John A. McClernand to Richard Yates, May 28, 1863, John A. McClernand Papers, Abraham Lincoln Presidential Library.

59. *Official Records*, vol. 24, part 1, 154–155 (McClernand's report), 617 (Carr's report), vol. 24, part 2, 20–21 (Osterhaus' report); John A. McClernand to Richard Yates, May 28, 1863, John A. McClernand Papers, Abraham Lincoln Presidential Library.

60. Sherman, *Memoirs of W.T. Sherman*, 352. Here Sherman stated that his corps had stopped fighting by the time McClernand made his request. In Grant's official report he wrote that he received McCler-nand's request at noon; see *Official Records*, vol. 24, part 1, 55.

61. See Simpson, *Ulysses S. Grant*, 203–204, and Marszalek, *Sherman*, 226.

62. *Official Records*, vol. 24, part 1, 155–156.

63. See John A. McClernand to Abraham Lincoln, February 14, 1863, Abraham Lincoln Papers, Library of Congress.

64. *Official Records*, vol. 24, part 1, 156.

65. John A. McClernand to Ulysses S. Grant, June 4, 1863, John A. McClernand Papers, Abraham Lincoln Presidential Library; see also John A. McClernand to Richard Yates, May 28, 1863, John A. McClernand Papers, Abraham Lincoln Presidential Library, and John A. McClernand to Abraham Lincoln, May 29, 1863, Abraham Lincoln Papers, Library of Congress.

66. *Official Records*, vol. 24, part 1, 159–161.

67. Ibid., 162–164.

68. Special Orders No. 164, June 18, 1863, John A. McClernand Papers, Abraham Lincoln Presidential Library.

69. John A. McClernand to Abraham Lincoln, June 23, 1863, Abraham Lincoln Papers, Library of Congress. McClernand's adjutant general had neglected to send a copy of the congratulatory order to Grant's headquarters, as required by regulations.

70. Quoted in Marszalek, *Sherman*, 227–228.

71. Quoted in Edward G. Longacre, *From Union Stars to Top Hat: A Biography of the Extraordinary General James Harrison Wilson* (Harrisburg: Stackpole, 1972), 82.

72. Ibid., 83 (italics in the original).

Chapter 11

1. *Official Records*, vol. 24, part 1, 166.

2. Ibid., 43.

3. John A. McClernand to Abraham Lincoln, June 23, 1863, Abraham Lincoln Papers, Library of Congress. See chapter 10 above for the June 4 letter to Grant.

4. Ibid.

5. Ibid.

6. John A. McClernand to Henry W. Halleck, June 27, 1863, John A. McClernand to Edwin M. Stanton, June 27, 1863, John A. McClernand Papers, Abraham Lincoln Presidential Library.

7. Ibid. (underline in the original).

8. *Official Records,* vol. 24, part 1, 167–168; *Chicago Tribune,* July 1, 1863.

9. John A. McClernand to John P. Usher, July 16, 1863, Abraham Lincoln Papers, Library of Congress.

10. John A. McClernand to Abraham Lincoln, July 18, 1863, Abraham Lincoln Papers, Library of Congress.

11. John A. McClernand to Henry W. Halleck, July 20, 1863, John A. McClernand Papers, Abraham Lincoln Presidential Library.

12. John A. McClernand to Abraham Lincoln, August 3, 1863, Abraham Lincoln Papers, Library of Congress.

13. Richard Yates to Abraham Lincoln, August 6, 1863, National Archives, RG 94, Generals Papers and Books, John A. McClernand.

14. Abraham Lincoln to John A. McClernand, August 12, 1863, Abraham Lincoln Papers, Library of Congress; Basler, ed., *The Collected Works of Abraham Lincoln,* vol. 6, 380.

15. John A. McClernand to Abraham Lincoln, August 24, 1863, Abraham Lincoln Papers, Library of Congress; *Official Records,* vol. 24, part 1, 168 (August 24 note to Stanton); John A. McClernand to Edwin M. Stanton, September 5, 1863, Edwin M. Stanton to John A. McClernand, September 14, 1863, John A. McClernand Papers, Abraham Lincoln Presidential Library.

16. John A. McClernand to Henry W. Halleck, September 25, 1863, John A. McClernand to Abraham Lincoln, September 28, 1863, Abraham Lincoln Papers, Library of Congress; for the statements of support from 13th Corps officers see *Official Records,* vol. 24, part 1, 169–186.

17. Lyman Trumbull to John A. McClernand, December 21, 1863, John A. McClernand Papers, Abraham Lincoln Presidential Library.

18. John F. Cowan to John A. McClernand, December 29, 1863, John A. McClernand Papers, Abraham Lincoln Presidential Library.

19. John F. Cowan to John A. McClernand, January 20, 1864, John A. McClernand Papers, Abraham Lincoln Presidential Library.

20. John F. Cowan to John A. McClernand, February 13, 1864, John A. McClernand Papers, Abraham Lincoln Presidential Library.

21. *Chicago Tribune,* June 30, 1863; *Jacksonville Journal,* July 2, 1863.

22. John A. McClernand to Abraham Lincoln and Edwin M. Stanton, January 14, 1864, Abraham Lincoln Papers, Library of Congress.

23. Special Orders No. 35, January 23, 1864, National Archives, RG 94, Generals Papers and Books, John A. McClernand.

24. John A. McClernand to Richard Yates, February 2, 1864, Richard Yates Papers, Abraham Lincoln Presidential Library; Richard Yates to Nathaniel P. Banks, January 28, 1864, John A. McClernand Papers, Abraham Lincoln Presidential Library.

25. *Official Records,* vol. 34, part 2, 134, 400–401.

26. Ibid., 425, 474, 482, 545, 563–564.

27. Ibid., 574–575.

28. Ibid., 701.

29. John A. McClernand to Nathaniel P. Banks, April 30, 1864, John A. McClernand Papers, Abraham Lincoln Presidential Library.

30. John A. McClernand to Juan N. Cortina, April 7, 1864, Nathaniel P. Banks Papers, Library of Congress.

31. Unsigned, unaddressed account of events, April 7, 1864, John A. McClernand Papers, Abraham Lincoln Presidential Library; *Chicago Tribune,* May 4, 1864.

32. John A. McClernand to Nathaniel P. Banks, April 8, 1864, Nathaniel P. Banks Papers, Library of Congress.

33. *Official Records,* vol. 34, part 3, 128.

34. Ibid., 244–245, 296.

35. John A. McClernand to Nathaniel P. Banks, May 5, 1864, National Archives, RG 94, Generals Papers and Books, John A. McClernand.

36. *Official Records,* vol. 34, part 3, 475, 557.

37. Henry C. Warmoth to Nathaniel P. Banks, May 18, 1864, Nathaniel P. Banks Papers, Library of Congress; Henry Payne to Lyman Trumbull, June 19, 1864, Lyman Trumbull Family Papers, Abraham Lincoln Presidential Library, for an extension of McClernand's leave of absence; *Alton* (Illinois) *Telegraph,* June 24, 1864.

38. John A. McClernand to Edwin M. Stanton, July 15, 1864, Abraham Lincoln Papers, Library of Congress.

39. Basler, ed., *The Collected Works of*

Abraham Lincoln, vol. 7, 473; John A. Mc-
Clernand to Lorenzo Thomas, July 28, November 23, 1864, John A. McClernand Papers, Abraham Lincoln Presidential Library.

Chapter 12

1. For Lincoln's thought processes in
choosing generals see T. Harry Williams, *Lincoln and His Generals* (New York: Knopf,
1952), 10–14, Herman Hattaway and Archer
Jones, *How the North Won: A Military History
of the Civil War,* 29–32, and David H. Donald, *Lincoln* (New York: Simon & Schuster,
1995), 313–314.
2. Robert McCormick, *Ulysses S. Grant:
The Great Soldier of America,* 95.
3. John A. McClernand to Abraham Lincoln, April 10, 1861, John A. McClernand Papers, Abraham Lincoln Presidential Library;
see also chapter 4.
4. John A. McClernand to Abraham Lincoln, September 28, 1862, Abraham Lincoln
Papers, Library of Congress; see also chapter 8.
5. David Dixon Porter Journal, David D.
Porter Papers, Library of Congress.
6. John A. McClernand to John A.
Logan, January 8, 1862, John A. Logan Family Papers, Library of Congress.
7. Jones, *"Black Jack,"* 133.
8. Mary Logan to John A. Logan, January 5, 1862, John A. Logan Family Papers,
Library of Congress.
9. *Official Records,* vol. 10, part 1, 250;
William T. Sherman, *Memoirs of W.T. Sherman,* 257.
10. Lloyd Lewis, *Sherman, Fighting Prophet*
(New York: Harcourt, Brace, 1932), 284.
11. William T. Sherman to John Sherman,
January 17, 1863, in *The Sherman Letters,* ed.
Rachel S. Thorndike (1894; repr., New York:
Da Capo, 1969), 181–182.
12. *Official Records,* vol. 32, part 3, 40.
13. William T. Sherman to John W.
Draper, November 24, 1867, John William
Draper Family Papers, Library of Congress.
14. John A. McClernand to Henry W.
Halleck, June 1, 1862, National Archives, RG
94, Generals Papers and Books, John A. Mc-
Clernand.
15. Henry W. Halleck to John A. McClernand, August 20, 1862, John A. McClernand
Papers, Abraham Lincoln Presidential Library.

16. *Official Records,* vol. 35, part 2, 48.
17. Ambrose, *Halleck: Lincoln's Chief of
Staff,* 207, 209.
18. See chapter 6 for a discussion of this.
19. *Official Records,* vol. 52, part 1, 314.
20. *Official Records,* vol. 24, part 1, 87.
21. Ibid., 37.
22. Ibid., 87, 37.
23. Brooks D. Simpson, *Let Us Have
Peace: Ulysses S. Grant and the Politics of War
and Reconstruction, 1861–1868* (Chapel Hill:
University of North Carolina Press, 1991),
xvii.
24. Welles, *The Diary of Gideon Welles,*
vol. 1, 387.
25. See Herman Hattaway and Archer
Jones, *How the North Won: A Military History
of the Civil War* (Urbana: University of Illinois Press, 1983), 30.
26. Philip S. Paludan, *The Presidency of
Abraham Lincoln* (Lawrence: University Press
of Kansas, 1994), 25.
27. John G. Nicolay and John Hay, *Abraham Lincoln: A History,* vol. 7 (New York:
Century, 1890), 136.
28. *Official Records,* vol. 24, part 1, 178.
This report was written in September 1863
in response to McClernand's request for accounts to support his claim.
29. Ibid., 179.
30. Journal of Captain R.B. Beck, Mrs.
Douglas W. Clark Collection, Library of
Congress.
31. Paul H. Hass, ed., "The Vicksburg
Diary of Henry Clay Warmoth," *Journal of
Mississippi History* (November 1969): 340.
32. Ibid., 346.
33. Mary Ann Anderson, ed., *The Civil
War Diary of Allen Morgan Geer* (New York:
Cosmos, 1977), 25. This happened on April
8, 1862.
34. Ibid., 31 (May 16, 1862).
35. Ibid., 50.
36. The information on Logan came from
Jones, *"Black Jack."*

Epilogue

1. See Richard J. Oglesby to John A. Mc-
Clernand, May 15, 1866, John A. McClernand
Papers, Abraham Lincoln Presidential Library.
2. See Richard J. Oglesby to John A. Mc-
Clernand, March 18, 1867, C.E. Lippincott

to Richard J. Oglesby, March 21, 1867, John A. McClernand Papers, Abraham Lincoln Presidential Library.

3. Rives to John A. McClernand, April 4, 1867, William H. Seward to Orville H. Browning, May 31, 1867, S.S. Marshall to John A. McClernand, July 15, 1867, John A. McClernand Papers, Abraham Lincoln Presidential Library.

4. Lyman Trumball to John A. McClernand, July 21, 1867, S.S. Marshall to John A. McClernand, July 21, 1867, John A. McClernand Papers, Abraham Lincoln Presidential Library. For Logan's role see James P. Jones, *John A. Logan: Stalwart Republican from Illinois* (Tallahassee: University Presses of Florida, 1982), 9.

5. *Arbor Day Exercises at Springfield, Illinois, April 25th, 1902, in Honor of Gen. John M. Palmer and Gen. John A. McClernand* (Springfield, 1902), 45. This address was entitled "McClernand as Lawyer," and was given by Charles A. Keys.

6. See statement of land purchase on Midland Town Company letterhead in John A. McClernand Papers, Abraham Lincoln Presidential Library. Nothing more was found on the Midland Town Company.

7. John A. McClernand to Grover Cleveland, January 17, 1885, February 24, 1885, March 7, 1885, January 14, 1886, March 1, 1886, Grover Cleveland Papers, Library of Congress.

8. U.S. Department of the Interior to John A. McClernand, April 19, 1886, John A. McClernand Papers, Abraham Lincoln Presidential Library.

9. John A. McClernand to Grover Cleveland, April 10, 1886, March 28, 1887, June 30, 1887, July 9, 1887, July 12, 1887, October 8, 1887, March 10, 1888, Grover Cleveland Papers, Library of Congress.

10. John A. Logan to John A. McClernand, May 3, 1886, John A. McClernand Papers, Abraham Lincoln Presidential Library.

11. *Illinois State Register*, September 20, 1900; *Chicago Tribune*, September 20, 1900.

12. Will of John A. McClernand, Will Book XI, 415–416, University of Illinois at Springfield Archives.

13. John A. McClernand to Richard Yates, January 26, 1863, Richard Yates Papers, Abraham Lincoln Presidential Library.

Bibliography

Primary Sources

Manuscripts

Abraham Lincoln Presidential Library, Springfield, Illinois:
Nathaniel P. Banks Papers
Ulysses S. Grant Papers
Benjamin Grierson Papers
Isham N. Haynie Papers
Charles Lanphier Papers
Lincoln Legal Papers
John A. McClernand Papers
James B. McPherson Letters
Richard J. Oglesby Papers
Schwartz, Adolph. "Biography of John A. McClernand." Manuscript.
Lyman Trumbull Family Papers
Jonathan Baldwin Turner Papers
Wallace, Joseph. "Sketch of John A. McClernand." Manuscript.
Richard Yates Papers
Chicago Historical Society, Chicago, Illinois:
Mason Brayman Collection
William Butler Collection
John A. McClernand Collection
Logan U. Reavis Collection
Walter B. Scates Collection
Delaware Historical Society, Wilmington, Delaware:
James Harrison Wilson Diary
Illinois State Archives, Springfield, Illinois:
Election Returns
Executive Record, 1832–1856

Library of Congress, Manuscript Division, Washington, D.C.:
Nathaniel Prentice Banks Papers
Alpheus S. Bloomfield Papers
Benjamin Helm Bristow Papers
Journal of Captain R.B. Beck, Mrs. Douglas W. Clark Collection
Grover Cleveland Papers
Cyrus Ballou Comstock Papers
John William Draper Family Papers
John Newton Ferguson Diary
Andrew H. Foote Papers
Manning Ferguson Force Papers
Peter Force Papers
Ulysses S. Grant Papers
Henry Wager Halleck Papers
Charles Smith Hamilton Papers
Hiram P. Howe Papers
John Griffith Jones Correspondence
Abraham Lincoln Papers
John Alexander Logan Family Papers
John A. McClernand Papers
William Franklin Patterson Papers
Ninian Pinckney Papers
David Dixon Porter Papers
Edward Paul Reichhelm Collection
William Tecumseh Sherman Papers
Bela T. St. John Papers
Lyman Trumbull Papers
James Harrison Wilson Papers
National Archives, Washington, D.C.:
Records of the Adjutant General's Office, Generals Papers and Books, Record Group 94

Records of the Department of the Tennessee, Record Group 393
Records of the Thirteenth Army Corps, Record Group 393
New York Historical Society, New York, New York:
John A. McClernand Papers
University of Illinois Archives, Springfield, Illinois:
Deed Records
Wills
University of Notre Dame Library, South Bend, Indiana:
William Tecumseh Sherman Family Papers

Government Documents

Atlas to Accompany the *Official Records*
Congressional Globe, 28th, 29th, 30th, 31st, 36th Congresses
Federal Census Records, 1820–1860
Journal of the Illinois House of Representatives, 1836–1843
War of the Rebellion: A Compilation of the Official Records of the Union and Confederate Armies. 128 volumes. Washington, D.C.: Government Printing Office, 1880–1901.
War of the Rebellion: A Compilation of the Official Records of the Union and Confederate Navies. 30 volumes. Washington, D.C.: Government Printing Office, 1894–1922.

Newspapers

Chicago Tribune
(Washington, D.C.) *Daily Globe*
Daily Jacksonville (Illinois) *Constitutionist*
(Washington, D.C.) *Daily Union*
Jacksonville (Illinois) *Journal*
(Shawneetown) *Illinois Republican*
(Jacksonville) *Illinois Sentinel*
(Shawneetown) *Illinois State Gazette*
(Springfield) *Illinois State Journal*
(Springfield) *Illinois State Register*
(Taylorville) *Independent Press*
(Jacksonville) *Morgan Journal*
New York Times
Ottawa (Illinois) *Free Trader*
(Shawneetown) *Southern Illinois Advocate*
(Shawneetown) *Southern Illinoisan*

Wabash (Illinois) *Democrat and Shawneetown* (Illinois) *Gazette*

Books

Anderson, Mary Ann, ed. *The Civil War Diary of Allen Morgan Geer*. New York: Cosmos, 1977.
Arbor Day Exercises at Springfield, Illinois, April 25th, 1902 in Honor of Gen. John M. Palmer and Gen. John A. McClernand. Springfield, IL, 1902.
Browning, Orville Hickman. *The Diary of Orville Hickman Browning*. 2 volumes. Edited by Theodore C. Pease and James G. Randall. Springfield: Illinois State Historical Library, 1925–1933.
Chase, Salmon P. *Inside Lincoln's Cabinet: The Civil War Diaries of Salmon P. Chase*. Edited by David Donald. New York: Longman's, 1954.
_____. *The Salmon P. Chase Papers*. Edited by John Niven. Kent, OH: Kent State University Press, 1993.
Dickens, Charles. *American Notes*. Gloucester, MA: Peter Smith, 1968.
Douglas, Stephen A. *The Letters of Stephen A. Douglas*. Edited by Robert Johannsen. Urbana: University of Illinois Press, 1961.
Force, Manning F. *From Fort Henry to Corinth*. New York: Charles Scribner's Sons, 1881.
Grant, Ulysses S *The Papers of Ulysses S. Grant*. Edited by John Y. Simon. 31 volumes. Carbondale: Southern Illinois University Press, 1967–2009.
_____. *Personal Memoirs of U.S. Grant*. Reprint, New York: Da Capo, 1982 (first printing, New York: C.L. Webster, 1885–1886).
Halstead, Murat. *Three Against Lincoln: Murat Halstead Reports the Caucuses of 1860*. Edited by William B. Hesseltine. Baton Rouge: Louisiana State University Press, 1960.
Illinois Election Returns, 1818–1848. Edited by Theodore C. Pease. Springfield: Trustees of the Illinois State Historical Library, 1923.
Jackson, Joseph Orville, ed. *"Some of the Boys...": The Civil War Letters of Isaac Jackson, 1862–1865*. Carbondale: Southern Illinois University Press, 1960.

Johnson, Robert U., and Clarence C. Buel, eds. *Battles and Leaders of the Civil War.* 4 volumes. Secaucus, NJ: Castle, 1887.

Lanphier, Charles H. *Glory to God and the Sucker Democracy.* 5 volumes. Privately printed by Frye-Williamson, 1973.

Lincoln, Abraham. *The Collected Works of Abraham Lincoln.* 8 volumes. Edited by Roy P. Basler. New Brunswick, NJ: Rutgers University Press, 1953.

Linder, Usher F. *Reminiscences of the Early Bench and Bar of Illinois.* Chicago: Chicago Legal News, 1879.

Logan, John A. *The Volunteer Soldier of America, with Memoir of the Author and Military Reminiscences from General Logan's Private Journal.* Chicago: R.S. Peale, 1887.

Palmer, John M. *Personal Recollections of John M. Palmer.* Cincinnati: Robert Clarke, 1901.

Porter, David D. *Naval History of the Civil War.* Secaucus, NJ: Castle, 1984.

Proceedings of the Conventions at Charleston and Baltimore of the National Democratic Convention. Washington: National Democratic Executive Committee, 1860.

Sears, Stephen W. *The Civil War Papers of George B. McClellan.* New York: Ticknor & Fields, 1989.

Sherman, William T. *Memoirs of W.T. Sherman.* Reprint, New York: Library of America, 1990 (first printing, New York: C.L. Webster, 1875).

Stephens, Alexander H. *A Constitutional View of the Late War Between the States.* 2 volumes. Philadelphia: National, 1868–1870.

de Tocqueville, Alexis. *Democracy in America.* 2 volumes. New York: Knopf, 1945.

Trollope, Frances. *Domestic Manners of the Americans.* New York: Knopf, 1949.

Wallace, Isabel. *Life and Letters of General W.H.L. Wallace.* Chicago: R.R. Donnelley & Sons, 1909.

Welles, Gideon. *Diary of Gideon Welles.* New York: Houghton Mifflin, 1911.

Whitney, Henry Clay. *Life on the Circuit with Lincoln.* Caldwell, ID: Caxton, 1940.

Wills, Charles W. *Army Life of an Illinois Soldier: Letters and Diary of the Late Charles W. Wills.* Washington, DC: Globe, 1906.

Wilson, James H. *Under the Old Flag.* 2 volumes. New York: D. Appleton, 1912.

Articles

Warmoth, Henry Clay. "The Vicksburg Diary of Henry Clay Warmoth." Edited by Paul H. Hasse. *Journal of Mississippi History* (November 1969): 334–347.

_____. "The Vicksburg Diary of Henry Clay Warmoth." Edited by Paul H. Hasse. *Journal of Mississippi History* (February 1970): 60–74.

Secondary Sources

Books

Ambrose, Stephen E. *Halleck: Lincoln's Chief of Staff.* Baton Rouge: Louisiana State University Press, 1962.

Ballard, Michael B. *Vicksburg: The Campaign That Opened the Mississippi.* Chapel Hill: University of North Carolina Press, 2003.

Bearss, Edwin C. *The Vicksburg Campaign.* 3 volumes. Dayton, OH: Morningside House, 1985–1986.

Catton, Bruce. *Grant Moves South.* Boston: Little, Brown, 1960.

Coleman, Roger. *The Arkansas Post Story.* Santa Fe, NM: Southwest Cultural Resources Center, 1987.

Cooling, Benjamin F. *Forts Henry and Donelson: The Key to the Confederate Heartland.* Knoxville: University of Tennessee Press, 1987.

Daniel, Larry J. *Shiloh: The Battle That Changed the Civil War.* New York: Simon & Schuster, 1997.

Davidson, Alexander, and Bernard Stuve. *A Complete History of Illinois from 1673–1873.* Springfield: Illinois Journal, 1874.

Dell, Christopher. *Lincoln and the War Democrats.* Cranbury, NJ: Associated University Presses, 1975.

Donald, David H. *Lincoln.* New York: Simon & Schuster, 1995.

Feis, William B. *Grant's Secret Service: The Intelligence War from Belmont to Appomat-*

tox. Lincoln: University of Nebraska Press, 2002.

Ford, Thomas. *A History of Illinois*. Chicago: S.C. Griggs, 1854.

Grabau, Warren E. *Ninety-Eight Days: A Geographer's View of the Vicksburg Campaign*. Knoxville: University of Tennessee Press, 2000.

Griess, Thomas E., ed. *Atlas for the American Civil War*. Wayne, NJ: Avery, 1986.

Hamilton, Holman. *Prologue to Conflict: The Crisis and Compromise of 1850*. Lexington: University of Kentucky Press, 1964.

Hart, B.H. Liddell. *Sherman: Soldier, Realist, American*. New York: Frederick A. Praeger, 1958.

Hattaway, Herman, and Archer Jones. *How the North Won: A Military History of the Civil War*. Urbana: University of Illinois Press, 1983.

Hicken, Victor. *Illinois in the Civil War*. Urbana: University of Illinois Press, 1966.

Hoehling, A.A. *Vicksburg: 47 Days of Siege*. New York: Fairfax, 1991.

Holt, Michael F. *The Political Crisis of the 1850s*. New York: John Wiley & Sons, 1978.

_____. *Political Parties and American Political Development from the Age of Jackson to the Age of Lincoln*. Baton Rouge: Louisiana State University Press, 1992.

_____. *The Rise and Fall of the American Whig Party: Jacksonian Politics and the Onset of the Civil War*. New York: Oxford University Press, 1999.

Hughes, Nathaniel Cheairs. *The Battle of Belmont: Grant Strikes South*. Chapel Hill: University of North Carolina Press, 1991.

Johannsen, Robert. *Stephen A. Douglas*. New York: Oxford University Press, 1973.

Jones, James P. *"Black Jack": John A. Logan and Southern Illinois in the Civil War Era*. Tallahassee: University Presses of Florida, 1967.

_____. *John A. Logan: Stalwart Republican from Illinois*. Tallahassee: University Presses of Florida, 1982.

Kiper, Richard. *Major General John Alexander McClernand: Politician in Uniform*. Kent, OH: Kent State University Press, 1999.

Lewis, Lloyd. *Captain Sam Grant*. Boston: Little, Brown, 1950.

_____. *Sherman: Fighting Prophet*. New York: Harcourt, Brace, 1932.

Longacre, Edward G. *From Union Stars to Top Hat: A Biography of the Extraordinary General James Harrison Wilson*. Harrisburg, PA: Stackpole, 1972.

Marszalek, John F. *Sherman: A Soldier's Passion for Order*. New York: Free Press, 1993.

McCormick, Robert R. *Ulysses S. Grant: The Great Soldier of America*. New York: D. Appleton-Century, 1934.

McDonough, James L. *Shiloh: In Hell Before Night*. Knoxville: University of Tennessee Press, 1977.

McFeely, William S. *Grant: A Biography*. New York: W.W. Norton, 1981.

McPherson, James M., ed. *The Atlas of the Civil War*. New York: Macmillan, 1994.

McPherson, James M. *Battle Cry of Freedom*. New York: Oxford University Press, 1988.

Miers, Earl S. *The Web of Victory: Grant at Vicksburg*. Baton Rouge: Louisiana State University Press, 1955.

Milton, George F. *The Eve of Conflict: Stephen A. Douglas and the Needless War*. Boston: Houghton Mifflin, 1934.

Nevins, Allan. *The Emergence of Lincoln*. 2 volumes. New York: Charles Scribner's Sons, 1950.

_____. *Ordeal of the Union*. 2 volumes. New York: Charles Scribner's Sons, 1947.

_____. *The War for the Union*. 4 volumes. New York: Charles Scribner's Sons, 1959–1971.

Paludan, Philip S. *The Presidency of Abraham Lincoln*. Lawrence: University Press of Kansas, 1994.

Pease, Theodore C. *The Story of Illinois*. Chicago: University of Chicago Press, 1925.

Potter, David M. *The Impending Crisis, 1848–1861*. New York: Harper & Row, 1976.

Sandburg, Carl. *Abraham Lincoln: The Prairie Years*. 2 volumes. New York: Harcourt, Brace, 1926.

_____. *Abraham Lincoln: The War Years*. 4 volumes. New York: Harcourt, Brace, 1939.

Shea, William L., and Terrence J. Winschel.

Vicksburg Is the Key: The Struggle for the Mississippi River. Lincoln: University of Nebraska Press, 2003.

Simon, Paul. *Lincoln's Preparation for Greatness: The Illinois Legislative Years.* Urbana: University of Illinois Press, 1971.

Simpson, Brooks D. *Let Us Have Peace: Ulysses S. Grant and the Politics of War and Reconstruction, 1861–1868.* Chapel Hill: University of North Carolina Press, 1991.

_____. *Ulysses S. Grant: Triumph Over Adversity, 1822–1865.* New York: Houghton Mifflin, 2000.

Smith, Timothy B. *Champion Hill: Decisive Battle for Vicksburg.* El Dorado Hills, CA: Savas-Beatie, 2004.

Sword, Wiley. *Shiloh: Bloody April.* New York: William Morrow, 1974.

Thomas, Benjamin P., and Harold M. Hyman. *Stanton: The Life and Times of Lincoln's Secretary of War.* New York: Knopf, 1962.

Walker, John W. *Excavation of the Arkansas Post Branch of the Bank of the State of Arkansas.* Southeast Archeological Center, National Park Service, 1971.

Walther, Eric H. *The Shattering of the Union: America in the 1850s.* Wilmington, DE: Scholarly Resources, 2004.

Warner, Ezra J. *Generals in Blue: Lives of the Union Commanders.* Baton Rouge: Louisiana State University Press, 1964.

Waugh, John C. *On the Brink of Civil War: The Compromise of 1850 and How It Changed the Course of American History.* Wilmington, DE: Scholarly Resources, 2003.

Williams, Kenneth P. *Lincoln Finds a General.* 5 volumes. New York: Macmillan, 1949–1959.

Williams, T. Harry. *Lincoln and His Generals.* New York: Knopf, 1952.

Wilson, James G. *Biographical Sketches of Illinois Officers Engaged in the War Against the Rebellion of 1861.* Chicago: James Barnet, 1862.

Woodworth, Steven E., ed. *The Art of Command in the Civil War.* Lincoln: University of Nebraska Press, 1998.

_____, ed. *Grant's Lieutenants: From Cairo to Vicksburg.* Lawrence: University Press of Kansas, 2001.

_____. *Nothing but Victory: The Army of the Tennessee, 1861–1865.* New York: Knopf, 2005.

Articles

Bearss, Edwin C. "The Battle of the Post of Arkansas." *Arkansas Historical Quarterly* (Autumn 1959): 237–279.

Brooks, Robert P. "Howell Cobb and the Crisis of 1850." *Mississippi Valley Historical Review* (December 1917): 179–198.

Crenshaw, Ollinger. "The Speakership Contest of 1859–1860." *Mississippi Valley Historical Review* (December 1942): 323–338.

Feis, William B. "Grant and the Belmont Campaign: A Study in Intelligence and Command." In *The Art of Command in the Civil War,* edited by Steven E. Woodworth. Lincoln: University of Nebraska Press, 1998.

Hamilton, Holman. "'The Cave of the Winds' and the Compromise of 1850." *The Journal of Southern History* (August 1957): 331–353.

Hicken, Victor. "John A. McClernand and the House Speakership Struggle of 1859." *Journal of the Illinois State Historical Society* (Summer 1960): 163–178.

Hodder, Frank H. "The Authorship of the Compromise of 1850." *Mississippi Valley Historical Review* (March 1936): 525–536.

Huffstot, Robert. "Post of Arkansas." *Civil War Times Illustrated* (January 1969): 10–19.

Kiper, Richard L. "Prelude to Vicksburg: The Louisiana Campaign of Major General John Alexander McClernand." *Louisiana History* (Summer 1996): 283–308.

Longacre, Edward G. "Congressman Becomes General: John A. McClernand." *Civil War Times Illustrated* (November 1982): 30–39.

Marszalek, John F. "Sherman Called It the Way He Saw It." *Civil War History* 50, no. 1 (March 1994): 72–78.

Meyers, Christopher C. "'Two Generals Cannot Command This Army': John A. McClernand and the Politics of Command in Grant's Army of the Tennessee." *Columbiad* (Spring 1998): 27–41.

Russel, Robert R. "What Was the Compromise of 1850?" *Journal of Southern History* (August 1956): 292–309.

Winschel, Terrence J. "Fighting Politician: John A. McClernand." In *Grant's Lieutenants: From Cairo to Vicksburg,* edited by Steven E. Woodworth. Lawrence: University Press of Kansas, 2001.

Unpublished Materials

Fehrenbacher, Don. "Illinois Political Attitudes, 1854–1861." PhD diss., University of Chicago, 1952.

Hicken, Victor. "From Vandalia to Vicksburg: The Political and Military Career of John A. McClernand." PhD diss., University of Illinois, 1955.

Lupton, John. "Lincoln's Law Practice in Macoupin County." MA thesis, Sangamon State University, 1992.

Melia, Tamara M. "James B. McPherson and the Ideals of the Old Army." PhD diss., Southern Illinois University, 1987.

Index